A Light Shone in the Darkness

The Story of the Stigmatist and Mystic Therese Neumann of Konnersreuth

A LIGHT SHONE IN THE DARKNESS

THE STORY OF THE STIGMATIST AND MYSTIC
THERESE NEUMANN OF KONNERSREUTH

By
Doreen Mary Rossman

Queenship

PUBLISHING COMPANY
P.O. Box 220, Goleta, CA 93116
(800) 647-9882 • (805) 692-0043 • Fax: (805) 967-5843

©1997 Queenship Publishing

Library of Congress #: 97-06 9916

Published by:
  Queenship Publishing
  P.O. Box 220
  Goleta, CA 93116
  (800) 647-9882 • (805) 692-0043 • Fax: (805) 967-5843

Printed in the United States of America

ISBN: 1-57918-044-2

To Our Lord's Mother, Mary, Our Mother
and to Msgr. James A. MacLellan
who patiently guided me into our beloved Roman Catholic Church

CONTENTS

LETTERS AND VISIONS

FOREWORD
BY AUTHOR

For many years, I have heard of Therese Neumann, the stigmatist and mystic, of her suffering of the passion and the mysterious phenomena surrounding her. Shortly after a visit to Konnersreuth and to Therese Neumann's only living brother Ferdinand Neumann, I decided to write a small pamphlet about Therese Neumann, for the English speaking world has had very little written about her since her death on September 19, 1962. As I progressed in my research, it soon became evident that the "small pamphlet" would have to be enlarged if the entire picture of her unbelievable life story was to be fully presented.

This book is written for the laity of the Church, to bring again to light the remarkable life of Therese Neumann. It is not a theological treatise.

The significance and magnitude of Therese Neumann is manifested in the hundreds of thousands of visitors to Konnersreuth who came to see Therese, and now come to visit her grave. The visitors range from the simple lay person who wishes to glimpse a small light of the wonder of God, up through all the ranks of our society. Hundreds of Bishops and Cardinals, and thousands of priests have paid their respects to her. Pope Pius XI sent his Apostolic Blessing to her in 1928 and 1931. He also gave her a relic of St. Francis of Assisi in 1938. Pope Pius XII sent Therese Neumann a relic of the True Cross in 1955.

Perhaps the miracle of God in His servant Therese Neumann was best described by Michael Cardinal Faulhaber, Patriarch of Bavaria, at a symposium in Munich, 1930, a few days after visiting Therese Neumann. He said: "Even before a definite judgment is pronounced, Konnersreuth can be for us a message of grace; men of modern times stricken with the sorrow of our days return to the pious Veneration of the Passion of Christ and take refuge in His Wounds. A child of the Fichtelgebirge, with complete resignation, becomes lost in contemplation of the sorrows of Jesus, especially on Fridays. In compassion she sheds tears of blood and has become a living image of the Crucified.....and the poor child having no other instruction then that she was given in the elementary school, has nevertheless learned to draw her knowledge from the book of the cross. Preaching without words, but by the force of example she has led the people of Europe to the foot of the cross of Christ and buried them in its wounds; thus rings out from today The Message of Konnersreuth."

My research has shown that the formal initiation of the Beatification Process for Therese Neumann is long overdue. On June 6, 1971, Bishop Rudolf Graber of Regensburg appointed the Rev. Dr. Carl Straeter to gather historical evidence of the life of Therese Neumann, and also to interrogate witnesses. Soon after he appointed a "postulator" and two "vice-postulators" to continue the assemblage and compiling of all information for the beginning of the first step of the Beatification Process, the "Ordinary Process."

Due to an ongoing intimidation by certain priests within the Diocese, the Beatification Process has come to a standstill. It is my opinion that the present Bishop, Bishop Mueller, abrogate any threat as soon as possible. Therese Neumann's life was truly an example which, in this age of spiritual barrenness, is desperately needed by society and more specifically the members of the Church.

I have drawn from the writings and direct quotes of persons who had personal and direct contact with Therese Neumann and who made accurate almost daily notations of their observations.

It is with the deepest of gratitude that I acknowledge the immense and untiring assistance received from Ferdinand Neumann. He had placed at my disposal all his personal pictorial, audio, and written documentation. Many hours I have viewed his private pictures and movies of his sister Therese. All enclosed pictures are from his archives. At the slightest request for information, Mr. Neumann would spend days and at times weeks on research for me. Without him there would be no book. Also to his daughter, Marie Therese, for her many hours spent helping her father and collecting and putting at my disposal the numerous pictures, visual and audio transcriptions from their personal records, I am deeply indebted. For his invaluable review and advice, I extend thanks and gratitude to Father Ulrich Veh, OFM. Cap., Altoetting, Germany.

To my husband Wendell, who was my translator and inspiration, I extend my heartfelt thanks. I am indeed grateful for his continual assistance and support. I am also most grateful to Carmel Linskey for the many hours she spent reviewing and typing the manuscript.

Therese Neumann was known by her family and her many friends under the nick-name Resl. After months of living and breathing the subject Therese Neumann, I feel that I have also become her friend. I pray that she will not be offended when she realizes that I have boldly used her familiar name "Resl" in the book (Resl is pronounced - Raysl.)

- Doreen Mary Rossman

The author and Ferdinand Neumann

FOREWORD
BY FERDINAND NEUMANN

I am indeed pleased to write a few lines for this book, *A Light Shone in the Darkness* by Doreen Mary Rossman.

Together with her, I endeavored to present the events and happenings around my sister Resl as objectively as possible. During Resl's life, Doreen's parents-in-law were most closely connected with my family. In particular, the common bonds between the two families in the fight against Hitler and his regime remain most vividly in my memory. Such as, when the parents of Doreen's husband, Wendell, responding to a direction from Resl, brought Fr. Ingbert Naab (who, together with Dr. Gerlich was the most significant opponent to the Third Reich), to safety into Switzerland. Willingly, they risked their lives in doing so. Although, perhaps unexpected by some, this book also speaks of Hitler's rise to power and of the first line of fighters against him. Many of these fighters could be counted among the friends of Resl and were often guided by her on a day-to-day basis.

It is for the first time that I have, for the publication of this book, made available the texts from the voluminous documents of the visions and extraordinary events of Resl.

My present work of assembling these documents and the translations of my audio recordings is not as yet complete. Therefore, the chapter on visions is somewhat of an advance publication. I truly wish this book all success.

-Ferdinand Neumann

RESL
A BRIEF STORY
OF HER LIFE

Konnersreuth, May 4, 1926

*"Excellency! Most Reverend Bishop! Your Grace!
Concerning: Therese Neumann of Konnersreuth*

*Remarkable events have taken place here at
Konnersreuth in the last few years around
(with) Theresa Neumann...."*

With this letter to his Bishop Antonius von Henle at Regensburg, Father Joseph Naber, pastor of St. Lawrence Roman Catholic Church, in the small village of Konnersreuth, not many kilometers from the Czechoslovakian border, officially announced to the Church and the world the unbelievable happenings in the life of Therese (Resl) Neumann. Resl was, without question, one of the greatest mystics of this century, and perhaps of all times. Much has been written, debated, and investigated concerning her. She was very much in the life of the world, not cloistered away in a monastery, but visible for all to see, hear and wonder about. Of course, she soon had ardent believers, skeptics, and outright hostility from non-believers. Dr. Fritz Gerlich, a noted writer and publisher of her times, went to see her for the sole purpose of proving her a fraud. He left believing, became a Catholic, her protector, and life-long friend.

1

Difficult it must have been, not only for her family but for all the people in Konnersreuth and the district to accept the fact of these strange happenings. All were forced into believing or not believing. If you are indifferent, that in itself is non-belief.

RESL'S EARLY YEARS, 1898 TO 1918

Resl was born sometime between the late hours of Holy Thursday, April 8, 1898 and early Good Friday, April 9, 1898. The exact hour is in question. However, it matters not. She was born the first of eleven children to a simple, uncomplicated, down-to-earth couple, Ferdinand and Anna Neumann of Konnersreuth, East Bavaria, Germany.

Ferdinand Neumann was a tailor by trade, and Anna was in charge of their small farm. As could be expected of farmers at the turn of the century, their lives revolved around the Church, her teaching, and the necessity of providing for their family.

April 10, 1898, Resl was baptized Therese, after her Aunt and in honor of St. Teresa of Jesus, of Avila. She attended the village school from 1904 to May 1911, followed by a Sunday School education to 1914, then she continued studies in Christian Doctrine at home. It was on April 18th, 1909 that she received her "First Holy Communion" at the age of 11. In September of the same year Resl had her first catechism lesson from the newly appointed parish priest Father Joseph Naber, who would become her spiritual director until her death in 1962.

Religious training started early in the Neumann household. They were brought up in a strict, but not puritanical, Christian atmosphere, practical and with a spirit of cooperation in the family. Above all, they were taught obedience to God, Church and parents. Disciplinary measures were administered when needed. Proper behavior was insisted upon, especially in Church.

Resl showed nothing beyond the devotion expected of a normal pious Catholic girl of her age. It must be remembered that a family unit, during Resl's early life, did not have the confusion and doubts of faith with which our present liberal teachings have bewildered our society.

One could depend on her to do her share, plus, in everything. Just as most oldest children of large families acquire a deep feeling of responsibility toward parents and family, Resl too became a type of surrogate mother to her siblings; a peacemaker, provider of counsel, and her parents' right arm. Life on a farm did not allow for much fantasy or daydreaming. As the oldest, she had her feet firmly planted and probably did not put up with laziness or pranks from her younger siblings.

She was a happy child, healthy and strong, normal, well balanced, outgoing and attractive.

The Neumann's life was a life of financial struggle. New children arrived every year or two. The last child, Hans, was born when Resl was 14 years old. At 12 years, she complimented her families' meager income by doing domestic work for the neighbors. She preferred work in the fields and with animals to work in the house, for she loved the outdoors, the plants, the flowers, and animals. Even in her last years she had a flower garden and birds in her room.

Her parental education showed itself early in her life. As Dr. Gerlich observed, she did not like fairytales, stories of magic, or exaggerated legends. Romantic or heroic fiction did not appeal to her; reality was of first importance. She enjoyed reading horticulture books, true stories, and biographies. *Introduction to a Devout Life* by Francis de Sales was also her reading material, as was Therese of Lisieux's autobiography *Story of a Soul*.

In her 10th year, Resl first made known her desire to join a community of sisters with missions in Africa. Later, she applied for entrance at a convent in Tutzing, Bavaria. Slowly, she saved money for her "Dowry". Suitors came, but Resel discouraged them all. She had set her sights on a different mountain.

Ferdinand Neumann, her father, served in France during WW I, thereby leaving greater responsibility on Resl. On one of his furloughs, her father brought Resl, who already had a little picture of Therese of Lisieux, some rose petals. He was well aware of her love and devotion to this simple, child-like Carmelite. Since there was very little or no money, her mother, Anna, asked her to postpone her entrance into a convent until the end of the war and the return of her father.

Three years old.   *L.P.*

With her parents after the healing in 1925.   *L.P.*

Resl continued working for a farmer, Max Neumann, (not related), a short walk from her home. The work was hard indeed. With the men off to war, she soon performed all the duties on the farm.

Until April 10, 1918, life at the Neumann household was business as usual. That day would change their lives forever, especially for Resl. A fire!

FIRE, PURGATION, STIGMATA; 1918-1928

Fires are always dreadful, but perhaps more so on a farm. The danger to the buildings, the animals, grain, hay and straw being stored, is terrifying. When the stubble on the fields catches fire, it can spread as fast as the wind will blow it. It's a farmer's continual nightmare. It was an unspoken commitment from every neighbor that they would instantly come to fight the fires with whatever equipment they possessed.

Ferdinand Neumann was home on furlough on that fateful morning, when a fire suddenly broke out on a neighboring farm. Resl helped lead the animals to safety. As the flames swept across the fields, the buildings on the Max Neumann farm were also in danger of being destroyed. Since all the firefighters and fire equipment were deployed at the original fire, the entire Neumann household and all the servants formed a bucket brigade to drench the buildings to protect them from the fire. The family and servants handed pails full of water to Resl, who was standing on a stool. She in turn would pass the pail over her head to the roof where Max Neumann was. Resl supported herself with her right arm while lifting the pail with her left. This continued for over two hours, without a break, drink, or breakfast. Suddenly, losing her balance, she dropped the pail, and leaned against the building, to prevent herself from falling. She said "I just could do no more. I felt a sudden pain in my back as if something had snapped in me." With great difficulty, numb legs, and increasing pain in her back, she eventually made her way back to her home. By then the pain had spread over her whole body. It was later found that she had dislocated two of her vertebrae.

Shortly after the fire Resl had fallen backwards on a flight of stone stairs. One hour later her sister found her unconscious and bleeding from her head. Resl described the pain of her head injury "...as though my eyes would jump out of their sockets."

Now began what theologians call "purgation." A time in life when "Holy men and prophets are cleansed and purified for God's greater purpose." "The metal is beaten into the dust from which it came."

The drenching with cold water while perspiring profusely on the day of the fire left Resl with lung trouble; first a cough, then pleurisy, followed by pneumonia. There were several other falls, mostly on her back, and after each fall, her eye sight deteriorated. A fall in August brought about convulsions, and a fall in October further deteriorated her eyesight plus leaving her paralyzed on one side. The fall on March 17, 1919, left Resl completely blind. The fire of the previous year had immediately affected her digestive system; first vomiting, then lack of appetite and distaste for any food.

Before the age of 21, this cheerful, strong young woman, was paralyzed and blind. Bedridden and motionless, her years of darkness had begun.

There were many who interrogated Resl regarding her illnesses. Two of the most thorough interrogators, who wrote precise documents of these sessions were Gerlich and Father Witt.

In his book *Mystical Phenomena* pp. 112-113, Archbishop Teodorowicz, who had witnessed it, described her most pitiable condition: "After a short ailment of the eyes, total blindness followed; never ending night surrounded poor Therese. Abscesses formed in the ears and throat. For some time she lost her hearing and the mere act of eating became a burden to her. Her sense of touch was also affected. Even breathing brought its difficulties. This arose from the nauseating odor of the foulness of her wounds. In her attacks of shortness breath, she became almost blue. The suffering was greatly increased through severe contractions of the muscles;....on the left foot, deep bleeding, painful wounds formed. 'The left foot,' says Therese herself, 'had no skin from the ankle to the sole. The ankle bone was exposed. On my back I had six or eight sores as large as a paper mark (currency), the width of the hand. Water, blood and matter oozed out of all the wounds.'"

For seven years she suffered. Physicians could provide no relief for any of her maladies. Things only got worse. Gone was the dream of entering the religious vocation, of being a Missionary Sister in Africa.

When all hope of recovery vanished, Resl accepted the Will of God and submitted herself to a life of suffering because with uniting her suffering with those of our Savior, she could help to win souls for God. Resl said, "I resigned myself to the Will of God because the duty of every Christian is to accept the cross which the Savior sends. It would be a sin to strive against the Will of God. I did not accept the cross because of the cross, but in devotion to the cross of the Savior......My pains by themselves are of no avail to save souls but only when united with the pains of Our Lord." Later in life, when she more fully realized the value of suffering patiently, united with Christ's suffering, she said: "If it were possible I would willingly accept suffering in heaven in order to bring more souls to the Savior."

During her sufferings Resl continued to be alert, lively, and never complained. She slept little and was often unconscious (this unconscious state later became known as "Exalted Repose"). For one year, an abscess in her head caused both eyes and one ear to bleed.

Near the end of 1923, she was unable to eat or drink for 12 days. Soon she could drink only one cup of liquid a day. Fifteen days before Easter 1925, she could neither eat nor drink except for her daily Holy Communion and progressed to complete inedia as of the Feast of the Transfiguration, 1925.

All medical means at their disposal were administered by the physicians and parents, but they were completely ineffective either to cure the ailments or to arrest their progress.

In this, her life in the darkness, her resignation to the will of God, her devotion to her "Savior," and her love of Therese of Lisieux, became her mental occupation. Five years into her sufferings, the first in a series of many miracles began to manifest themselves.

On April 19, 1923, the day of the beatification of Therese of Lisieux, Resl's mother and sister Creszenzia heard her vehemently pounding the floor with a stick (her signal to her family that she was in need) and they rushed to her room. To their utter amazement, they realized that Resl had regained her eyesight. She explained that she had felt a hand touching her and she suddenly was able to see.

On May 17, 1925, two years later, the date of Therese of Lisieux's canonization, Resl became aware of a beautiful light and then a voice which spoke to her, asking her twice if she would like to be healed of her remaining ailments. Because the voice was loving and reassuring, she was unafraid. Twice Resl replied that "God's Will and what is from God are the only things that would make me happy." The voice told her that she would now receive some joy and healing but "Through suffering you can best exercise your devotional convictions and call as Victim-Soul. You can in this way save souls and support priests." Resl responded with "Everything the Good Lord wants is fine with me."

"The metal is readied for the Maker's hand." Resl has now accepted and the announcement has been made of her role "Victim-Soul".

The healing consisted of instantaneous return to normal of her pinched and dislocated vertebrae, her crippled legs were healed, so were her bed sores, her muscle cramps and paralysis. After seven years of being bedridden, she was able to walk with the aid of a cane.

September 30 of the same year of 1925, the anniversary of St. Therese of Lisieux's death, at 11:30 PM, while in prayer, the same light she had seen in May appeared again, and the same loving voice spoke to Resl, telling her of sufferings yet to come, and to "Follow your father confessor in blind obedience and trust him in everything! Always remain childlike simple!" From then on, Resl Neumann was able to walk without any help.

November 13, 1925, Dr. Otto Seidl was called to see Resl who had, for a week, steadily become more and more ill. The diagnosis was "acute appendicitis", and immediate surgery was necessary. Resl called for her father confessor, Fr. Naber, and in the presence of Dr. Seidl said "You know, if I tell it to the little Saint, she could help without the cutting." Upon hearing this request the doctor said: "Do you really think St. Therese works nothing but miracles for you?" Resl replied that if it was God's will then she would be most willing to submit to the surgery. However, since her mother was so very distraught, could she not beg St. Therese to help, if it were all right with God? With Father Naber's permission the rose petals from St. Therese of Lisieux, which Resl's father had brought from France during his stay there in WWI, were placed on the afflicted area, and all prayed to St. Therese. Resl was healed. This was the fourth miraculous healing with the aid of St. Therese of Lisieux. A more detailed account of this healing appears in Fr. Nabers letter Chapter 8 of this book. In a booklet published in 1929, Dr. Seidl stated "There was no natural explanation for the extraordinary cures and the phenomena that followed them."

At the beginning of Lent 1926, with watery and pussy eyes bleeding, plus painful ear trouble, Resel was diagnosed as having the flu. Two to three weeks into Lent, March 4-5, while meditating on the Agony in the Garden, she became aware of blood flowing from a wound which appeared just above her heart. One week before Good Friday, March 28th, 1926, the wound of a nail appeared on her left hand. Late Holy Thursday night, April 1, 1926, Resl began a long, almost continual vision of the Passion of Our Lord. It started with the Last Supper, followed by the Agony in the Garden and the arrest. On April 2, 1926, she witnessed and followed, in her visions the entire terrible events leading to His Crucifixion and His Death. On this same Good Friday, while witnessing the Passion of our Savior in a vision, her right hand and both feet received the wounds of our Lord. Her eyes, which from 1923 had bled only drops of blood, now bled profusely. Her sufferings, both physical and spiritual, were so great that Father Naber was ready to administer the Last Rites, but 3:00 PM brought a change in her condition. For the rest of the day, through Saturday, until Easter, she slept with little discomfort. On Easter Sunday she appeared to be a changed person from the previous days.

Her hands, feet and heart had received the wounds of the stigmata.

On this "Good Friday" she, for the first time, experienced and saw the entire Passion of our Lord, from the Agony in the Garden to the Crucifixion and Death. She went with the crowd, as though walking with them, being a person in that time; experiencing all; smells, heat, and hearing everything. In these visions Resl was never aware of the outcome. She was always hoping that what she was witnessing would somehow not come to pass. Resl was an actual participant—a co-sufferer. Never aware of her own being but only of what she was witnessing. Her reactions were simple and straightforward.

While being absorbed in the visions, Resl's body experienced all the agony, spitting, buffeting and pain our Savior suffered. She experienced the scourging, the crown of thorns, the weight of the cross, the many falls under the cross, the nails of the crucifixion on her outstretched hands, the raising of the cross, the jolt as it fell into the hole provided to stabilize it, the excruciating pain, muscle cramping, heat, abandonment by men and by "God", the great physical thirst, the terrible pangs of death, then death itself.

An attempt was made to heal Resl's wounds, or more precisely stigmata, with ointments which brought only pain to her. She soon discarded the bandages with the salves. Fr. Naber told her to reapply the medication, but her hands, feet and side swelled and were very painful. After 10 hours he permitted the treatment to stop. The wounds continued to bleed. Not continuously, but moist enough to be lightly bandaged. Saturday, April 17th, there appeared a transparent membrane, a skin like overlay, somewhat like gelatin over the reddish wounds. She could now wash her hands. They remained closed until Thursday, April 22, 1926. On that night, the vision of the Passion of our Lord started to appear to her again. She again suffered the entire Passion, however not as severely. Her wounds, which opened and bled Fridays, were closed and dry on Saturday

From this time onward, Resl saw and suffered the "Passion of our Savior" an incredible 760⁺ times, from Thursday evening 11:00 p.m. to Friday 3:00 p.m., Holy Land time. She also took neither nourishment nor liquid. Her sole food was the Holy Eucharist for the rest of her life. There were no Passion sufferings on Fridays between Easter and the Feast of Corpus Christi.

Resl gradually received the wounds of the Crown of Thorns. She had begged that they not appear on her forehead. By the first Friday of November 1926, she had received eight wounds on her scalp which could only be seen when they bled on Fridays. Later, the wounds of the scourging appeared on her back as well as the shoulder wound from the cross. However, these two stigmata soon disappeared, only to reappear during Lent and Passion time.

Resl lived an open life, among her friends and the whole community. Events such as these would be impossible to be kept secret. Almost immediately, streams of people began beating a path to the little village of Konnersreuth. It is still quite a small village,

Neumann family and friend, 1947. Seated, mother Neumann, Fr. Naaber, *L.P.* father Neumann, Resl at center, flanked by her six sisters and four brothers. At extreme left is Hans, right, Ferdinand.

but at that time it must have been much more so. This phenomenon which happened to a young neighbor created quite a stir.

Religious and clergy, government observers, the media, self appointed observers, believers and skeptics, royalty, and the simple ordinary folk flocked to her home. Of course she was a curiosity and an object to explore. Resl was particularly baffling to the "intellectuals" and "scientists." However, as Ernest Renan in *Life of Jesus* (1863) said, "No miracle has ever taken place under conditions which science can accept."

Soon, the government and all persons who considered themselves as part of the intelligentsia demanded statements from all the physicians who ever treated her, concerning the medical phenomena. People who knew her well were questioned regarding her character, mental stability, etc. The mystery of the miraculous offers no answers. They (the scientists and intellectuals) will never be satisfied. Accusation of fraud were made, never proven. To continue a fraud for thirty-six years, a fraud involving a large family and a village, would be a miracle in itself. A two week medical observation was made under the auspices of the Diocese of Regensburg. However, some scientists and adversaries were not satisfied, and wanted examinations under their direction and control, to do as they pleased.

A Brief Sketch of Hitler's Rise to Power; 1928 to 1945

In light of some of the first resistance to the Nazis, which was mainly by Roman Catholics, with Resl as their center, and in order to understand just how this unbridled power-grab by Hitler could occur in such a short time, it is necessary to give a brief historic sketch of events leading to and during the actual take-over by the Nazis, a take-over in an especially greedy and indifferent society. This type of take-over, by a political despot, needs only an apathetic and complacent citizenry to be repeated again. This lesson must be taught to and relearned by every generation and Hitler's take-over is an excellent example.

November 1923 brought the "Beer Hall Putsch" in Munich, an uprising lead by General Erich Ludendorff and the head of the National Socialist Party, Adolf Hitler. Poorly organized, it was quickly put down. Hitler was sentenced to five years in prison where he wrote his book *Mein Kampf.* He was released within one year and quickly resumed his political career. In the German elections (Reichstag elections) of May 4 1924, the National Socialist Party gained 12 seats. By the election of 1930, September 14, they became a major party with 107 seats. The Socialists retained their 143 seats, communists 77 seats, with the moderates losing heavily. The rapid gain of political power by the National Socialists (Nazi) and the Communist parties, ushered in a period of disorder. The financial collapse of central Europe in May of 1931, including Germany, brought on the economic depression. By 1932, 6,000,000 in Germany alone were unemployed, bringing about social tensions and the growth of both Communism and National Socialism.

Two elections were held in early 1932, and on April 13th a ban on the activities of Hitler's (National Socialist Party) storm troops was imposed. This ban in turn was lifted by mid June and from then on the National Socialists gained great momentum. Rowdiness and clashes were the order of the day. By July, Berlin and Brandenburg, where the Nazi storm troops had made it difficult to maintain order, were placed under martial law. A further election on July 31, 1932 gave the National Socialists 230 seats, the Socialists 133, the Center Party 97, and the Communists 89. Since neither the National Socialists nor the Communists would enter into a coalition, no majority was possible. From then until March 5, 1933 there were several elections and attempts at establishing a majority.

The National Socialist Party appealed to the prejudices in Germany against the Jews, intellectuals, gypsies, pacifists, communists, socialists, and liberals. Hitler exacted unquestioned obedience from his followers, and promised in return to make Germany strong, self-sufficient, respected, an Aryan nation purified of all Jewish elements, able to revive the traditions of early Teutonic heroism. The middle class, which had been ruined by the economic crises, were offered the end of Jewish competition in business and also in the professions. Thousands of unemployed young men were put into uniform as storm troopers. With the aid of his lieutenants, such as Goebbels and Goering, Hitler was able to get an extremely efficient propaganda machinery into motion and many impressive demonstrations were held. With his extraordinary powers of an orator, his fanatical patriotism and nationalism, Hitler secured the backing of many who were discontent with their present social conditions.

A violent confrontation between the National Socialists and the Communists culminated in a fire which partly destroyed the Reichstag building. Hitler, of course, denounced it as a Communist plot. President von Hindenburg issued emergency decrees, suspending the constitutional guarantees of free speech, free press, as well as other liberties, thereby opening the door for the Nazi storm troops to intimidate and bully their opponents with impunity.

On March 5, 1933 the Reichstag elections gave the Nazi Party 288 seats, the Socialists 120, the Communists 81, the Central Party 74, the Nationalists 52, and others 23. These results of the election gave the Nazis 44% and their ally, the Nationalists (Party of big business and of the old aristocracy) 8% - totaling 52%. Hitler was now in power.

Eighteen days after the elections, the crucial "Enabling Act" was passed, with only 94 votes cast against it. The act gave the governing party dictatorial powers until April 1, 1937. Now Hitler's dictatorship was affirmed. The passing of the act enabled Hitler to establish his policies, which affected almost every phase of life, in only a few very brief years. The changes included:

Constitutional changes: Gradually the states were stripped of their effective power, changing Germany from a federal state to a national state..

Administrative changes: By the Civil Service Act, April 7, 1933, all non Aryan (i.e. Jewish) government officials could be retired, also teachers, notaries, and other semi-public servants.

Judicial changes: Entire legal systems were overhauled with traditional concepts of law discarded. The sole deciding consideration was the welfare of the state and Nazi regime. The "Peoples Court" was established on May 3, 1934, to try "treason cases" and was given an extremely wide definition. Proceedings were secret, with no appeal possible except to the "Fuehrer." Summary execution of sentences were usual. Concentration camps sprang up. Opponents detained in these camps without a trial, became a standard procedure.

Political changes: All opposing parties were liquidated under Nazi pressure. The other dissolved themselves. On July 14, 1933 the National Socialist Party (Nazi) was declared the only political party.

Racial changes: Then began the persecution of Jews, including those of 1/4 Jewish extraction, and of Gypsies; boycotts of their businesses and of professionals. On Sept. 15, 1935, the Jews and partial Jews were stripped of rights of citizenship, and intermarriages with Jews forbidden.

Economic changes: Strikes and lockouts were forbidden (May 17, 1933). Employers were given extensive control. Unemployment was eliminated through labor camps, public works, rearmament, etc. Costs were met by internal loans, mostly forced. Industry was gradually controlled by the government. Peasants were held to their land.

Military Changes: Compulsory service was instated on March 6, 1935, and rapid rearmament began. By 1938 the Nazis had an impressive army and an air fleet superior to that of any other country. The Western front was heavily fortified against an "attack by France."

Religious changes. It was soon evident that the Nazi regime planned to coordinate all religious organizations with state machinery. Neo-Pagan movements were encouraged, while Christian churches were exposed to great pressures from the government.

The Protestants were amalgamated into a state Evangelical Church (July 11,1933) with a government appointed national bishop. Those who broke away formed the German Confessional Church and were soon in conflict with the state. Many were arrested, tried, and imprisoned in concentration camps.

The Catholic Church fared equally badly. The Bishops had spoken against Hitler and most Catholics did not vote for him. On July 30, 1933, a new concordat was signed with the Vatican. All future diocesan appointments were to be made by the Holy See only after consulting the German government. Catholic clergy were forbidden to take part in politics. Religious societies were allowed only if they did not "meddle" into public affairs. Children were brought into the Nazi Youth Movement where doctrines, objectionable to many Christian parents, were taught. Many Catholic leaders protested, but again to no avail. On the contrary, the government in retaliation, in 1937, brought many monks and clergy to trial on trumped up immoral charges, etc. and in general did all in their power to discredit the Catholic Church.

Even before England's Prime Minister Lord Chamberlain sought an agreement with Italy and Germany, known as the "Policy of Appeasement" (It seems that such is still attempted, even by our own government), Hitler and his National Socialists were well into their executions and tortures at their concentration and labor camps.

By the time England declared war on Germany on Sept. 3, 1939, thousands of Germans, both Jew and non-Jew had already been incarcerated, tortured and annihilated. This terror spread through Austria in 1938 and into Czechoslovakia between September 12, 1938 and March 15, 1939. On March 31, 1939, Britain ended the "Policy of Appeasement" when Britain and France guaranteed aid to Poland "in the event of any threat, direct or indirect, to the independence of either." Guarantees were given to Greece and Romania, along with an assistance pact with Turkey. Now Britain had the arduous task of bringing Russia into the "Peace Front."

The Germans marched into Poland on Sept. 1, 1939. Great Britain and France declared war on Germany on September 3, 1939. On September 5, 1939, the US declared neutrality in the European War. On May 10, 1940, the German army invaded the Netherlands, Belgium, and Luxembourg. By June of the same year, France fell to the Germans. Now the Battle of Britain began (June 1940). Sept. 27, 1940, the German, Italian, Japanese Pact was concluded in Berlin. With the invasion of Russia on June 22, 1941, the incessant air attacks on the British Islands subsided somewhat. On December 7, 1941, the Japanese attacked Pearl Harbor in Hawaii, and the US Congress declared war with Japan. (This was two years and three months after the British declaration of war on Germany). On Dec. 9, 1941, in conformity to their pact with Japan, Germany and Italy declared war on the USA.

By this time, Hitler had squelched almost all interior dissension. Whoever had been or still was against the Nazis was either already killed, in concentration camps, out of the country, or completely underground.

With the continual threat of Japanese invasion of the sub continent of Australia; the wars in Europe, Asia, the Pacific and Africa; the uncertain loyalties of Argentina; the world was soon afire as never before! There was either war or the building up of defenses on every continent on earth. From March 23, 1933, with the passage of the Enabling Act and thereby the firm establishment of the Nazi dictatorship, until the end of the war in the Pacific, August 14, 1945, millions of people were killed; property damage in the untold billions of dollars. When a potentially evil member of the human society presents a threat to mankind as a whole and his criminal conduct goes unchecked, it is a grave error of omission on the side of society. How was it possible that such atrocities could sweep the globe at such a terrifying speed! And yet, upon closer examination the nations could or should have known of the possibility of a World War II. The indications were there, but the indifference of mankind allowed Hitler to become what he was. Many countries even praised him! Was not our Diplomatic Service receiving and studying the goings on in Germany? It is for certain that the U.S. paid no attention to the screaming voices of warnings which came from Germany itself.

RESL THROUGH THE NAZI TIMES; 1928 TO 1945

Years before Hitler's rise to power, a group of Catholics, opposed to the Nazi philosophy and ambitions, formed a group later called by its enemies the "Konnersreuth Circle." They clearly saw, as early as 1926, the dangerous and terrifying intentions of the Nazis, intentions which the Nazis planned to put into practice. Resl, who was the spiritual center of this group, gave them counsel, encouragement, and at times directives.

By 1930 the Konnersreuth Circle consisted of:

Dr. Fritz Michael Gerlich; who was the owner and publisher of a newspaper *Der Gerade Weg,* or *The Straight Way,* the most profound anti-Nazi publication. Dr. Gerlich also wrote two volumes concerning Resl Neumann.

Father Ingbert Naab OFM Cap, 1885-1935; from the cloistered monastery at Eichstaett.

Dr. Franz Xaver Wutz; Priest and professor of the Old Testament, and specialist of oriental languages at the Phi-Theologischen Hochschule in Eichstaett.

Father Cosmas; Father Ingbert Naab's close associate.

Pfarrer Joseph Naber; Pastor of St. Lawrence Church in Konnersreuth and Resl's pastor and confessor.

Fuerst Erich von Waldburg-Zeil; Financial base for Dr. Gerlich's newspaper *The Straight Way.*

Maria Benedikta von Spiegel; Abbess of the Abby of St. Walburg at Eichstaett.

Dr. Joseph Lechner; Professor for Canon Law at Eichstaett Hochschule.

Erwein Freiherr von Aretin; associate of Dr. Gerlich.

Dr. Franz Xaver Mayer; Professor of chemistry, biology and geology at the University of Eichstaett.

Johannes Steiner; Gerlich's associate.

Sister Walburga O.S.B.; sister of Fuerst Erich von Waldburg-Zeil.

Dr. Emslander;

Anni Spiegl;

Therese Neumann (Resl)

Ottilie Neumann; Resl's sister at age 31.

Ferdinand Neumann; Resl's brother at age 22.

Hans Neumann; Resl's brother at age 21.

There was also a smaller group around Father Naab (the "Eichstaett Circle") which partook in anti-Nazi activities. The group included Bishop Dr. Alois Brems, Prof. Dr. Joseph Kuerzingen, Dr. Emslander, Supreme Court Judge Fackler, Professor Friedrich Doerr, Alfons Fleischmann, Dr. Schorer, Dr. Hans Hutter, Bishop Of Eichstaett, Leo von Mergel O.S.B. (Bishop from 1905 - 1932), and Konrad Graf Cardinal Preysing. The two above bishops had direct connections to Resl. Many were members of both Circles.

The Konnersreuth and Eichstaett Circles had many sympathizers and helpers, in Eichstaett, Konnersreuth, and in other parts of Bavaria, who were ready to risk their lives. Baroness Elizabeth von Guttenburg (who's husband Baron Enoch Guttenburg started his anti Hilter activity as early as 1925), Erwein Freiherr von Aretin, Friedrich Ritter von Lama, and Gerda and Rudolf Rossmann and

Ernst Rossmann are but a very few. Most of them were persecuted, and many were killed by the Nazis.

In 1932, Dr. Gerlich's newspaper *The Straight Way* printed an open letter to Hitler which was written by Father Ingbert Naab, exposing the treachery and dangers of Hitler and his followers. Over 20 million copies were eventually printed. In March 1933, only days after Hitler gained power, Dr. Gerlich was arrested, imprisoned and continually tortured. He was taken to Dachau and there brutally killed on June 30, 1934, without ever having a charge brought against him or having had a trial. His last article to appear in *The Straight Way* on March 9, 1933 was "The End of Democracy."

Because he was the author of the "Open Letter" to Hitler, Father Naab was now in grave danger. It was agreed that he must leave Germany immediately. Resl sent Professor Wutz to Gerda and Rudolf Rossmann, who lived in Gauting just south of Munich, to help in getting Father Naab out of the country. Rudolf's brother, Ernst Rossman, gave his passport for Father Naab. Gerda and Rudolf then went to the Capuchin Monastary Ave Maria to pick up Father Naab. They shaved and disguised him to look as much as possible like their brother Ernst. Just minutes before the gestapo arrived to arrest Father Naab the three left for Constance, smuggling him across the Swiss border. They proceeded to Lucerne and brought him to the Franciscan Monastary of Wesemlin. From here, he was shuffled from one monastary to another. Later, in 1935, Father Naab died of a heart attack at Koenigshofen in France. His remains now rest at Eichstaett, Germany.

Fredrich Ritter von Lama was also arrested for his anti Nazi activity, sent to Stadelheim Prison, and finally to the gallows on Feb. 6, 1944, carrying a rosary around his neck. His son Franz, a correspondent from Vienna, died in Dachau.

Dr. Franz Xaver Wutz died in 1938, also of a heart attack, only two days before the SS arrived to arrest him.

Hitler had a fascination with the occult and all spiritual phenomena. He was both attracted to and yet afraid of Resl. She was always under surveillance and threatened. Several times, she was even declared dead in the Nazi press in a hope that she would somehow disappear. Her visions, Passion sufferings, etc. continued as before. Her brothers, Ferdinand and Hans, were repeatedly imprisoned; tortured, and eventually released. Because Resl's father allowed a few French prisoners to visit Resl, he too was imprisoned for a few months.

From March 5, 1933, until the end of the war on May 8, 1945, life was always a frightening uncertainty. News of the imprisonment and often death of family members and friends was very frequent. The scare tactics of the Nazis were of course calculated and deliberate. With almost no medical aid for civilians, Resl helped the sick and the dying as much as she could. Shortly before the end of the war Resl was to be arrested, however, a high officer in charge just couldn't see how this simple farm woman could be of national danger. No arrest was ever made.

As the American troops neared Konnersreuth, the SS troops deliberately shelled the town of Konnersreuth, damaging the Church and the rectory. Counter shelling by the advancing American forces damaged the Neumann house. However, this was the last of the Nazi terror.

With the arrival of the US forces, peace, order and safety had at last returned to Konnersreuth.

AFTER WORLD WAR II UNTIL RESL'S DEATH; 1945 TO 1962

American servicemen came to Konnersreuth in great numbers. From the low ranks of the private to the top, the Generals. They came to see the Mystic of Konnersreuth, and left with impressions which would remain with most of them until their death.

When asked to reflect on this time, Ferdinand Neumann relayed the following heart warming story: With the arrival of so many foreigners, the German visitors to Konnersreuth soon complained to the Pastor and the people who controlled the crowds, that preferential treatment was given to the American soldiers and to the "Auslaender" (foreigners), religious or lay. To satisfy their grumbling it was decided that two visitor lines would be formed; one with the German populous, while the other line consisted of

On the family farm with a sister.   *F.N.*

With her horse "Lotte'   *F.N.*

Resl working in the fields   *F.N.*

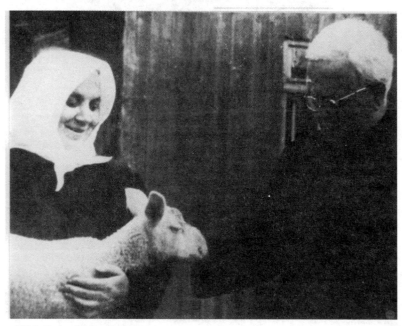

With Father Naber in 1932   *F.N.*

Prof. Franz Xaver Wutz of Eichstaedt. The first to
identify Resl's use of Aramaic. Approx. 1928.

F.N.

A meeting of friends. L to R: Fr. Naab, Resl, Prof.
Wutz, Ferdinand and Ottila Neumann. (1927)

F.N.

Benedikta von Spiegel, Abbess of St. Walburg of   *F.N.*
Eichstaett (an Abbess has Bishop's rank). The
Abbess was one of Resl's closest friends.

Resl with General Farrell   *H.N.*

Resl with U.S. forces   *H.N.*

Resetting of the cross on the steeple of St. Lawrentins church in Konnersreuth. Ferdinand Neumann is hidden in the steeple scaffold to receive and anchor the Cross.

HN.

the foreigners. All visitors were allowed to come in to see Resl while she was in the "Passion," alternately, a few from the German line, followed by the exact number from the foreigner's line. Mr. Neumann commented that it was almost immediately observed that the Germans pushed and shoved and were generally very vocal while they waited in line and as they viewed Resl in the Passion Sufferings. The foreign soldiers, religious, and lay, were quite the opposite. They lined up quietly, prayed or read the Holy Scriptures, and most, after viewing Resl and the Passion, left with tears running down their faces, if not actually weeping!

General Farrell, top brass of the American Occupation Army, also paid his respects to Resl. He orchestrated, with the aid of a giant US helicopter, the resetting of a new cross at the top of the Church steeple, which had been destroyed during the shelling. Encapsulated in the sphere at the base of the new cross is a particle of the "true cross of Jesus." Resl, in gratitude, gave her Rosary to the General, who in turn took his Rosary out of his pocket and gave it to Resl. The General's driver told that the General would often pray the Rosary when they drove.

From the end of the war to her death, Resl's life primarily consisted of the continuation of her Passion sufferings and her sufferings as a "victim-soul." She received on the average 100 visitors per day. Many of these visitors brought their personal worries, sorrows, and requests to her and she dealt with them as conscientiously as she could. She took care of a substantial correspondence, but her joy was the decorating of the Church. Resl also undertook the arduous task of establishing two major religious building complexes.

The first was a school for people who late in life were called into the Holy Orders. The respective buildings and farm lands, known as Fockenfeld, were originally the summer residence of the Abbot of Waldsassen. When the new owner, a Saxonian industrialist made known his intentions to sell the property to the Protestant Church who wished to convert it into a school, Resl managed to stop the pending sale. Ferdinand Neumann and his American friend Morris Verner, obtained a restitution fund for Earl Erich von Zeil, who in turn gifted the money to the Salesian Order. The Salesians then purchased Fockenfeld and established a religious school for 350 students. To date, Fockenfeld, in its 30 years of existence has produced 350 priests and one Bishop (of Eichstaett installed in 1996).

The second project was the building of the Theresianum, named after St. Therese of Lisieux, and essentially a Monastary. The impetus of this project was Bishop Graber of Regensburg's request to Resl to help him in the establishment of a place for perpetual adoration and a prayer house for the intentions of the Bishop. Characteristically, Resl went into action and persuaded an industrialist from Ragensburg to fund the project. He did donate the funds but not without causing Resl some terrifying anxiety, which only in part was later corrected by the good donor. The Theresianum is a large, stately, two-wing, multi-storied building, occupied by Carmelites for the purpose it was intended and it is in Konnersreuth. Resl died before it was completed.

RESL'S DEATH—THE LIGHT IS EXTINGUISHED

The prelude to her death is contained in the following transcription from a tape given to the author by Ferdinand Neumann:

I would like to narrate, from the many events of life and dying as witnessed by my sister Resl, which evolved into a firm conviction on my part.

Resl was frequently called to the dying. When death occurred, Resl spontaneously fell into a vision. She saw the person in bright light, fully recognizable as in real life. Suddenly, the Savior appeared, transfigured, before this person. Also, those members of the family who had died before and were transfigured, appeared in luminous form. The Savior looked at the person fully and then vanished. Likewise, the family members also vanished. The deceased remained behind, in sadness and his brightness changed to more or less dark.

In all of the 36 years, Resl had a close relationship to the deceased. They frequently appeared to her in luminous form, but absolutely recognizable. Their bodies were as they will be "beyond." Any disfiguration of this life no longer existed.

Resl throughout and to the end of the war (WWII) cared for the sick in the community, since there was no medical help here. In this work, it happened not infrequently that she promised to help them in the "beyond." Such deceased frequently appeared to her with strong reproaches, mostly in this form: "You promised to help me, why didn't you?" Resl often told me (F.N.) in tears, of such contacts. She commented that she suffers and offers herself for the souls in purgatory but cannot make the decision to whom the suffering is given, only the Savior decides that!

Resl continuously accepted atonement suffering, predominately in the time around All Souls. The whole of Advent was usually filled with very severe atonement sufferings. In this connection, I would like to tell of my last meeting with my sister before her death.

It happened on Thursday, Sept. 13, 1962. I was called on the telephone by my sister Resl for an immediate visit to Konnersreuth. Subject: the site for the new Monastery of Adoration needed to be surveyed. After taking care of the survey, I wanted to leave immediately to fulfill another obligation, but my sister would not let me go. I pushed to leave. At that moment, Resl climbed into the car and took a hold of my jacket sleeve. She gave me encouraging advice regarding my business existence. I stepped on the gas to leave. Then Resl said: "No! By the time you get back it will be too late." And she continued with emphasis....here are the deciding words she spoke to me explicitly, and also for those remaining on this earth:

"FERDL, DO NOT FORGET THOSE WHO HAVE DIED. PRAY FOR THEM, EVERY DAY AND OFFER UP FOR THEM ALL DIFFICULTIES WHICH WILL COME UPON YOU, BECAUSE WE DO FAR TOO LITTLE FOR THE DEAD. AS LONG AS THEY ARE ALIVE, WE CARE FOR THEM AND TRY TO HELP THEM. NOW, WHEN THEY NEED OUR HELP WE HARDLY THINK OF THEM ANY MORE. THEY WAIT FOR AND NEED OUR HELP. THEY CANNOT HELP

THEMSELVES AND AS IS, THEY ARE CLOSER TO US NOW THAN THEY WERE IN THIS LIFE.

(And in a more relaxed tone she continued:)

YOU KNOW, IT IS ALSO NOT SUCH A BAD DEAL. THE HELP WE GIVE THEM WILL BE RETURNED BY THE SAVIOR ONE WAY OR ANOTHER, PLENTIFULLY. THEY DO NOT EXPECT SOMETHING FOR NOTHNG.

(Then at the end - spoken with special emphasis:)

WHAT I HAVE SAID TO YOU DO NOT KEEP TO YOURSELF, BUT TELL IT TO ALL PEOPLE WITH WHOM YOU COME IN CONTACT." (End of tape.)

On Thursday, September eighteenth, Therese Neumann died. The day after the interment, Fr. Naber dictated this account of the last days and hour of Resl to J. Steiner:

On Sept. 13, 1962, she decorated, with greatest dedication, the Mission cross in the Church and the Mater Dolorsa which is placed beneath. On the following day, the feast of the Elevation of the Cross, after a three-hour suffering, she again had the vision which repeated itself annually on this day: She saw how Emperor Heraklius, ornately attired and with a large following, attempted to carry a cross up the mount of Calvary, but was unable to continue beyond the city gate. Only after he followed the advice of Bishop Zacharias to remove crown, jewels and shoes, was he able to continue to carry the cross up to Golgotha and to erect it there before a deeply touched crowd. This, The Triumph of The Cross, was Resl's last vision.

On Saturday morning, the feast of the Seven Sufferings of Mary, while getting dressed, Resl experienced a severe stab of pain of a heart infarct, which soon thereafter lead to her sudden death. Therese suffered the most excruciating pain, so that she had to be sat up in bed and be supported by stacks of pillows. In this position, on Thursday, Sept. 18, in the arms of her sister Marie, who was summoned in the last minute, she died without even being able to say goodbye.

At 10:30 that morning she received Holy Communion for the last time. I think back on this last Communion of Resl: On this Thursday of her death, she had asked me humbly to bring her Holy Communion at noon. But at 10:30, she sent word she wanted to receive Communion now. I brought her Holy Communion forthwith. She was very weak. Then she asked Marie to bring her some water because her mouth was so dry. Since 1927, she did not take even one drop of water with Holy Communion. With this Communion only, did she ask for water. We considered this to be unusual, but neither Marie nor I thought of her dying, since we had seen her so very often in such pitiable conditions. I then put a few drops of water into a spoon and placed the Host on it. This, I brought near her mouth, where it disappeared without a swallowing motion as I approached her mouth with the spoon. Now, it had always been like this, that the bread-form did not dissolve in her until shortly before she received Holy Communion again. She was thus conscious of: "The Savior is with me, in me." This, naturally, filled her with great joy and strength. When I asked her: "What do you live on?" she replied, simply, "On the Savior." So it gave the impression that the Savior wanted to come to her yet again before her death.

I then heard confession of someone and was eventually called to lunch. Then, the bell suddenly rang, from Resl's room. Marie went up right away and in short while she yelled, "Father! Father!" I went up immediately.

But as I came up, it was all over, life had already left. Marie said "This looks just like her dying the passion ecstasy" and for some time we could not accept that it was death indeed. For, five to six hundred times one had witnessed this: Resl in the Friday Passion suffered the agony of death with the Savior, and then simply collapsed and lay there seemingly dead." Marie continued to wait, for she might come back to life, but it did not happen. Thus, Resl died in her arms.

Within hours the news of her death had spread over Germany and much of the world. Telegrams started to arrive from places as far as the United States and even Japan. People began to arrive at Konnersreuth to once more see

Therese Neumann, the stigmatic servant of God. Visibly moved, they came to say goodbye to their friend Resl.

"Laid out on the bier, she looks just like every time after the Passion of our Lord, when she saw the death of Jesus. We saw her so very often in this condition. Now we are all surprised that she should not awaken to life again," said Resl's sister Marie.

The head cloth with the blood spots from the crown of thorns from one of the earlier visions of the Passion was draped around her head. In her hands, which still bore the square stigmatic marks of the nails, she grasped the cross of the dying and her Rosary. Her countenance was that of peaceful sleep. Not a trace of the agony of death. No sign of the great suffering which always plagued her, or any sign of the last suffering, the heart infarct.

Letters and telegrams of condolence from friends and strangers, who wished to say goodbye, increased day by day.

Resl was laid out in the living room of the Neumann house. The bier was decorated with greenery and autumn flowers. Yellow wax candles finished the simple yet graceful decorations. Because of the crowds and lack of air circulation, the small room was warm and stuffy.

Into the late evenings the mourners filed past her bier. Some came with scissors in order to cut off a memorabilia or relique; so the family inserted a large glass panel into the then locked door, thereby affording plenty of vision of Resl and still having security from the overly zealous.

The Diocese of Regensburg, who foresaw the possibility in the future of the moving of the body into the Church, requested that Resl be placed into a tin coffin. To make a tin coffin took time, and therefore the burial was delayed for four days.

The day of interment, in the presence of her sister Marie and her brothers Ferdinand and Hans, three physicians examined her body for the last time. All the stigmata were still there. They were amazed that there were no signs of death. After four days in a warm, stuffy room the body should have had definite odors of decay. Examination of the mouth found it to be slightly moist with a fresh odor.

She appeared youthful and quite beautiful.

Four men from the undertakers service arrived to prepare the body for the burial. They expected the body, which was dead for four days, to be stiff and easy to lift. However, when they lifted Resl's body off the bier to place it in the coffin, it slipped out of their hands and fell. The body was not stiff, but limber, as though it was alive! No rigor-mortis had set in!

The day of the interment, a dark and sometimes rainy Sept. 22, 1962, fell on a Saturday. All roads leading to Konnersreuth were lined with cars. The police wisely kept the interior of the village free of cars so the people could move with greater ease.

An estimate of the number of people who arrived at Konnersreuth was set by the police to be at least seven thousand. The license plates showed the arrival of visitors from all over Europe. The media, radio and TV, arrived from as far as France.

At 10:00 in the morning, a Solemn Requiem Mass, as fitting for a servant of God, was celebrated at the church. The church was filled and the people lined the street all the way to the Neumann house.

When Mass was finished at 11:30 A.M., in drenching rain students from Fockenfeld carried the coffin into the square before the Neumann house for the blessing of the body. After the blessing, the rain suddenly stopped. Now began the procession to the cemetery.

The media had positioned themselves on the cemetery walls, some even on neighboring roofs. At the crypta, which was lined in white tile and decorated with many flowers, the pastor with the support of a choir recited the usual liturgy in Latin. The sun suddenly appeared, and the congregation prayed the "Our Father." A representative of the Third Order of Franciscans, laid a wreath on the crypta of their sister Resl.

The mourners walked past the crypta, and sprinkled Holy Water, as was the custom. The cemetery slowly emptied. Quiet came back to Konnersreuth and the people returned to their everyday lives.

MYSTICAL
PHENOMENA

I f we are to understand and appreciate how great a "mystic" Resl was, we should first inform ourselves of what constitutes a "mystic". What must be present and what are the qualifications of a "mystic"? It is true, mystics are found inside and outside the Catholic Church. Here, however, we are concerned and shall deal only with mystics within the Roman Catholic Church. Jean Gerson defined mysticism as "knowledge of God through experience arrived at through the embrace of unifying love." Would this indicate that we do at times, knowingly or not, experience "Mystical Phenomena." Are we not all called to know and love God? So what elevates a mystic over the ordinary, faithful person? What is the difference between Teresa of Avila, Catherine of Siena and John and Betty Smith who live across the street?

The *New Catholic Encyclopedia* is used as a reference throughout this chapter when describing mystical phenomena.

DEFINITIONS

The *New Catholic Encyclopedia*, Vol. 10, P 171 puts mystical phenomena into two categories:

"(1) those internal and external manifestations that ordinarily proceed from authentic mystical activity of a soul (concomitant mystical phenomena); and (2) the extraordinary graces, charisms, or miracles that sometimes accompany mystical activity but are not essentially related to mystical operations (Charismatic mystical phenomena)."

The *concomitant* mystical phenomena is truly God's work in our souls, His guidance and His leading of souls as He wills. All experience this phenomena, conscious or not, some more than others, depending on the work and gifts of the Holy Spirit. Even though these gifts are supernatural, they are classified as concomitant mystical phenomena. The individual may open himself to the Holy Spirit in his search for God and his desire to be close to God, but the Holy Spirit is the worker, we respond or not, by our own free will.

The *charismatic* mystical phenomena, as well as the concomitant phenomena proceeds from a supernatural cause. However, it is different from the gifts, virtues and sanctifying grace of the Holy Spirit and it need not occur in the normal spiritual growth of the average person. It is a charism, an extraordinary phenomena. Pope Benedict XIV, while still Prospero Lambertini, in his treatise "De Servorum Dei Beatificatione et de Beatorum Canonizatione" said "No phenomenon is to be attributed to a supernatural power until all possible natural or diabolical explanation has been investigated and excluded." Extraordinary phenomena does not pre-suppose sanctity of the individual and is not necessary for the attainment of sanctity. It is principally for the good of the people and not the receiver. Here the discernment of spirits is of greatest importance. It consists less in judging the origin than by the fruits it produces. If it is oriented toward good, then the spirit is good; if toward evil, then the spirit is evil.

It must be remembered that in private revelation the Church will only confirm them as to whether they contain anything contrary to the doctrine of the Church, faith or morals. We are then at liberty to believe or not to believe without committing heresy or sin against faith. To quote Benedict XIV from the same treatise "There is no duty, or even a possibility, of accepting them by an act of Catholic Faith. One can admit them only by an act of human faith according to the rules of prudence which presents them to us as probable."

The normal Christain belief is that this world of time, material, substance, and rational activity is but the barest surface of an unimaginable existence of energy and reality, a reality that is incomprehensible to our human reasoning. There is what Dean Inge describes as "the raw material of all religion, and perhaps of all philosophy and art as well, namely that dim consciousness of the beyond, which is part of our nature as human beings." Into this "beyond" a mystic travels, but only by the gift of the Holy Spirit.

Charismatic phenomena are not wished for and thereby received. If they do come as a result of a wish, the phenomena just may not be from God but from self delusion or evil spirits. God gives as He wishes, not as we wish, for His Glory, not the worldly glory of the receivers.

It is true that some alleged experiences from God are in reality self-deception, hallucination, hysteria etc. However, it would be absurd to suggest that all mystics deceive all the time. Once established that mystics may be right sometimes, that they genuinely experience God sometimes, there is grounds for claiming that they are witness to the ultimate truth, the truth that we can only dimly grope for. The only question is whether the experiences are from God.

To summarize: Charismatic mystical phenomena are primarily (1) for the good of others, (2) not a proof of sanctity of the receiver, (3) not to be desired or sought for. In the case of concomitant phenomena (the works of the Holy Spirit within ones' soul) the phenomena is for the benefit of the receiver and these may be desired and sought for.

However, we, due to our "dim consciousness of the beyond" find the mystic fascinating! So what are these mystical phenomena that completely absorb the mystic to such an extent that the phenomena may be more real to them than life itself? There are many acknowledged phenomena but let us only cover the ones that were evident in Therese Neumann.

MYSTICAL PHENOMENA AND RESL

Visions

"A supernatural vision is a charism (gratia gratis data) through which an individual perceives some object that is naturally invisible to man." Visions are divided into three groups, corporeal, imaginative, and intellectual. *Corporeal* visions which are perceived by the eye may be caused by God, angelic powers, the devil or by natural phenomenon (optical illusion). *Imaginative* visions are in the imagination without the aid of eye sight. It can be during sleep or when awake and often accompanied by ecstasy. They produce great virtue in the soul, cannot be produced or dismissed at will and leave the soul in great peace. In the *intellectual* visions intuitive knowledge is supernaturally produced without the aid of internal or external senses. It may occur at any time. Only God can produce them for only He has access to the intellect. It can be a simple mental intuition of something without any form, words, or image."

In the Old Testament; Moses on Mount Sinai, Jacob and the ladder, Daniel and the many prophets, etc. all had visions. The New Testament is also full of visions; Zachary in the Temple, Mary at the Annunciation, Joseph in his dream, etc. Since then many people and of course Saints have been privileged with visions sent by God. To name only a few; St. Teresa of Avila, one of the greatest mystics in the Church; St. John of the Cross - friend of St. Teresa of Avila and Priest and Doctor of the Church; St. Catherine of Siena; St. Gertrude, a Benedictine nun who wrote down her visions of our Savior in a book called *Revelations* or *The Herald of Divine Love;* St. Francis of Assisi; St. Margaret Mary Alacoque, and so many others through the centuries. Some of the more recent visionaries were St. Bernadette, the children of Fatima, Anna Catherine Emmerich, Maria Valtorta and Sister Faustina.

Resl's visions began in 1926 and continued until her death on Sept. 18, 1962. Her visions followed the liturgical calendar, the entire New Testament and the early Church. She saw Jesus' glorious entry into Heaven; Mary's life, death, assumption into Glory; the lives and events of saints; heaven, and purgatory. Her visions of Creation, the angels and all events in the Bible, Resl heard spoken in Hebrew. Everything pertaining to Jesus and His life, she heard spoken in the old Aramaic language. However, Peter's speech to the devout people in Jerusalem on Pentecost, Resl heard in German. The lives and events of the saints were in the language of the saint, e.g. St. Therese of Lisieux - French, St. Anthony of Padua - Portugese. Though she knew only her own Bavarian dialect, she comprehended the meaning, but not the abstract language. On All Saints Day 1934, she saw Dr. Fritz Gerlich enter into the glory of

heaven with the martyrs. She also witnessed the entrance of Pope
Pius XI into heaven and the election of Pius XII in Rome, March
2, 1939. But by far the most heartrending visions were the "Passion of our Lord." In these amazing visions, Resl is present, as an
on-looker in the crowd and follows along through all the scenes of
the Passion. At the same time, she was quite unaware that her
body was going through the same torture and crucifixion that she
was witnessing happening to Our Lord.

Stigmata

"These phenomena are the spontaneous appearance of wounds
and bleeding which resemble the wounds of Christ. Sometimes
the entire body is covered with wounds, as if from a scourging, or
the head is punctured as if by thorns. These wounds usually appear
during ecstasy and the wounds do not become inflamed or infected.
Stigmatization could be produced by natural causes (autosuggestion, hypnosis, fraud), by the devil or by supernatural power."

In determining whether the stigmata are of demonical or divine origin, Catholic theology, provides the following test. The one
on whom the stigmata is bestowed by God will reflect Him. The
receiver will live in complete submission to His will and to the
spiritual authority of the Church. The receiver will be constantly
drawn closer and closer to God, and has a deep love of God with
an almost fanatical desire to please Him, and humbly submits, with
resignation to His Will. The demonical will try to make men of-
fend and resist God, the spiritual authority of the Church and become proud.

It is suggested by some that St. Paul was the first stigmatist. "I
bear the marks of the Lord Jesus in my body" (Gal 6.17). However
this doesn't necessarily indicate stigmata, visible or invisible. It could
well mean the markings of the suffering for Christ, not the crucifixion. St. Francis of Assisi received the stigmata while in ecstasy
two years before his death on Oct. 3, 1226. Other stigmatists include: St. Lutgarde, 1182-1246, a Cistercian mystic; St. Gertrude
the Great, 1256-1303, the Benedictine mystic; St Catherine of
Siena, 1347-1380, Dominican mystic, (declared in 1970 by Paul
VI as Doctor of the Church) is said to have had invisible stigmata;
St Catherine of Genoa, 1447-1510, mystic who wrote "Treatise

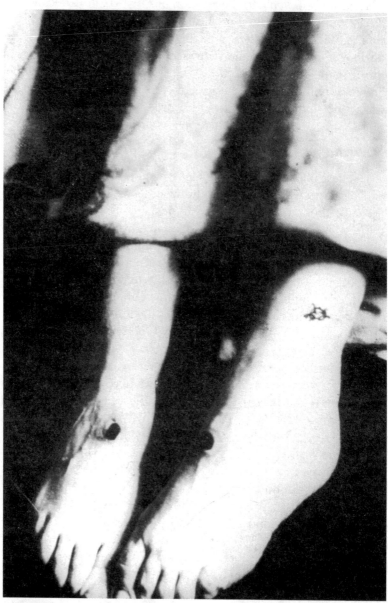

This page and facing page; Resl's stigmata.
(Medical pictures by Dr. Seidl, photographer
Hoelzl) 1927.

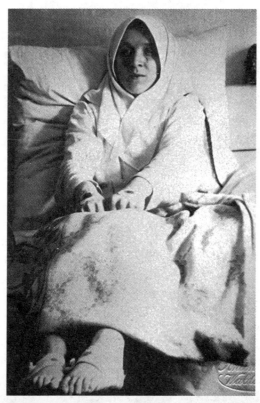

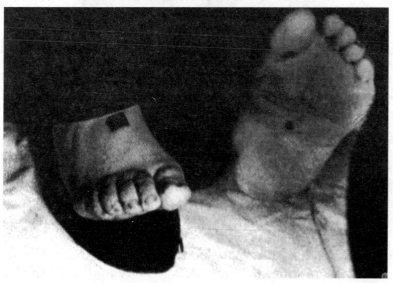

on Purgatory" and "Spiritual Dialogue"; St John of the Cross, 1542-1591, Discalced Carmelite, mystical theologian, priest and Doctor of the Church; St Catherine of Ricci, 1522-1590, Dominican mystic, a most interesting saint, experienced the Passion every Thursday evening until Friday 4:00PM for 12 years, worked for Church reform; St Teresa of Avila, of the Discalced Carmelites, Doctor of the Church, invisible stigmata. More recently, Anna Catherine Emmerick, 1774-1824, Augustinian nun and mystic; Louise Lateau, 1850-1883, Belgian mystic; St. Gemma Galgani, 1878-1903, Italian mystic; Padre Pio, May 25, 1887 - Sept. 23, 1968, Italian Capuchin mystic, bore the stigmata from Sept 20, 1918 until his death 50 years later, when they disappeared.

Resl received the stigmata in 1926. She took them into her grave. The stigma were on her hands, feet, side, her head from the crown of thorns, plus bleeding from her eyes. The stigmata from the scourging and the shoulder stigmata from the carrying of the cross, were visible only during Lent and Good Friday. An amazing observation of the bleeding during the crucifixion scene is that the blood flowed as it did on Calvary, down her body and her feet, even though Resel was laying down. The blood flowed against gravity.

Her stigmata are an admonition to a society which has rejected God; that He had been on earth and had suffered for our salvation out of love for us. This suffering is not something in the past but is still here, now, in the present.

Locutions

"These are interior illuminations by means of words or statements, sometimes accompanied by a vision and seeming to proceed from the object represented." Locutions fall into three categories, corporeal (auricular), imaginative, and intellectual. Auricular or corporeal locutions are generally caused by a supernatural acoustical vibration which is heard by the ear. It may come from a vision or an object such as a crucifix, cross, or statue. It can be caused by God, natural causes or by the devil. Imaginative locutions are words perceived awake or asleep. These locutions may be caused again by God, natural causes or the devil and therefore the outcome must be discerned as to their source. "Locutions of supernatural origin cannot be produced at will; they are distinct, causing fervor, peace, humility, and obedience." Intellectual locutions are words or statements perceived by the intellect without the aid of the sense of hearing or the imagination. They are directly infused upon the intellect. The devil can produce sounds that the individual can hear or imagine but he cannot enter the intellect, therefore he cannot produce truly intellectual locutions.

The definition of the mystical phenomena of locution is so broad that it opens many avenues. Perhaps of all the mystical phenomena, locutions must be most scrutinized. Locutions should not be accepted without much reflection and counsel. One can easily be deceived. The discernment of its effects on the individual and the contexts must be thoroughly subjected to study.

In the Bible many examples of locutions appear. God asked Cain "Where is your brother Abel?" God told Noah how to build the ark, and made His covenant with him. He called to Abraham to offer his son as a holocaust. And so on. In the New Testament John the Baptist heard a voice from heaven saying "This is my beloved Son. My favor rests with him." (Matthew 3:17) Paul on the road to Damascus heard a voice saying "Saul, Saul, why do you persecute me?" (Acts:9-4). Later, mystics and the saints experienced locutions. St. Teresa of Avila carried on conversations with the voice of the Lord.

Resl began to experience the mystical phenomena of locutions when she first heard St. Therese of Lisieux's voice on May 17, 1925. It was the date of St Theresa's canonization. From then on she often heard her voice, giving instructions or encouragement. After the appearance of the stigmata, locutions and visions were a daily occurrence.

Revelations

"These are manifestations of hidden truths that are not normally accessible to man. Truly mystical revelation is usually accompanied by the gift of prophecy and its interpretation requires the gift of "discernment of Spirits." Revelations may be; *absolute* (simple statement of a truth or mystery); *conditioned* (usually a threat or promise based on some condition); or *denunciatory* (a condemnation or threat of punishment). "They may proceed from a natural, diabolic or supernatural source. In its interpretation, the individual may distort the meaning."

According to St. Thomas of Aquinas, the purpose of private revelation or prophesy is not to prove the truth of Christian doctrine or add anything to it but to offer men of a certain time, because of the circumstances of that time, a direction for human action. They are not, like the public revelations of the Bible and the Apostolic Tradition, intended for all men at all times. Fatima would fall into private and conditional revelation for though it was for all people, it was for a specific time in the history of man and the admonishment was based on the spiritual condition of society.

The prophets of the Bible, Isaiah, Jeremiah, Daniel and all the other prophets in the eighteen prophetic books were ecstatic persons. Their revelations and prophecies, preserved in the Sacred Scripture, focused on: Monotheism, the One God with whom Israel lived in a sort of sacred partnership or covenant; Morality and its relation to religion, be good and you are rewarded, be evil and you shall be punished; God restoring "His Kingdom" after man has destroyed it through sin; the "Messiah," His life, suffering, His "New Covenant" and His reign in the "New Kingdom of God."

The New Testament is full of Jesus's prophecies for the future of man, to the end of time. The book of Revelations is just that, a book with prophecies only.

Toward the end of 1959, Padre Pio sent a message, through Alberto Galletti who lived in Milan, to the Archbishop of Milan, Cardinal Montini, that he would be the next pope and added "Do you understand what you are to say? Tell him so, because he must get ready." In 1963 Cardinal Montini became Pope Paul VI. Resl had told Rev. Michael Rackl that one day he would become Bishop of Eichstatt and to Rev. Dr. Rudolf Graeber he would be Bishop of Regensburg. And so it was.

Reading of Hearts

"The knowledge of secret thoughts of others or of their internal state without communication is known as reading of hearts. The certain knowledge of secret thoughts of others is truly supernatural, since the devil has no access to the spiritual faculties of men and no human being can know the mind of another unless it is in some way communicated."

Jesus, of course, is the prime example of Reading of Hearts. All through the four gospels there are many examples of this wonderful phenomena.

St. John Vianney, 1786-1859, confessor, mystic, patron Saint of Priests, also known as Cure d' Ars, who on certain days heard confessions for up to 16 hours, was known to be able to bring to the memories of the penitents events which they had forgotten. He also had the knowledge of future events. He became renowned as a preacher, confessor, and director of souls and thousands flocked to Ars year after year. The most recent known example of Reading of Hearts is Padre Pio. It is he who would scold the penitent if he wasn't sincere, repentant or not confessing as he should. He too, would remind the penitent of past, forgotten misdeeds.

With Resl it wasn't only the sins of a person but the spiritual state of the consecrated religious. Fallen away priests were special candidates for her rebuke when they visited her in Konnersreuth. Fr. Naber speaks of one, posing as an artist, who came to Resl and had to listen to a barrage of his transgressions. "It almost toppled him over!" Dr. Hynek, a physician and convert, tells in his book, "A well-dressed man, posing as a physician, asked to examine the hands of Resl. Suddenly she put her hand on his shoulder and said "Oh! Reverend Sir, what have you done?" He turned pale, fiery red, and left the room. Later it was found that he was an apostate priest.

In an address given (Feb. 12, 1928) by the Right Reverend Joseph Schrembs, Bishop of Cleveland, Ohio, the Arch-bishop relates the following amazing incident which occurred when he and his Chancellor, Msgr. McFadden, visited Resl in December 1927. It was a Friday morning after Mass, and Father Naber (the pastor), Resl's father and mother, a soldier at the door, the Bishop and his Chancellor were in Resl's room during her Friday sufferings.

The Bishop stated, "Resl suddenly spoke to her mother. 'Mother, dear, you know that man who is sitting next to you (that was myself), he comes from this country. He used to live round about here, but now he lives in the far distant land across the big water, and oh, oh, he works so hard, he spends himself without any care or thought to his health. He works so much for Our Lord; (and for my consolation she added.), and Our Lord loves him very much. And you know, Mother, I have something to say to him but I can only say it to him all alone. You must all leave the room' .

"So everybody started to leave the room. Father McFadden was sitting near. Of course, he had the disadvantage of not understanding what was going on, except when I would interpret it. He rose and turned to go towards the door, when the girl (Resl) spoke to me and said, 'Oh, no. That other man that is sitting next to you, he can stay. It won't matter. He won't understand anything anyway.'

"So Father McFadden came back and he became the only witness to that strange conversation that took place between that girl (Resl) and myself. For three quarters of an hour that girl (Resl) reached into the innermost depths of my soul. She told me things that remained locked in my breast but I cannot forget to my dying day. She spoke even of conditions of my Diocese. She delineated certain things to me concerning the persons with whom I daily work. She described some persons so minutely that I could place my fingers on them and know exactly whom she was talking about. Father McFadden was the only witness to it. He saw the effect it had on me, as I knelt more than once in tears."

Tears of Blood and Bloody Sweat (Hermatidiosis)

"The effusion of blood from the eyes, as in weeping or from pores of the skin, as in perspiring, could be caused by supernatural powers, the devil, or it could be the effect of some physical or psychic pathology."

"And being in agony, He was praying very fervently; and His sweat became like drops of blood, falling down upon the ground." (Luke 22.44) Our Savior in the Garden of Gethsemane on the Mount of Olives, in His anguish sweat blood. St. Gemma Galgani, 1878-1903 mystic and stigmatist, experienced the phenomena of Hematidiosis (bloody sweat).

It was in November of 1924 that Resel first experienced some pus and blood coming from her eyes. She had a bad cold which affected her ears. This effusion did not impair her eye sight. When the suffering of the Passion started in 1926 her eyes bled profusely.

From then on, her eyes along with the stigmata of the nails, the scourging, the crown of thorns, the shoulder wound from the weight of the cross and the lance wound over her heart, bled every time Resl went through the Passion of Our Savior.

Hierognosis

"The ability to recognize a person or object as holy or blessed and to distinguish what is genuinely so from what is not."

While in the state of exalted repose or prepossession (states which occurred after the passion suffering, esctasies or after receiving communion) Resl had the ability of discernment of people and relics. She was able to say whether the relic was genuine or not, whether it was a 1st class relic (a part of the body of a saint) or a 2nd class relic (a piece of saint's clothing or something that was touched by a 1st class relic). She was especially moved by the presence or the touch of the particles of "the True Cross". When a Benedictine monk brought two of his relics, she affirmed one to be a particle of the True Cross which was under the Redeemer's feet. The second relic was of a holy Pope and martyr. (Though she did not give the name, it had the name "Linus" on it. Linus was St. Peter's successor.) She recognized the relics of St. Clare, St. Odilia, St. Cecilia, St. Stephen the first martyr, St. Lawrence, St. Elizabeth, and many others. When presented with a relic of St. Nicholas von der Flue, the Swiss mystic, she said "Oh My! That was a good man, for he loved the Savior much, and do you know that he ate nothing, just as I? But he had it much better than I, for he was in the woods and the 'lighted-man' (her designation for an Angel) brought him our Lord."

The following incident was told to the author by Gerda Rossmann. When Gerda, and her husband Rudolph Rossmann brought a relic to Resl, which they believed was a Cross particle, she became quite excited and said "Yes, it is, but there is more! There are fibers from Mother Mary's veil on it!"

As to a relic of Father Liberatus Weiss, a Franciscan, born in Konnersreuth, who went to Abyssinia, now Ethiopia, and was martyred by stoning in 1716, she asked for prayers for his speedy beatification. "This Saint went to heaven without going to purgatory."

When traveling through towns she would be aware of where the Blessed Sacrament was; church, chapel, or private residence... and where it had been in the past but was no longer held.

Bilocation

"An extraordinary mystical phenomenon in which the material body seems to be simultaneously present in two distinct places at the same time. Since it is physically impossible that a physical body completely surrounded by its place be present in another place at the same time, this could not occur even in a miracle. Therefore, bilocation is always an apparent or seeming bilocation. When bilocation occurs, the true and physical body is present in one place and is only apparently present in the other by means of a representation of some kind."

The following saints have traditionally been said to have had bilocation phenomena: St. Clement I, Pope (99-102), martyr, 3rd successor to St. Peter; St. Francis of Assisi, confessor, died 1226, founder of the Franciscan order; St Anthony of Padua, confessor and doctor, 1196-1231; St. Francis Xavier, confessor and great missionary in the Far East, 1506-1552, one of the founders of the Society of Jesus (Jesuits); St Joseph Cupertino, confessor, 1603-1663, Franciscan mystic; St. Martin de Porres, confessor and mystic, 1579-1639, Dominican brother at Lima, Peru, (friend of St. Rose of Lima); St. Alphonus Mary de Liguori, Bishop, confessor, doctor, Patron of Theologians, 1696-1787, founder of the congregation of the Most Holy Redeemer (Redemptorists); St. John Bosco; St. Teresa of Avila; and St. Catherin of Ricci, 1522-1589. It is said that St. Martin de Porres had been seen in five places at the same time. His reply was, "If Christ multiplied the loaves of bread and the fish, then why cannot he multiply me?"

With Resl, there are many known incidences of bilocation. It was soon realized that she would be present at Mass at her local church while actually being at home in bed! She would repeat the homily and even name children who were not behaving during Mass. Father Ingbert Naab, the Capuchin monk whom she later helped escape from the Nazis, related an incident which occurred when he was celebrating Mass and giving a homily during a retreat for young people at the Palatinate. Resl was at the rear of the church for 3/4 hour. There she was in her usual attire while at the same time she was at the home of Dr. Wutz in Eichstatt.

A priest from the Diocese of Campinas in South America was startled when he visited Resl in Konnersreuth for he recognized her as being the person who had spoken to him previously in South America.

The wife of a chauffeur in Zwiefalten, whose husband was to have his foot amputated, wrote to Resl for help. Two nights later Resl, in her usual attire, appeared before the chauffeur and his wife. She touched the sleeping man's foot, prayed and vanished! When the doctor examined the foot later, he found it completely healed. The wife told him what had happened. The doctor withdrew from the case for he did not want his colleagues and certain scientists to know that he had been an accessory to the miracle.

These are only a few of many cases involving Resl and bilocation.

Levitation

"The suspension of a material body in the air without visible support, in apparent opposition to the law of gravity. There seems to be little doubt concerning the fact of levitation, but it has not been scientifically proven that this type of bodily suspension surpasses the psycho physical powers of nature. Levitation of human bodies or of inanimate objects has been reported in the lives of the saints, in cases of diabolical intervention, and in spiritualistic seances. Levitation is not admitted as one of the miracles required for the canonization of a saint, though it may be considered a testimony of a person's heroic sanctity."

At times St. Teresa of Avila would levitate at Communion. She would try to hold herself down by grasping the Communion rail so as not to attract attention of others present. Other saints who experienced this phenomenon are St. Dominic, St. Frances Xavier, St. Catherine of Siena, St. Martin de Porres, St. John Bosco, St. Gemma Galgani, to name just a few. Also, Louise Lateau of Belgium and the most recent mystic Padre Pio.

Maria Benedikta von Spiegel, Abbess of the Abby of St. Walburg at Eichstaett (also a member of the Konnersreuth Circle,) told of witnessing Resl levitating at least 1/2 meter above the ground during a vision. The priests of the Monastary of Tirschenreuth also reported seeing Resl levitate during a vision.

Inedia

"This is an absolute and total abstinence from all nourishment beyond the limits of nature. Some investigators are not convinced that inedia is necessarily miraculour." It is believed, that 60 days of fasting is the limit without food. In the case of Fakirs, who can fast for longer periods, and who fall into a deathlike sleep, if not awakened in time they do end up in death.

There were quite a number of people who did not eat or drink but existed only on Holy Communion. It usually occurred over a period of time. First, solid food was no longer possible to consume, then any form of liquid. Louise Lateau, 1850-1883, was unable to eat solids from the spring of 1871. By 1876 she only existed only on Holy Communion. St. Nicholas von der Flue, a Swiss, lived 20 years without food, except for Communion. At one time a 24 hour guard was placed before his hut "the ranft," to determine whether he was a fraud. For over three weeks they observed no food or water what-so-ever. Some of the others who were sustained only on Holy Communion are: St. Catherine of Siena, St. Lidwina of Schiedan, Blessed Angela of Foligno, and in the last century, Venerable Anna Catherine Emmerick and St. Gemma Galgani, who died in 1903.

Next to her stigmata, Resl's inedia created the most interest. The first time she was unable to retain any solid food was for 12 days in December of 1922. Dr. Seidl of Waldsassen, her physician, attributed this to a "paralysis of her swallowing muscles." Then, a few weeks before Easter 1925, she no longer could take any solids or any form of liquid, only daily Communion. Under the direction of the Bishop of Regensburg, Resl underwent a 15 day observation, which was considered a sufficiently long period to establish her inedia beyond a doubt. The specialists, together with Dr. Seidl, were of the opinion that a fast of two weeks without food could be possible, but 15 days without any form of nourishment and liquid was impossible. Four Mallersdorfer Sisters, under oath, stayed with her day and night. They bathed her with a sponge and even mea-

Left: 1925, during
her 15 day observation with
Sr. Registuudis (one of the
four observing Mallersdorfer
sisters) and Fr. Naber in the
background

L.P.

F.N.

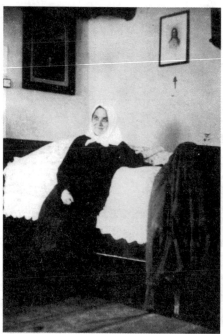

F.N.

In the "Taylor's" room, on the parental bed.

F.N.

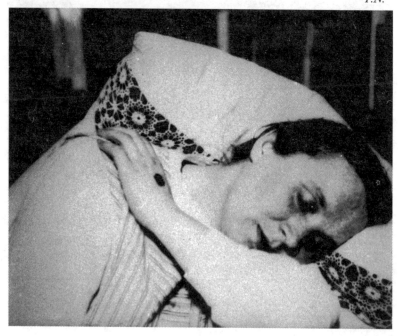

sured before and after all water used for mouth wash. Periodic weighing, pulse and temperature were taken. She was not allowed even confession. She should have lost considerable weight, and during the Friday ecstasy she did loose 3 to 8 lb., but gained it back as quickly as she had lost it. At the end of the observation, Resl was the same weight as at the beginning of the 15 days.

Dr. Fritz Gerlich, in his writings about Resl quotes Dr. Professor Ewald of Erlangen, one of the participators of the observation, and an opponent of any supernatural explanation of this phenomena: "Throughout the observation period there was the greatest and most intense attention given that the instructions regarding bathing, mouth water etc., were strictly observed. Despite the strictest watchfulness, it could not once be observed that Therese Neumann, who was not alone for one second, took any food or water or tried in any way to take anything. The bed of the observed was not only examined with the utmost carefulness at the beginning of the observation, but it was made each day, not by a relative, but by the Sisters. Neither the physician, Dr. Seidl, nor the Sisters were of the opinions that any mistake in their observations could have been committed in regard to the taking of nourishment or water."

Dr. Deutsch, an avowed Nazi, was not satisfied and demanded another observation of four weeks. This observation would have to be away from Resl's natural surroundings with other sisters (nurses) and not under the direction of Dr. Seidl, who as a Catholic man refused to deny the possibility of a supernatural explanation.

Dr. Hoehn, writing in the "Straight Way" said "Since Dr. Deutsch demands a period of four weeks for a new observation of the stigmatized, a further word would be in order here about the length of the 15 day observation by the Sisters." After consulting experts, the Ordinary of Regensburg agreed. Celebrated physicians with a philosophy of life entirely different from Dr. Seidl examined the records made by the Sisters very critically, and published the following conclusion; "The Sisters' daily record, according to Dr. Ewald, was kept conscientiously, exactly, without prejudice, and with sound judgment." It was determined that neither food nor water were ever taken by Resl during her observation. On the whole, most doctors accepted the findings, only a handful (mostly Nazis) were against. Resl's inedia continued for the rest of her life.

Behind the altar, vision during Holy Mass. At
the stigmata at her left hand a light ray
appeared.

F.N.

Mystical Aureoles and Illumination

"Resplendent light may emanate from the body of an individual, especially during ecstacy or contemplation. It is considered an anticipation of the radiant splendor of a glorified body."

In Exodus 34:29-35, Moses came down from Mt. Sinai with the second set of tablets "the skin of his face had become radiant," (New American Bible - St. Josephs Edition,) "the skin of his face shone," (King James Version.)

The Transfiguration of Jesus - Mathew 17:2 "His face became as dazzling as the sun, his clothes as radiant as light" (New American Bible), "His face did shine as the sun, and his raiment was white as the light." (King James Version.)

One morning after Mass, Resl fell into ecstacy and stood up with her arms fully outstreached toward the ceiling. Suddenly, the stigmata on her hands were filled with light, almost like a lighted bulb. A picture was taken of this phenomena and is included in this book.

Blood Prodigees, Bodily Incorruptibility and Absence of Rigor Mortis

"These phenomena are well attested to in the line of the saints. Many cases could possibly have a natural explanation or be caused by diabolical powers. Some are accepted as true mystical phenomena and testimonies from God concerning the holiness of an individual."

The day after the death of St. Teresa of Jesus, the evening of Oct 4, 1582 in Alba, Spain, her body was put in a coffin and buried. Afraid that her body may be stolen, they piled many rocks, bricks etc. on top of her grave. Her coffin soon gave way to the weight of the rubble and a wonderful fragrance issued from St. Teresa of Jesus's tomb. Secretly, nine months later, the rocks and etc., were removed and her body was observed to be as fresh and whole as on the day she was buried. In November 1585, three years after her death, her body was exhumed and again found to be incorrupt. It was secretly taken to Avila, to the great joy of Avila and the anger and sorrow of the people of Alba. However, St. Teresa's body later took a secret journey back to Alba and never returned to Avila again.

Two others, whose bodies are still incorrupt are St. Elizabeth, Queen of Portugal who died in 1336, and St. Mary Magdalen dei Pazz who died 1607.

After Resl's death on Tues., Sept. 18, 1962, her body was under continual medical observation until her burial on Saturday, Sept. 22. The last examination found the following: no death odor or spots, no rigor mortis, her lips and mouth were fresh and moist.

Resl's
Spirit

Throughout the history of mankind, God has used his people to fulfill special roles in His revelation of Himself to all His people. The larger roles, e.g. Moses, were always for the benefit of all God's people and for all times; the smaller roles were for smaller groups, specific times or for only the individual. God is continually revealing Himself to his people. The working of the Holy Spirit continues incessantly. We are not orphans. So, how was Resl's life a revelation of God, to God's people in her time?

Compelled to do "God's Will"

During the many years of illness Resl's spiritual life developed to such a high state that she became totally focused on the Savior. Her pains, discomforts, desires, etc., were no longer of importance to her. She had overcome her concern for herself and became completely submissive to His Love and His Will. Her desire was only to love, serve and obey her Savior. No sacrifice was too great. If it would please the Lord, she would have gladly remained for ever, a bedridden invalid. Her willingness to suffer with the Savior was the absolute submission of her will to God. This submission became a power and strength within her, and "God's Will" became her only purpose in life.

This power and strength may be witnessed in the prophets and saints. They possessed an unbelievable drive or energy to do just that…"God's Will," to the point, as with Resl, of it becoming an obsession. Moses, wandered in the wilderness, not knowing where he was going or why, only that a greater power moved him to do so. After the expulsion of the Israelites from Egypt, he led them for 40 years, a people he barely knew, led them to the ever evasive "Promised Land of Milk and Honey." How about Noah; building a huge boat, miles from water and incurring the ridicule of the people for his obedience to God's Will. I have often wondered why more credit has not been given to Mrs. Noah. Can you imagine a woman of our present times of the feminist movement going along with the lunatic antics of her husband whom everyone called insane? What about Noah's sons and their wives? Times have truly changed! Noah, in these days, would be committed by his family to "Happy Acres"! This same driving force was experienced by Elijah, Isaiah, and again in Christ's time by John the Baptist, plus many, many, more.

When Therese of Lisieux asked Resl twice if she would like to be healed and have her sight restored; twice she answered that only "God's Will," and what is of God would make her happy. It is hard indeed for us to fully comprehend the total commitment of this young woman, having spent years blind, bedridden, and in pain, to not have jumped at the chance of recovery.

After the appearance of the stigmata, Dr. Seidl put an ointment on the wounds in an attempt to heal them. The wound began to give her great pain so she removed the applications to get relief. When Father Naber saw what she had done he insisted she have them reapplied. Since Father Naber was her Father confessor, she obediently reapplied them. It was not until ten hours later, after viewing the escalating agony the medication was inflicting on Resl that Father Naber agreed to their removal.

HER DEVOTION TO THE BLESSED SACRAMENT

The Real Presence of our Savior in the Holy Eucharist was a fact to Resl. He was her life's purpose, love and strength. She truly lived for, by and in Him. He was her life.

This total awareness occurred for the first time at her First Holy Communion on April 18, 1909. The pastor, who had given

Resl receiving Holy Communion, administered by Fr. Naber. (mid fifties)   *F.N.*

Vision, not identified.   *F.N.*

the children their instructions gave Resl an F for her inattentiveness during the Mass. She just did not pay attention and follow the Mass as the other children did. Later Fr. Naber asked the child Resl, why did she behave so? She answered that she could not pay attention to the Mass but only to her Savior. She did not realize that only she and not the other children saw the Savior. It is not known whether this seeing of her Savior also occurred between her First Communion and the time of her receiving the stigmata.

After her stigmatization, Resl was always aware of the presence of the Savior in the Holy Eucharist in her. It was a continual awareness extending from one Communion to the next. If the Mass was late, or if the Holy Eucharist was not brought to her at the appointed time, she would truly get weak and had a burning desire to receive the Host. At times she would almost become aggressive.

Without the Holy Eucharist, Resl could not have lived. It was her strength and sole nourishment. Resl (Palm Sunday 1930) said to Father Helmut Fahsel of Berlin, "The Savior sustains me. He said 'My body is food indeed,' so why shouldn't it be actually true for once, if He Wills it?"

People who witnessed her receiving the Holy Eucharist were awed at her humility and devotion. Never did she receive it in a casual manner, but only with great reverence and excitement.

Normally Resl received the Eucharist as we all do. However, on Saturdays after the Passion suffering, on special feast days, or after expiatory sufferings, as she received the Host she saw the Savior in the Transfigured state. During these Ecstatic Communions, the Host immediately disappeared as soon as it touched her tongue, even before she could close her mouth. There was also no swallowing motion of her throat and jaws. Her brother Ferdinand had taken movies of this beautiful phenomena which are still in existence, and which I had the grace of viewing.

RESL, THE VICTIM-SOUL

"Through your suffering you can best exercise your devotional convictions and call as Victim-Soul. Follow your Father Confessor in blind obedience and entrust to him everything. Always remain childlike and simple;" were the words of Therese of Lisieux to Resl.

"Everything the Good Lord wants is fine with me." was Resl's repeated answer. We are all called to a life in Christ, called to suffer and thereby become "Christ-like" or "Christians" or small-scale co-redeemers. We are called to sanctity, some as victim-souls.

The life of a victim-soul is a life of complete, voluntary subjugation to the will of our Lord out of love for Him. The victim-soul's life is a constant giving of oneself and of being incessantly on fire with love, a life consisting of adoration, expiation, and continuous prayer. They live with the one thought of consoling the Lord. Our Savior is consoled by love and by the redeeming of souls. He is consoled by love especially where love has been enkindled in hearts that have grown cold. Souls are redeemed by sacrifice. Expiation requires great courage, great generosity, great love and great faith. Just as our Savior was a Willing-Victim for the redemption of mankind, so are the victim-souls who offer themselves as a holocaust for the redemption of their brethren. "There is no greater love than this, to lay down one's life for one's friend." (John 15:13)

The victim-soul knows that every time they expiate for a specific sin, it is one less suffering for our Savior. Resl said "We ought to pray for everyone, especially for those who ask for our help or tell us their troubles. I am not forced to suffer. If I wished, I could say 'I will not suffer', and it is surely true that nobody likes to undergo pain. But when I know that it pleases the Savior, then I am ready. Then I say 'Savior, let the pain come!' And often He lets me know for whom I suffer and how it ends."

These expiations lasted from a few hours to three or four days. Once it lasted for eight years.

She suffered physically, when she offered to suffer that someone may be physically cured. Her suffering was spiritual when she suffered for someone of spiritual illness. It was both physical and spiritual when she suffered for someone with an afflicted soul as well as body. She suffered the identical physical or spiritual ailments as the person suffered.

A young seminarian's priesthood was threatened because of a throat disease. Resl asked the Savior to allow her to take his suffering so that he would be able to continue his studies. The seminarian was instantly cured and Resl acquired the throat disease. While in a state of exalted repose, which followed Passion sufferings, she was told that she would suffer the throat pain until the seminarian had celebrated his first Mass.

Her expiatory sufferings extended to groups as well as individuals, to people who afflicted pain on her, to all souls and people in general in this life who suffered illnesses, temptations, or were far from God. She most frequently expiated for souls in purgatory and especially for priests, both living and deceased.

While suffering the Passion, if a person who had grievously sinned, or if an unbeliever entered the room, she would immediately suffer for them. This person instantly felt something happening within him, something happening to his soul.

People wrote letters to her pleading for advice or her prayers. She would very frequently take on their sufferings and the letter writer would feel the lifting of their problems.

One day, Father Naber was summoned to her room by her family. There was Resl, acting in a very foreign manner to her, and reeking of alcohol. It was soon learned that in a neighboring village a man was suddenly cured of his alcoholism.

The following is a list of Victim-Soul Sufferings, from the diary of Fr. Joseph Naber, over the time span from 3-18-28 to 3-3-29:

Victim-Soul Sufferings of Therese Neumann

DATE	FOR WHOM	TYPE OF SUFFERING
3-20/21-1928	not stated	great pain at shoulder wound and joint rheumatism
3-23-1928	someone who was here today and would not accept Jesus' shoulder wound	excruciating pain at shoulder wound
3-27/28-1928	not stated	previously foretold pneumonia, shoulder pain, and joint rheumatism

3-30-1928	Fr. Stiglbauer, released today from purgatory through Resl's suffering	suffocation attacks
4-3/4/5-1928	not stated	great pain, weakness and joint rheumatism
4-15-1928	for the conversion of a priest	suffering not told, continued through six days
4-29-1928	not stated	serious inflammation of a shinbone
5-2/3-1928	for a deacon	suffering not told
5-20/25/26-1928	for the convert and the deacon who is at end of despair	kind of suffering not told
6-3 to 9-1928	a protestant scissors sharpener	kind of suffering not told
6-10 to 16-1928	not stated	kind of suffering not told, every night
6-17/18-1928	one in total despair, who was here last Thursday and Friday	kind of suffering not told
6-27-1928	for a young man near death as the result of a car accident	kind of suffering not told
6-29-1928	for the same young man	agonies of death
7-6-1928	for a diocesan priest	severe suffering

7-14-1928	for a former communist	kind of suffering not told
7-20-1928	for the soul of an old priest who has been in purgatory for over 100 years and is now in utmost desolation, who's release from purgatory and assumption into heaven is seen by Resl	kind of suffering not told
7-26-1928	for a deathly ill lady convert	kind of suffering not told
8-10/24-1928	for an alcoholic priest, who fell back again and in despair took poison	severe blood poisoning from an insect sting
9-14-1928	not stated	excruciating pain of the stigmata
10-7/13-28	not stated	"as usual, atonement sufferings"
11-9-1928	for the redemption of a soul from purgatory; also for activities in Vienna	kind of suffering not told
9-30-1928	an officer who is near despair	kind not told, suffering for the entire week
Advent 1928	not stated	continuous sufferings, not told as to kind
1-1-1929	not stated	suffering ceased during Christmas but started again Jan. 1. Kind not told.

1-6-1929	for a man from Bruenn	suffering for entire week, kind not told
1-27-1929	for a priest who engaged in an immoral relationship with two women teachers	kind of suffering not told
3-3-1929	a man in the Rhine country, a non-believer, deathly ill of stomach and intestinal diseases	stomach and intestinal cramps

For the time span of 54 weeks, as recorded by Father Naber, Resl suffered as a victim-soul for 94 days and nights, slightly more than a quarter of the time. Since she continued to do so for her entire stigmatic life of 36 years, her victim-soul sufferings added up to 3530 days, or nearly 10 continuous years. These are the sufferings recorded, they do not include her Friday Passion sufferings or unrecorded ones.

At the end of August 1962, within days of her death, Resl, in the company of Father Naber and her brother Ferdinand, was for a week a guest of the industrialist Goetz at Ravensburg. The purpose of this visit was the funding of the Theresianum. For three days, Cardinal Bea from Rome and the Bishop of Laira (Fatima) were also guests. The Cardinal had just received the directive to be the principal organizer of the forthcoming Vatican Council II. He spoke with Resl about his concerns, the impact of the Council on the Church, on its theology and about Church history. As Resl was leaving he begged her for her prayers for the success of the Council. She promised Cardinal Bea that he will have her prayers and if God willed it to be so, she was prepared to give her life.

For the following two weeks Resl's life had an urgent quality about it, as though the clock was ready to strike. She was eager to complete all that she could so she would not leave anything undone. By September 18, only 18 days after leaving Ravensburg, Resl was dead.

Soon after her death, Father Naber received a letter from Cardinal Bea in which he told of his last conversation with Resl in Ravensburg, where she stated her willingness to offer her life as a sacrifice for the success of the forthcoming Vatican Council.

One would deduce that God took her up on her offer! Perhaps this willingness to die for the Church was truly the submission of a martyr!

RESL AND THE POLITICAL POWERS OF HER TIME

The political powers, the governments of countries of the Western world, are said to base their laws on the Ten Commandments. This is particularly the case of England and since the United States based their laws on the English system, we, too must have the Ten Commandments as our foundation. However, upon close examination, this is not so anymore. The Sabbath is a far cry from being "Holy" and the commandment "Thou shall not kill" has been overthrown by Roe vs. Wade. To lie is only wrong if you get caught!

Let us now briefly examine the political attitude toward Resl as written by Dr. Fritz Gerlich in his writings *Die Stigmatisierte Therese Neumann von Konnersreuth*. He tells us that by the summer of 1927, only 1 1/2 years after the appearance of the stigmata, public discussion and debate over Resl had reached a high pitch. It was demanded by several parties, that the Bavarian State Government, (1) in the name of reason and science would take action against the stigmatist; (2) the stigmatist be interned in a neutral clinic where she would be observed and investigated as seen fit; (3) close her away from public life because the visits to Konnersreuth are leading to the stupefaction of the people. The Communists threatened with force if the state would not submit to the desires of these political entities. Dr. Gerlich continues that everyone being party to these demands could not have cared in the least as to how the laws of the country would protect a harmless female citizen who had done no harm to anyone and requested no one to visit or look at her. At this time Dr. Gerlich was the Chief Editor of a major

German newspaper *Muenchener Neusten Nachrichten* and in that capacity felt that he must familiarize himself with this young woman who had so stirred the country. He soon became one of Resl's staunchest supporters and defenders.

It was during this time that the "Konnersreuth Circle" (so called by its enemies) was formed. (See Chapter 1 - D.) Resl herself was not on the fighting end of this organization. She was its spiritual center and offered advice, encouragement and many times gave directives to individuals. She was its heart.

Resl and the Konnersreuth Circle were very much aware of the evil within their country. The atrocities of the Nazis weren't realized by most of the people. Those who heard rumors could not believe them to be true. Surely not! Not in our beloved Germany! Some knew the truth but did nothing or were afraid. A few put their lives and the lives of their loved on the line to make the horrors known and to help the victims of the Nazi persecution. One of these was Resl, also the Neumann family, friends and members of the Konnersreuth Circle.

One typical example of her continuous involvement in the "Circle" was her sending an urgent message to Erwein Freiherr von Aretin soon after Hitler was in power. "Destroy immediately, - whatever dangerous papers you might have in your home. They are going to search your house." A few days later the Gestapo did search his house but found nothing. Aretin had twice been in the Dachau concentration camp. No one considered how Resl knew of such things. She just did. Past experiences showed that such directives from her were not to be questioned.

RESL'S
CONTEMPORARIES

I s there a pattern in God's revelation through the mystics? Was there, and is there, a reason why they appeared and received these gifts, graces, and phenomena at their particular time in the history of mankind? Before comparing the three mystics, Venerable Anna Catharina Emmerick, Maria Valtorta and Padre Pio to Resl, let us quickly review a few mystics of the past whose tremendous influence on the Church was felt during their lives and continues in the Church to the present day.

Saint Francis of Assisi, 1171-1226, the famous and most beloved mystic, stigmatist and founder of the Franciscan Order, lived during the Crusades, the rise of bourgeoisie town life and the anticlericalism of the cities. St. Francis in Italy, as did St. Dominic in Spain, preached; the beauty of humbleness; poverty; devotion; simplicity in life; and the brotherhood of man, man and animal, of man and all creation. His impact on society in his days and ever since has been most profound.

Saint Catherine of Siena, 1347 - 1380, a Dominican Tertiary, declared a "Doctor of the Church" by Paul VI in 1970, was a mystic who experienced invisible stigmata which became visible upon her death. She was asked by the many cities of Italy who were in league against the Papacy, Pope Gregory XI and his French legates who were at Avignon, to become an arbitrator in their dispute. For peace, she agreed, but without immediate success. However, she did manage to convince Gregory XI to return to Rome. After the death of Gregory XI and the installation of Urban VI in 1378, the Church became divided and a second pope was installed. Catherine, who's health was deteriorating, offered herself as a victim for the Church. Soon, at the age of only 33, she died in Siena.

The great Saint Teresa of Avila, 1515-1582, suffered the presence and the persecution of the Inquisition. Saint John of the Cross, 1542-1591, not only had the Inquisition on his neck but was imprisoned by his fellow "Carmelites" for 9 months. Both Teresa and John of the Cross had branched off from their Mother homes, and formed a group, Discalced Carmelites, and returned to the original rules of the Hermits of Mt. Carmel in the Holy Land. This reform was not at all appreciated by the Carmelites for they found the new group an affront to their way of comfortable living in their monasteries.

During this time in Church history lived Saint Catherine of Ricci, 1522-1590, a Dominican and a most interesting saint. She was a great mystic who experienced the Passion every week for 12 years. The Church and the general political situation in Europe was full of intrigue, and many of the Popes were outright ruthless. The beginning of the Reformation in 1517, the ban of Luther in 1521, the Borgia Family with their ambitious control of both state and Church; the Borgia and Medici Popes; the terrible Sacking of Rome in 1527; the Universal Inquisition, (established in Rome 1542) all made for much upheaval. During Catherine's life, there were eleven true Popes. The Council of Trent opened in 1545. Pope Paul IV 1555-1559 was one of the chief and vigorous inspirers of the Counter-Reform. Pope Saint Pius V, 1566-1572, a very devout and ascetic priest, anathematized Queen Elizabeth I (1570). In all this turbulence, Catherine was deeply involved in Church reform.

As did the above five examples, Venerable Anna Catharina Emmerick, Maria Vallorta and Padre Pio, mystics closer to and during our and Resl's time, again offered people a direction and example of human behavior and action.

VENERABLE ANNA CATHARINA EMMERICK

Venerable Anna Catharina Emmerick's similarity to Resl is quite startling! She was born in 1774 to poor farmers in Westfalia, Germany. For a number of years she worked on a farm followed by being a servant girl and then a seamstress. In 1802, at the age of 28 she entered the Augustinian convent in Duelmen near Muenster.

This was the terrible period in the history of Europe of the Napoleonic Wars. In 1811, Joseph Bonaparte, Napoleon Bonaparte's eldest brother, suppressed all religious communities in Western Germany, confiscating their properties, forcing the communities to disperse and find refuge wherever they could. This was called "The Age of Enlightenment" and was the beginning of secularization in Europe, especially in Germany.

Shortly before Anna Catharina Emmerick took her vows, she received the stigma of the "Crown of Thorns." A few months after the convent closed, the stigmata of the hands, feet and side appeared, plus a cross on her breast. She had been given refuge by some people in town where she remained bedridden until her death.

Slowly, she too, lost the ability to eat solid food and could not drink except for a few drops of water. Because of the pain from the "Crown of Thorns" she rarely slept.

During her lifetime, many writers, (mostly from Germany) wrote, under the appearance of intelligent and scientific objectivity, treatises which tried to pass Jesus off as a minor historical person if not actually a fabrication by calculating people who then formed his Church. These writers denied the existence of the supernatural and denied the Bible as being God's revelation. The Frenchman, Voltaire, wrote his *Bible at Last Explained* at this time.

In this atmosphere, Anna Catharina Emmerick, mystic, stigmatist, and victim-soul, presented to the world her visions of the life of Jesus, of Mary, events in the Old Testament, the creation, and the beginning of the Church.

Clemens Brentano, a noted and popular writer of her day, realizing the importance of her vision, dedicated the rest of his life to the writing of these visions. It was an almost daily process until her death. Then, for the remainder of his life (18 yrs.), he sorted out the information he had collected and put them in a chronological order. Part of this information is in the work *Life of Christ* which has recently been reissued.

Anna Catharina Emmerick underwent two long and extensive investigations of her stigmata and related phenomena. One was conducted by an antagonsitic civil commission, which tried unsuccessfully to heal her wounds.

From the time of the appearance of the total stigmata, in 1811, and due to her being bedridden, Anna Catharina Emmerick lived in semi-seclusion (13 years), until her death at age 50.

As with Resl, her stigmata, visions and sufferings as a voluntary victim-soul, brought to light the historic reality of the Incarnation and the Redemption.

MARIA VALTORTA

The mystic Maria Valtorta, was born one year before Resl, March 14, 1897, and died one year before Resl, October 12, 1961. She was a visionary and victim-soul, but not a stigmatist.

Her father, Joseph Valtorta, a non-commissioned officer of the Italian 19th Calvary, was a loving, gentle father. Her mother, Iside Fioravanze, a French teacher, was quite his opposite. She was calculating and outright despotic; Maria suffered much from her. Her mother's scheming destroyed Maria's relationships with two young men whom Maria loved.

Early in 1920, a young juvenile struck Maria on her back with an iron bar. As the years went by, her suffering from this injury increased to such a degree that by January 1933, she could no longer walk out of her home. By April 1, 1934, at the age of 37, Maria was permanently confined to her bed. In that year, she suffered yet another blow, the death of her beloved father.

Her spiritual director requested that she write her autobiography. In the same year 1943, after completing her autobiography and under a supernatural calling, she began to put on paper the visions she was having. She received "dictations" from Jesus, Mary, her guardian angel and a inner voice. This inner voice was also her prompter. When she wrote something that was not as "dictated," she was immediately corrected by the inner voice. She wrote intensely from 1943 to 1947, after which her writing slowly decreased, and ended in 1953. She wrote through the dark war days in Italy. Some of the "dictations" from Jesus and Mary touched on World War II, and also on the future and end times. The "dictations" filled almost 15,000 notebook pages. Less than two-thirds are in the monumental work *The Poem of the Man-God,* which begins at the conception of Mary, Her life, the entire life of Jesus, Mary's assumption and ends with beginning of the Church. Also included are numerous "dictations" by Jesus and Mary; comments about their lives; Jesus' teaching; comments relating to our times; and further explanation of the happenings Maria Valtorta saw in her visions. The "dictations" from her guardian angel were commentaries on the Sunday Masses of the liturgical year.

Maria Valtorta belonged to the Third Order of the Servants of Mary and also to the Third Order of St. Francis.

From approximately 1956, when her writing was coming to an end, she started slowly retreating mentally from the world. And as though it were her last act of obedience, when the priest at her deathbed said "Depart, O Christian soul, from this world," Maria Valtorta breathed her last breath. At the age of 65, after 28 years of illness, on October 12, 1961 at 10:35 A.M. she went home to her beloved "Jesus." "I have finished suffering, but I will go on loving." is her epitaph.

As with Resl, Maria Valtorta suffered not only the physical pains of her infirmity, but also the unbelief and ridicule of many people. She would weep and tell Our Lord of the suffering inflicted on her by their cruel remarks.

Both Maria Valtorta and Anna Catharina Emmerick lived in semi-seclusion. Resl on the other hand was in daily contact with people and even traveled extensively in European countries.

Though Resl and Maria Valtorta lived at the same time, they had not met or even heard of each other. That is, except for one incident found in Volume 1, page 262 of the German translation of *The Poem of the Man-God.* The following is the text translated into English:

Quote: Jesus speaks to me: "What you have written on January 30, might give cause for the distrustful to offer their 'Yes, but!' I will respond for you, therefore.

"You wrote: 'When I begin to look and see, my physical strength and in particular that of my heart, dissipate.' There are then the great "scholars of the supernatural" who will say: 'Here is the very proof that the phenomenon can be explained as natural occurrences which lends the phenomena strength, yet never weakens it!'

"I would like to have them explain to me why the great mystics upon termination of the vision in ecstasy, during which the limits of humaness were being surpassed and thus the pain has been removed, and in spite of internal injuries, experience bliss and remain in a condition which shows a separation of soul from the body. They should, furthermore, explain to me why these mystics, only a few hours following the most terrifying agonies, which are but a repeat of my agonies, such as in the case with my servant Therese (Therese Neumann) and my sainted Gemma (Gemma Galgani), and also with many other souls, who through My love and their love were made deserving to live through my passion, who regained their strength and physical balance or have received it to the extent not even the most healthy human possesses."

PADRE PIO

P adre Pio, the great Italian mystic, stigmatist and confessor, was born in the small Italian village of Pietrelcina near Benevento on May 25, 1887, and given the name Francesco. His parents, Orazio Forgione and Maria Giuseppa De Nunzio, were poor farmers and had eight children of which only five lived. His father, Orazio, twice went to America to work as a laborer so that Francesco could be educated for the priesthood. At the early age of 7, Francesco's abhorrence of sin was so great that he could detect its presence in people. Early in life, he entered a school run by Capuchin Friars. The Superior remarked that "This child observes the rule better than we do!" He became a good negotiator and mediator at the school. In 1902, at the age of 15, he entered the Capuchin Monastery of Morcone near Benevento to begin his novitiate. Because of ill health, Fra Pio was sent to S. Elia in Panisi. Even though he stayed there four years, his health did not improve. He was plagued with frequent fever and nausea but continued to observe the rule of the community.

He was tormented by the dark powers and the vicious attacks of evil spirits. Another confessor of the Church who experienced such attacks was St. John Vianney (Cure d'Ars). Fra Pio's health continued to deteriorate and he was diagnosed as having tuberculosis. Even so, he was ordained a priest on Aug. 10, 1910 at the age of 23, and stationed in Foggia. When his health did not improve he was sent home for a rest.

It was at home in Pietrelcina, on Sept. 20, 1915, the Feast of the Stigmata of St. Francis of Assisi that the first signs were given, showing his future role as a victim-soul. He told his mother "I have stinging pains in my hands."

With the infamous assassination at Sarajevo, Italy entered the First World War. Padre Pio was called into the military. Again, because of ill health he was sent home. Eventually his Capuchin Superior transferred him to San Giovanni Rotondo.

Sept. 20, 1918, two days after the Feast of the Stigmata of St. Francis of Assisi, after hearing a piercing cry, the monk Padre Leone, found Padre Pio unconscious on the floor of the choir, bleeding profusely from his hands, feet and side. Padre Pio had received the "Stigmata," the wound of our Lord and Savior. He was the first known priest to receive the visible stigmata, for St. Francis of Assisi was not a priest but a brother.

From Sept. 30. 1918, his stigmata never closed, always bled, never became infected, caused constant pain, made it impossible to close his hands, and walking was most painful. He suffered constantly, day and night, from this phenomena. It is believed that his tuberculosis was healed at the time he received the stigmata.

For the next few years, as with Resl, it was a constant procession of people, inquiry, investigations, tests, attempts at healing the wounds, pictures and continually being subjected to the curiosity of the general public and scientific community.

From 1924, due to the almost hysterical crowds, Padre Pio was silenced. His superiors forbade him to preach and/or write letters. From now on, he could only celebrate Mass and hear confessions.

When the scientific investigations became a great hardship, his Capuchin Superior put a stop to them. In this way the Capuchin Order was able to protect Padre Pio and see that he received the peace necessary for him to perform his duties. Resl only had her parents and family to protect her. The authorities demanding investigations and proof would not give up insisting and pestering her and her family. They wanted to know how the phenomena occurred. The answer that it was of God and not answerable in our ways was never sufficient for them. That it was miraculous was not an acceptable answer.

Ernest Renan in 1863, *Life of Jesus* said "No miracle has ever taken place under conditions which science can accept." So it was, and is, with Resl, Padre Pio, Anna Catharina Emmerick and all stigmatists and mystics.

Padre Pio was most famous as a confessor. His common sense and practical attitude to life gave him the approach necessary when dealing with the thousands of penitents. As did Resl, Padre Pio had the simple and descriptive vocabulary of a farmer, expressive, down to earth and to the point. Both were direct and very frank.

Several mystical phenomena were experienced by Padre Pio. He was very familiar with his guardian angel who would at times instruct him and interpret foreign languages for him.

Food intake was between 300-400 calories of food per day and an occasional beer in the evenings. He slept 3-4 hours at night and rose at 3:30 a.m. There were so many who wished to go to confession to him that people had to register their names and sometimes it took many days before they could make their confession.

By the time of his death on 10/12/1968, at the age of 81, Padre Pio had received many famous visitors; religious and secular. The most famous was the then Cardinal Karol Wojtyla, now Pope John Paul II.

CONCLUSION

So what have all these mystics in common? Is there a pattern? Was it that they lived in times of political upheaval? Or was it that their times were of spiritual and moral conflict and the demoralization of society and Church?

History shows that the political and the spiritual (the Church) were basically one and the same during the lives of St. Francis, St. Catherine of Sienna, Saints Teresa of Avila and John of the Cross, and St. Catherine of Ricci. Moral decay was within and without the Church.

In the time of Anna Catharina Emmerick, the secularization of religious communities, (especially in Germany) was brought about by political powers, and this secularization in turn had devastating consequences on the Catholic Church. It is to be remembered that this was the beginning of the "Age of Enlightenment" movement, a movement begun by the "intellectuals" of that period.

The three mystic examples of this 20th century, Padre Pio, Maria Valtorta, and Resl, lived through two World Wars, and through the budding fruits of the "Age of Enlightenment." Now, the political powers directly attacked the spiritual (Church), however, in a most insidious manner. On the whole, the Church fights back only seldom. Here I must give exception to our present Pope John Paul II. His courageous and almost single handed defense of the Church and its teaching is positively inspiring! Many a Protestant has remarked to me how wonderful it is to hear him call the issues by their real name. What a tragedy that some clergy and Bishops of our beautiful Church have become so blinded that they can no longer even fulfill their vow of "obedience" to the Pope.

Could it be that the majority do not even recognize this confrontation which is directed at our Church? Has the enemy done such a tremendous job that we Catholics cannot see how we have been duped? Catholics in general, which includes the clergy, apparently do not understand and therefore cannot recognize the nature of the enemy. Heydrich, head of the Gestapo said "The only real enemy we have is the Catholic Church."

God sends his messengers and his mystics when the Church and mankind are about to enter a period of great peril. This period is inevitably brought about by the demoralization of society, followed by political upheaval. An excellent example is Fatima and its message of warning to the world.

But you can of course say, "O.K.!! Yes! A messenger, as in the three children at Fatima, but don't give me all this about mystics. That's only for old women and dreamy children! We all know better now. We don't live in the middle ages any more." How can anyone call himself a Christian, let alone a Catholic Christian, if there is no room in their belief for the mystical?

Our Lord's life was full of the mystical. Jesus came to teach us God's Ways and showed us how to live our lives. He repeatedly instructed and showed the apostles and His followers that our lives must be filled with love and with love comes suffering. Jesus, the infinite lover, was ridiculed, called a blasphemer, scourged; He the King of Kings was crowned by this world with thorns, and then suffered the most horrifying death of crucifixion.

To bring His people back to Himself, we are repeatedly shown through His mystics, how to live with a consuming love for God, and in this love accept the suffering which life brings. Over the centuries, by their sufferings, His mystics show to our unbelieving hearts how much our Savior suffered and how to love God and thereby all His creation. When we, like sheep, go astray, the lives of the mystics remind us what life is about and show us the road to be traveled.

When the world threw away the centuries of monastic and Church culture during secularization, the visions of Anna Catharina Emmerick, her life as a stigmatist and victim-soul, was a reminder to societies that Our Savior really did live and suffer for everyone of us and that we were shying away from the teachings of our Savior. Society's concept of "enlightenment" meant to do away with what it considered to be the primitive idea of God. This was, perhaps, the embryo of the "God is Dead" age.

The stigmatists Resl, Padre Pio, and Anna Catharina Emmerick brought to the world a most vivid picture of our Savior's Redemptive Act. The re-living of His passion is a reminder of the great price paid for our salvation.

The visions of Resl, Anna Catharina Emmerick and Maria Valtorta expanded on and brought to all the world a freshly detailed and extended picture of the life of Jesus, Mary and the early Church. Anna Catharina Emmerick's visions were "dictated" and transcribed by Brentano. Maria Valtorta wrote her own visions which were dictated by Jesus, Mary, her guardian angel and the inner voice. Resl told her visions to Father Naber and her brother Ferdinand Neumann, who when possible recorded these visions. These recordings are still in existence.

Padre Pio, by the example of his suffering and role of confessor, presented to us that through love, suffering and repentance one receives "Mercy" and "Redemption" from God.

All four mystics, in their own individual way, were the instruments of the Lord. They were all very human, each with their own character and personal anxieties. They learned early how to love

God, with their whole heart, their whole strength and with their whole being. Because of their love of God they:

1) Were completely obedient to His will.
2) Accepted their suffereings.
3) They were all victim-souls.
4) They all suffered the disbelief of the people, especially the "intellectuals." Resl, to this day is viciously attacked. (Mainly by Fr. Hanauer - Chapter 6).

These four lived their lives truly heroically! We too, are asked to be heroic, however the little way of the Little Flower - Therese of Lisieux, though her life was anything but easy, is the example most of us are able to follow. The four, Resl, Padre Pio, Maria Valtorta, and Anna Catharina Emmerick, were the giants and that life is reserved for only a few chosen souls.

Mystical Phenomena of Resl, Padre Pio, Maria Valtorta, and Anna Catharina Emmerick
(To the best knowledge of the author)

	Resl	Padre Pio	Valtorta	Emmerick
Stigmata	*	*		*
Visions	*	*	*	*
Locutions	*		*	*
Revelations	*	*		
Reading of Hearts	*	*		
Tears and Sweat of Blood	*			
Hierognosis	*			
Bilocation	*	*		
Levitation	*	*		
Inedia	*			*
	Eucharist only			Eucharist and Water
Mystical Aureoles and Illumination	*		Her right hand after death	
Absence of Rigormortis	*			
Gift of Tongues	*	*		
	In Visions			

Other Significant Comparisons

	Resl	Padre Pio	Valtorta	Emmerick
Remarkable Conversions	*	*		
Miraculous Cures	*	*		
Method of Delivering Visions	Her voice was recorded, then transcribed by Ferdinand Neumann	None recorded or written	Written by seer as dictated by Jesus, Mary, her guardian angel, an inner voice	Written by Brentano as told by seer
Religious Order	3rd order Franciscan	Capuchin	3rd order Servants of Mary 3rd order Franciscan	Augustin Nun
Voluntary Victim-Soul	*	*	*	*

RESL'S
ADVERSARIES

T he adversaries of God's graces and miracles would appear to be directly proportional to the greatness of the miracles. The ultimate of God's miracles, the presence of His Son on earth, was met with ultimate adversity and continues to our present time.

God's graces and charity, as manifested in His servant Therese Neumann, one of the greatest mystics of all time, was also confronted with bitter hostility from the outset; lock her up; no, not good enough, the firing squad; discredit her; defame her; threaten her; slander her, her family and her spiritual advisor. A small army has come to the fore to do the job; many men of the cloth and an assortment of medical experts. The chorus was completed by political factions in Germany.

Three major defamatory works appeared on the market, two by priests and one by a woman. The earliest is by Hilda Graef, about 1950/51 in Ireland and then in the US. This was followed shortly by Fr. Siwek, S.J. and more recently by Fr. Hanauer, a diocesan priest of the Diocese of Regensburg.

Each one borrowed from the other. Each one copied the other's falsehoods, deceptions, and preposterous theories. Above all, each one exhibits the same deep hatred and hostility toward Resl.

All this, 34 years after Resl's death would not matter if it were more or less forgotten. But it isn't. The fact remains, that the Neumann Press published Graef's story, the Bruce Publishing Co. of Milwaukee that of Siwek, and a German publisher, Hanauer's writings.

But most regrettable of all, the *American Catholic Encyclopedia* contains a totally distorted, largely untrue thumb nail account about Resl, penned by Siwek. The effect of this over the last 30 to 40 years has been one of rejection of God's miracles through His servant Therese Neumann by the Roman Catholic Church in America. It is inexcusable for the editorial board of the *American Catholic Encyclopedia* to offer such a preposterous falsification, especially in the face of absolutely overwhelming data for and on behalf of Theresa Neumann. Maybe this book will be a challenge to correct this grievous error. As to Hilda Graef, the *American Catholic Encyclopedia* offers her derogatory and largely false recital of Anna Catharina Emmerick, whose cause of beatification has since been opened.

It is therefore necessary, to aquaint the reader with the substance and personalities of the three principal adversaries; Graef, Siwek, and Hanauer.

HILDA (HILTGUNDE) GRAEF: "THE CASE OF THERESE NEUMANN"

Hilda Graef was born (1907 or 1908) and educated in Berlin, Germany. She received the standard German liberal arts education, including Latin and Greek. She states in her autobiography that in 1933 she did vote for Hitler. Although not threatened by the Nazis, she immigrated to England in 1936 since she had Hebrew blood in her ancestry. Her concern was over whether or not she would, under the circumstances, be employable in Germany. At some time after her move to England, she officially became an Anglican and studied theology.

At about that time, while in front of an Anglican Monstrance, she was overcome by emotion and made a vow of chastity until death with the caveat of not knowing how she could keep this vow.

In 1941 or 42, she converted to Catholicism. Somewhere in 1943, 44 or 45, she undertook what she called "the Carmelite Experiment." She formally entered the Carmelite order at Nottinghill Carmels. She describes her three weeks as a novice as utter shock, meeting unreasonableness at every turn, personal cleanliness was shunned, receiving a lecture on the virtues of sweeping floors to which she responded with her stunning counter lecture. She found the preparation, counting and packaging of eucharistic hosts as being utterly degrading. When she dropped an inkpot on the white wooden floor she was aghast over the notion that she should ask for permission to clean it up with her wash cloth. At the task of cleaning her own cell, she resorted to ridicule, cattishness and swearing. This attitude was further amplified in consideration over the Prioress' chicken. Everyone talked to her in baby language. Bad tasting herring finally made her leave to return to "the wicked world, and I loved it."

Her "Carmelite Experiment" may be found in its entirety in her autobiography *From Fashions to the Father, the Story of My Life,* Neumann Press, 1957.

Due to the continued indefiniteness of times and places in her writing, dates can only be approximated. However, in 1946 she did obtain a British citizenship and had taken a secretarial job with a publishing firm.

Probably around 1947, Graef was approached by Mercier Publishing in Ireland to write a book, in a positive but also objective format, about Resl. Hilda Graef delighted at this due to the anticipated handsome returns.

To inform herself about this Bavarian peasant woman, she purchased Archbishop Teodorowicz's *Mystical Phenomena in the Life of Therese Neumann.* Upon reading this book she decided that there was something "fishy" about Therese Neumann. To complete her analysis, she undertook to travel to Konnersreuth.

Of this visit she gave a full account in her original manuscript. The publisher, however, objected to its inclusion due to its lack of objectiveness and also its offensiveness. It can therefore only be found as an inference in her book. The account of the visit was however published in the American periodical *The Josephainum Review,* G-1-51 under the title "Personal Impressions of Therese Neumann" by Hilda Graef. She did elect to publish, in her autobiography, the entire incident, including the otherwise omitted act of her shameful intrusion into the church at Konnersreuth, with the sole intent of exposing Resl's so called "fraud."

Here is a summary of her description of her visit to Konnersreuth, 1947 or 1948. She devoted 15 pages to getting there, and only 2 pages at Konnersreuth itself.

People were awful everywhere, especially the G.Is. At Regensburg she found a nun of kindred spirit who told her no one around here believes in Resl. Upon arriving at Konnersreuth, she went to the "Presbytery" and pounded repeatedly on the door, as well as rang the bell, until a woman appeared to rudely tell her not to make so much noise. She had to wait 45 minutes for Father Naber who then gave her a canned talk on Resl. On the way out she met a stout woman with red blotches on her hands (Resl). Hilda Graef says she "was not impressed." She then went into the church, and with no one around, climbed over the altar rail (this was pre-Vatican II), went behind the altar, ripped away a curtain and exposed "the whole contraption," an electrically heated cushioned chair for Resl, while the arthritic old women, whom she examined at morning Mass, had to use the wooden pews.

Next day she foiled some GIs and snuck up on Resl to test her with a "poser." The question was: "People who were trying to lead a contemplative life in the world were often exposed to criticism. What should these do, give themselves to prayer, or sacrifice their inclination for the sake of activities?" According to Hilda Graef, Resl promptly fell into her trap, hook, line and sinker, by giving her the answer: "Work by day and pray by night." With that "poser," Hilda Graef left, having learned all she needed. Her sum-total time spent with Resl was less than 10 minutes.

Everything then went against her; Resl's revenge, as Hilda Graef put it!

In the preface of her book *The Case of Therese Neumann* she gives several references, almost none of which visited or spent any time with Resl. She does quote Dr. Gerlich, only to discredit him for not having an imprimatur. (Since his two volumes are about his observations and findings of Resl and not a religious work about the faith and morals, no imprimatur was needed.) She claims of not having had access to Father L. Witt's book *Konnersreuth im Lichte der Religion and Wissenschaft,* (1930), one of the most conscientious witnesses and chroniclers of Resl. She writes that he too did not receive an imprimatur. (An instant's examination of his book will reveal that the Vice-General of Regensburg states that an imprimatur was not needed since so much had already been written on Resl to that date.)

Hilda Graef has three principal witnesses to support her opinion of Resl. Two were avowed antagonists and the third she continually quotes out of context, so that the opposite is presented in her book. The three are as follows:

Dr. Waldmann, who would have loved to write a similar book on Resl as Hilda Graef, but his Bishop was opposed to it. His position was absurd, overbearing, dishonest, and based on the most questionable "Nazi" doctors like Dr. Deutsch. In the light of all objective reports and new data, some of which only as late as 1995 has come to light, he can in no way be taken seriously.

Dr. Bolesas de Poray-Madeyski (a Polish army physician) is passed off by Hilda Graef as the medical expert from the Sacred Congregation of Rites. A check with Rome in 1951 revealed, that they had never heard of him. It is Poray-Madeyski's medical diagnosis of hysteria which is one of Hilda Graef's most cherished tools with which to dismember Resl.

Archbishop Teodorowicz (author of *Mystical Phenomena in the Life of Therese Neumann*) is her principal source of the happenings at Konnersreuth. Hilda Graef, throughout the pages of her book, has quoted Teodorowicz, almost without exception, out of context, has in fact produced a montage of his writings which make him say the opposite of what he intended.

The following is only one example of Hilda Graef's misinterpretation and misuse of her sources. She had proposed, as an argument against any sign of sanctity or tendency toward holiness in Resl, that Resl did not go through any form of "purgation," which she said would be needed to precede the existence of sanctity or holiness. In the first chapter of this book, I have quoted a translated passage from Archbishop Teodorowicz's book *The Mystical Phenomena* (p. 112-113), which completely refutes her accusation. One of the most descriptive and pitiful examples of "purgation" given to us comes from "Job." He had lost all his temporal possessions and became covered with horrible sores. Resl, too, lost all that she valued; her health, strength, her ambition to become an African missionary; she too received suppurating sores with their foul odors, plus many more diseases. What more would Hilda Graef want God to inflict on His servants?

Minor Hilda Graef witnesses, like Doctors Killermann and

Martini and the like, were all enemies of Resl. Hilda Graef most studiously bypasses the many real chroniclers. She also lacks the scientific background to be creditable.

In consideration of her past, her caustic character, her Carmelite Experiment, her choice of exclusively hostile and antagonistic references and witnesses, she was totally unsuited to produce an objective account of Resl. Her book smacks of both academic and German superiority from the introduction to the conclusion ".....we have formally examined......"

Hilda Graef's tactic of discreditation of Resl is two-pronged. Prong one states that Resl was basically evil, untruthful, rude, impatient, uncharitable, conceited and deceitful. Therefore, her stigmata were false, her visions incredible, her inedia untrue, and her vision - bleeding a hoax. Ergo - Resl deserves oblivion. Prong two states that she was hysteric, diagnosed so by her personal physician and many other learned experts. Her hysteria therefore, accounts for all her mystic phenomena. According to the experts of Hilda Graef, hysterics can generate stigmata on themselves at will, can live without food and water any length of time, can produce sudden illnesses and wounds and equally rapid healing, all of which applies to Resl. The trouble with this is that Hilda Graef has not made a decision which it shall be - therefore overkill is best.

With the penetrating mind of her superior intellect, Hilda Graef had determined Resl's evilness in totality during her 10 minute visit with her at Konnersreuth. To conclude scientifically from this briefest of visits that all else is false, is so preposterous as to be an insult to the reader.

Next, the "diagnosis" of hysteria by Dr. Seidl, is the central pillar of Hilda Graef's theories. To obtain a disability pension, he diagnosed Resl's condition as the result of hysteria, (Resl's fire accident had left her disabled). Dr. Seidl later, under oath (1929) said and we quote: "The phenomena of Konnersreuth are medically inexplicable. They must be considered as a whole." In an interview in August 1931 he stated, "Had I then known Therese Neumann as I knew her afterwards — I would not have committed this stupidity. But how was I to foresee the importance which would be attached to a certificate whose only objective was to carry out an administrative condition. At that time I lacked the personal observations which would have allowed me to make a real diagnosis. In the circumstances hysteria seemed plausible. The subsequent use of the certificate is unjustified, after the proof that Therese Neumann was certainly not hysterical and her cures, at least the principal as well as later phenomena, cannot be explained scientifically or naturally." Unquote. Hilda Graef's other experts had either never seen Resl or did not conduct professional examinations.

Prong two is typical of Hilda Graef - her entire treatise is based on spurious witnesses, concocted conclusions, and downright dishonesties. Above all, she is a person totally hostile to Resl.

Shortly after her book issued in Ireland, the Rev. Dr. Alfred O'Rahilly, President of Cork University, took her to task. It is beyond the scope of my book to deal in detail with his precise and conscientious rebukes. In 27 full page installments in the Irish newspaper "The Sunday Press" 1958, Dr. O'Rahilly states the case of Resl in admirable clarity and objectivity, totally exonerating her.

So much for Fraeulein Graef.

PAUL SIWEK, SJ: "THE RIDDLE OF KONNERSREUTH"

"Therese Neumann -
New Catholic Encyclopedia, V 10 P 365-366"

S iwek's *The Riddle of Konnersreuth* begins with a conscious act of reader intimidation. On the very first page, he lists 24 of his books, written in 6 languages.

This is followed by a second act, surely intentional, of deception, if not outright fraud. The issue is an initial letter of Archbishop Carinci, dated Rome, April 8, 1952. The letter is essentially an effusive endorsement of a book titled *Une Stigmatisee de Nos Jours,* by Siwek, but not of the book in which it appears. The author later explains the discrepancy in most unconvincing words. The fact remains that the unsuspecting reader takes Archbishop Carinci's letter to apply to *The Riddle of Konnersreuth.* The second, and perhaps more disconcerting matter is that Archbishop Carinci was at that time the Secretary of the Sacred Congregation of Rites, and signed the letter in that capacity. The unsuspecting reader, again, cannot but conclude that, with the endorsement of Siwek's book, it's contents, it's conclusions, and all it's references and witnesses, Rome has, in fact, ruled on the case of Therese Neumann. Nothing could be further from the truth. Nonetheless, the triple whammy, as an opener, gives notice to the knowledgeable reader that Siwek is entirely capable of intentional deception and intellectual intimidation, and has here practiced this art unabashedly.

Siwek's use of sources is remarkable. In all cases of comparison, Siwek's portrayal and source used distorts history, often to the point of unrecognizability. And always, to Resl's discredit. To illuminate where Siwek hails from, most revealing is his statement "Among the publications on Therese Neumann which have appeared in English, that of Hilda Graef certainly is the best." I.e., Siwek has bought all of the incredibility's of Graef.

Among some of Siwek's own discoveries, he claims that Resl owned a rather large house at Eichstatt. Absolute fantasy! Next, he purported that Archbishop Schrembs of Cleveland, Ohio, a most ardent supporter of Resl, renounced her (some 8 years after their meeting in Konnersreuth) in the presence of diocesan priests, (this libel was published in Germany). As the Archbishop had died earlier, this was most sharply denied by diocesan officials, and was, without the slightest question, untrue. Archbishop Schrembs, in his letters, referred to Resl as a "living crucifix in a scoffing world." So why did Siwek pull that one?

Siwek, copying Graef, also bought the concept of menstrual blood, "surpressed menstrual blood" and added the term "complimentary menstruation." Dr. Waldmann's crew, Doctors Killerman and Martini, were to have obtained a blood sample and established it was menstrual blood! To make things work for Siwek and Graef, the females of the family must have, with further contributions from women in the village, mastered the clinical mechanics of collecting up to 3 quarts of menstrual blood per week, and possessed a hidden refrigerator for storage. Then no less than 760 times Resl was "prepared," in Hollywood fashion, by smearing the unclotted uncontaminated menstrual blood, (they would have needed a blender) on her eyes, her hands, her feet, her head, her chest, and her back. And to keep the show rolling, all this several times during every Friday Passion suffering. For whom do Siwek , Graef, and their fellow antagonists of shame, take their readers?

Most fortunately, Siwek's writings were virtually annihilated by the Rev. Charles M. Carty in his *A Reply to the Apostles of Hysteria,* as well as the work of Dr. Alfred O'Rahilly. Both authors having adequately responded to Siwek, there is no need for details here. By the way, Siwek had never visited with Therese Neumann or gone to Konnersreuth.

A word must also be said about Siwek's contribution to the *New Catholic Encyclopedia,* Vol. 10, P 365-366, which has, by and large, shaped the English speaking clergy's opinion of Resl.

When his treatise was analyzed on a line for line base for truth, it showed to be colored, distorted, untrue, absent of knowledge of facts, with innuendoes and unsupported opinions. 20%, primarily deals with place, time and general description of events. Colored (10%.) include out of context, shifted emphasis, and /or significance. Distortions which contain sequences of events in various misquotes of first hand reports of others and general untruths are 28%. Fully untrue are 8%. Without exception, untruths are Siwek's "authoritative" statements of events and conditions, which simply were not so. These untruths are inexcusable for a person of his academic stature, since at the time of his writing, the facts were publicly known and accessible to any scholar of Therese Neumann; that portion of unsupported opinions, all of which are derogatory and discreditive of Resl, comprise of 26%; the category of ignorance covered up by guesswork is 6%, which might be excusable since much new information has accrued since his writings. Since Siwek is subjective, he also indulges in innuendoes: 2%. This grouping is somewhat summarizing since most often distortions and untruths are intertwined with built-in opinions and insinuations.

As to the text, Siwek does violence to almost everything. Resl's childhood and early adulthood is reduced down to virtually a blank, with an early illness "which left her somewhat irritable and nervous, and she was moreover, subject to frequent attacks of vertigo." Witnesses and chroniclers tell us otherwise; a healthy, happy child, with the usual childhood illnesses, but bright, lively and athletic.

Next, Siwek spends an inordinate portion of his treatise on "the fire" and lifting of pails, and one other accident. This is followed by a relatively factual account of increasing illnesses. He relates that on May 19, 1919, a "severe convulsive attack that left her 'blind.'" Fact; she suffered all along from muscle cramps which were particularly sever in the middle of March 1919. On May 17, 1919, by noon, she became totally blind. Siwek belittles and distorts the illnesses and even more so, the sufferings of Resl. Of course, at no time does he enter the issue of her state of willingness to suffer for the Savior. He summarizes, in less than a dozen words, his conclusions of how Resl was healed from her numerous and horrible diseases. The interplay of God's grace, through St. Therese of Lisieux is completely omitted, although to all observers, including the attending physicians, the healing was a major supernatural event.

Siwek then addresses the phenomena. A major distortion appears almost immediately by his statement "These visions did not constitute a continuous spectacle, but was broken down into about 50 separate episodes (stations.) The duration varied between 2 to 15 minute intervals." Was Siwek there, as Father Naber was? Siwek did not ever consult chroniclers who had first hand reports at their disposal. He states "In the intervals between particular stations she would first fall into a state of 'absorption' (a word only Siwek uses) in which her mind resembles that of an infant and the simplest notions were unintelligible to her." No such thing has ever been observed or reported by any of the many eyewitnesses. The statement is purely the product of Siwek, who had never even seen Resl. He continues: "This was regularly followed by a state of 'exalted repose,' in which Therese may speak, perhaps using unaccustomed turns of phrase, or she might communicate Christ's counsel and orders to others or announce future events." To his excuse Siwek did not have access to the most comprehensive and accurate accounts of this subject, namely the *Diary of Father Naber* since this only appeared in 1987. His statements do not agree with facts, and were by necessity his own fabrication.

It must be added, that Resl, only on the rarest of occasions, knew future events and certainly not as Siwek indicates as a frequent occurrence while in the 'exalted repose' state.

Nonetheless, he could have obtained accurate information from Father Naber, had he chosen to do so. What is, however, published in the *New Catholic Encyclopedia* is a serious distortion of facts. His concluding sentence on the subject of phenomena, reads "The Friday ecstasies were associated with stigmata on her hands and feet and her left side." This statement is a combination of distortions and untruths. Facts: Her stigmata began in Lent of the year 1926, starting with the wound of her side, on Good Friday, 1926, the stigmata on her hands and feet appeared; November 19, 1926, the head wounds of the crown of thorns appeared; March 8, 1929 the shoulder wound; and on Good Friday, March 29, 1929 she received the wounds of the flagellation. Resl took all stigmata into her grave. If her stigmata was due to hysteria, one must therefore conclude that the stigmata would have disappeared at death when her mental conditioning would no longer be functioning! It was the stigmata more than anything else which caused the world to raise it's head and look toward Konnersreuth. To relegate this phenomena into insignificance is, to the faithful, almost blasphemous. But it would seem that the learned professors are exempt from such sins. Again, it is a mad distortion of fact of which Siwek is guilty.

Siwek then addresses the issue of interpretation. At the outset, he separates "——the possibility of sanctity....." from the occurrences of "...the strange phenomena.... ." He discounts any miraculousness of Resl's cures on the basis of rules set down by the Congregation of Rites. This statement is wholly presumptive, since it would be the congregation's privilege, and not his, to pass such judgment. He claims: "There is insufficient existence either that alleged organic illnesses existed or that the cure could not have been effected by natural forces." (Cures could possibly, in the course of years come about naturally, however, the issue here is spontaneous healing). Siwek either did not know the facts or brushed them aside. "The supernatural character of Therese's Friday ecstasies cannot be affirmed according to the rules laid down by Benedict XIV and by mystical authorities such as St. Teresa of Avila and St. John of the Cross." This is an opinion of Siwek, and I beg to differ in principal. Again, Siwek did not possess nor cared to obtain facts. Lastly, he is wholly disproven through the current audio transcriptions of Resl's recountals of her visions.

Siwek adds, that for this reason a number of ascetical theologians, and he lists Westermayr, Mager and Bruno (?), "....have rigorously opposed what they called mysticism of Konnersreuth..."

To this it must be said that while these men are entitled to their opinions, we need not share them. Moreover, even their opinions have by now been neutralized through the above mentioned transcriptions.

Siwek: "Again stigmatization carries no guarantee of its miraculous origin. It could well have been, it seems, a natural effect of her 'ecstatic emotion'". "...could, it seems," are unsupported statements. But most of all, had Siwek seen Resl's stigmata, held her hands, looked at her feet or even studied photographs? Has he ever consulted the numerous medical reports, all stating absolute UNEXPLAINABILITY? He had the opportunity of going and visiting Resl, for she was still living, of consulting medical reports, but chose not to.

He furthermore states, "The first appearance of her stigmata, their gradual evolution, their changing of shape, their strict dependence upon the emotion, the manner in which Therese treated them, etc., all seem to favor this theory." We have mentioned above the sequence of the appearance of her stigmata. From that time they remained, 24 hours a day, year after year, unchanged. Resl never treated them or did "etc." to them. Siwek's discourse on Resl's stigmata shows an almost obsessive monomanic compulsion to disprove them. He cannot be excused because of lack of knowledge, the stigmata were there, pure and simple.

Siwek says that "Her visions also are susceptible of a natural psychological explanation, and indeed there are elements in their content that give rise to theological objections to attributing a divine origin to them." As above, the statement is, preemptive to the Congregation of Rites. Siwek does not offer any "natural psychological explanation." In his book, he goes into contortions to prove Resl was hysteric, the cause of it all.

As could be expected, Siwek has something to say about Resl's inedia. First off, he refers to it as a prolonged fasting, claimed to have started from Sept. 1927. No one claimed that the inedia started in Sept. 1927, nor is inedia the equal to prolonged fasting. Siwek should have been aware of these distinctions! He further asserts that "....Therese's family never allowed the thorough examination of this point that the Catholic hierarchy insistently demanded." This statement contains two untruths and a distortion. At the request of Bishop Henle of Regensburg, Resl's father did allow the well known 15 days, (1927) test with the diocesan promise that there shall be no further tests. The test was designed, executed, and supervised by two physicians, the avid atheist Dr. Ewald and Dr. Seidl, who acted on behalf of the Diocese of Regensburg. The results, through the indiscretion of Dr. Ewald, became public knowledge. The diocese then published a summary simply stating that inedia (total abstinence from water and nourishment) had been established to the diocesan's satisfaction.

There were further demands for tests in 1937, but Resl's father declined permission. The circumstances around one particular request from Rome were almost sinister, (see Chapter 7). Furthermore, of the veritable army of professors who came to Konnersreuth, many offered and even demanded that Resl be admitted in their clinics for their observation and their scientific study. Some had the brazenness to conduct on-site tests on her, like shining a carbonarc light of 6000 watts into her face to see whether she would become blind or not. Another, grabbing her hand and squeezing it until Resl yelled in pain. Upon the questioning by the indignant father, the doctor replied, he just wanted to see whether he could get the stigmata to bleed. Shades of Dr. Mengele!

Siwek and every other adversary of Resl are strangely silent about the fact that these were the years of Nazism, and that she was one of their prime targets. Nothing would have suited these people better than to have Resl put away in some maximum security asylum. The Neumann's knew all this, both of her younger brothers, Ferdinand and Hans, were repeatedly imprisoned and severely mistreated. The Neumanns did not prep their daughter and sister for sainthood: Siwek's last paragraph, therefore, is born of lack of knowledge and contains several untruths and innuendoes.

JOSEPH HANAUER

Father Joseph Hanauer, a most recent adversary (1990's) is a priest of the Diocese of Regensburg. He was a seminarian student of Father Waldmann, an arch-enemy of Resl. Father Waldmann, referred to by both Hilda Graef and Siwek, was a classmate of Father Naber.

Hanauer is a self appointed policeman of the "true" faith. In his self appointed capacity, he has traveled in the footsteps of his teacher by rejecting, attacking, discrediting, ridiculing, and condemning Resl from the outset. In his most recently published books (all published in Germany) he has refined his theories.

His earlier work, *Miracles or Miracle-Craving?*, published in 1991, deals with mystics, miraculous apparitions, "Marianism," religious movements, and a host of related subjects. He rejects the notion of mysticism almost in its totality, telling the reader it is invariably the figment of sick and/or hysteric minds, mostly occurring in women.

He rejects Fatima as a complete fable, especially Lucia. The "alleged" miracle of the sun never happened. He likewise claims that: Saint Margaret Mary Alacoque's visions were based on prior knowledge; Padre Pio predicted the future after it happened; the same was true for St. Catherine Laboure "saint or no saint!". Garabandal is a complete hoax. Here the Holy Mother of God got herself crossways with Padre Pio, leaving both losers. Medjugorie, according to Hanauer is the ultimate fraud; an ingenious fabrication of the Franciscans to appear important, especially in the face of the wise and well meaning Bishop of Mostar. He comes close to accusing the Gospa of all the trouble in the former Yugoslavia. Hanauer's discourse on Medjugorie is so full of hatred and perversity, that it overshadows even his ridicule of Lourdes! There, he claims, never were any healings. The problem lays with the world of medicine which only now is able to conclusively diagnose before and after. Ergo - no more healings! He tells us that there were eventually 20 (and maybe more) children who saw the Lady and Bernadette was all but forgotten!

Of course, Hanauer attacks all Religious Movements. His prime target is the Marian Movement of Priests. He begins with a blast at Father Gobbi; referring to him as an obese man in a cassock. More serious is Hanauer's repulsive and alarming involvement of the Holy Mother of God. For almost a full page in his book, he cited expressions of consuming love (of the Virgin Mary) for Father Gobbi, edited and misquoted so as to produce undertones of physical attractions.

He then runs down the "Charismatic Movement" and "Opus

Angelorum," followed by a healthy slap at the Venerable Anna Catharina Emmerick.

His ordinary, the late Bishop Rudolph Graber, is the author of a book on Marian Apparitions. Hanauer devotes substantial quantities of printers ink to ridicule and discredit this work in totality. Considering his viewpoint on all Marian Apparition, (these of course include La Salette, Beauraing, Banneux, and the Weeping Madonnas in Europe and many most of us have never heard of) Hanauer gives the reader the impression of a personal rejection of women in general, and the Mother of God in particular. His knowledge, incidentally, stops at Europe's Atlantic Coast. He is totally ignorant of all the Americas, Ireland, Asia, Japan, or Africa!

His sources, 425 suffixes, are first of all Hanauer himself, then a Spanish Jesuit by the name of Staehlin, quite a bit of Karl Rahner, the Regensburg Diocesan newspaper plus other periodicals. His most interesting source is undoubtedly the German grocery store tabloid "Neue Bildpost."

Needless to say, he takes a swipe at Resl at every possible occasion, always showing her as a cardinal example of deception.

His second recent book, *Konnersreuth; Lie and Deceit with Ecclesiastical Blessing?* deals exclusively with Resl. It was triggered by a two hour talk given by Toni Siegert, a reporter of the Bavarian Broadcasting System. The talk was presented on the 30th anniversary of Resl's death, and dealt mainly with her inedia. Since Hanauer, in a most hateful manner decries this phenomena, Siegert takes him to task with truly Bavarian charm. He presents a factual, well researched counter-position which all but annihilates all of Hanauer's theories. Of course, Hanauer reacted. True to his personality, his response begins with "....the yapping of a mongrel at the moon, not worthy even of notice..." Yet, he meekly attempts to defend himself in the first 86 pages.

The second half of his book is solely devoted to Resl and the potential of a beatification. As can be suspected, it is one continuous slander against her, her brother Ferdinand, her family and his own Ordinaries. His representation of the rules for beatification is deficient and often falsified. Interesting though is his obsequiousness, lamenting that nobody likes him anymore. His Ordinary saw to it twice that his writings were not translated into English or would reach our shores. How could any informed Catholic possibly take Father Hanauer seriously?

SUMMARY

A ll three above adversaries have common ground and features. They express themselves in an attitude of supremacy, condescending to the subject and also the reader. All are willing to distort and misquote in order to support their own view points, using references of the same mold as themselves. Those who were of different viewpoints had their words taken out of context to read what was not intended. Their sole witnesses are (a) avowed enemies of Resl and (b) people who have had, at the most, only a cursory knowledge of Resl. Their medical witnesses were invariably prominent Nazis, like Dr. Deutch and Dr. Aigner. All three studiously avoided any mention of the horrors of the times.

Lastly, one cannot excuse their obvious tone of naked hatred for Resl, upon whom God's finger drew His design for the return of His children to Him. Each one had the chance to observe this gift to us, and to believe, but chose not to.

'ET LUX IN TENEBRIS LUCET, ET TENEBREA EAM
NON COMPREHENDERUNT.'

(And the light shone in the darkness; and the darkness
grasped it not.)

BEATIFICATION AND CANONIZATION PROCESS

REQUIREMENTS

There are two categories under which the Church considers a person as a candidate for beatification: 1.) Martyrdom or 2.) Heroic virtue.

1.) Martyrdom: The early Church believed that by their supreme sacrifice of their lives for the faith, martyrs were perfect Christians or saints. Their sufferings united them to Christ. The people invoked the intercession of the martyrs, begging them to intercede before God, to obtain the grace to imitate the martyr in the profession of the faith.

2.) Heroic virtue: Heroic virtue is found in a person whose life far exceeds the ordinary virtuous life, whose life becomes a perfection of virtues to such a degree that it becomes "heroic" in its exercise. Heroic virtue is based on the Cardinal and Theological Virtues being lived to a heroic perfection and intense charity brought to a high degree. A beautiful example is found in St. Therese of Lisieux, and her "Little Way" of perfection in the little things of life. Pius XI said that "heroic virtue was to be sought in the ordinary things of daily life." St. Elizabeth Ann Seton in the many struggles in her life, manifested heroic virtue.

Toward the end of the Roman persecution, the veneration of martyrs was extended to those who, even though not martyrs, did defend and suffer for the faith. Within a short time this veneration was extended to persons who lived exemplary Christian lives, especially in austerity, penitence, and charity, and also to those who excelled in Christian doctrine (Doctors of the Church) or in apostolic zeal (bishops, missionaries.)

The Episcopal Canonization, a diocesan process, was not as thorough as in later centuries and the judgment of approval was quite often given hastily. Over the centuries, the criterion used to ascertain the person's holiness became more exacting. Gradually recourse to the Pope became a practice which prompted canonization decrees by the Pope. The first Papal Canonization recorded was St. Udalricus in 973. With these interventions by the pontiff, the Papal Canonization received a more definitive structure and value and such processes became the main source of investigations into the saint's life and miracles. By 1234, under Gregory IX, this practice of Papal Canonization, became the only legitimate form of inquiry. In 1588, Sixtus V, developed the guidelines for the division of the work of the Roman Curia and established dicasteries to take charge of Papal affairs. The Congregation of Rites was given the task of preparing the Papal Canonization. The Congregation formed the process and method of action for beatification and canonization. In 1642, Urban VIII, ordered the publication of all the decrees and interpretations issued on canonization during his pontificate.

Benedict XIV (1740-1757) while still Prospero Lambertini, wrote his treatise "De Servorum Dei Beatificatione et Beatorum Canonizatione." (1734-38). While this treatise does not possess Papal authority, the Church has used it as a guide. He illustrated in a precise manner the points that had previously been used in these processes and explained the concept of heroic virtue. This work remains the norm which is followed by the Congregation of Rites in the beatification and canonization process. This procedure, on May 19, 1918, entered the *Code of Canon Law, Book 4, Canons 1990 to 2141*. Benedict XIV, stated among many other points, that a certain period of time must be lived in heroic virtue, though this time period may vary depending on the height of holiness achieved. Venial sin, even if committed deliberately, after a person has achieved a level of heroic virtue, is not reason for exclusion from beatification if the person has provided satisfactory compensation for these sins and has taken steps against its reoccurrence. No proof of infused contemplation, miracles or mystical phenomena during the persons life are necessary for beatification, however, they should be taken into account. "A gratuitous grace" is a supernatural gift conceded gratis by God. It does not by itself make the possessor pleasing to God, but it is principally directed to the good of others....Gratuitous graces are common to both sinners and the just.....Account is taken of these graces in investigations for beatification and canonization, if apart from these graces, the heroic virtues and innocence of life of the servant of God are verified. For their association with virtue shows that they were conferred not only for the good of others, but also as a witness of the sanctity of the servant of God. - De Servoruim Die Beatification iii 42.

THE PROCESS

The procedures of beatification and canonization of saints according to the "Code of Canon Law" are as follows:

Ordinary Process

After the death of a person who has lived an exemplary Christian life and/or whose "fame of sanctity" or "fame of martyrdom" has been generally acknowledged, the bishop of the diocese where he or she died may deem it opportune to institute a process. This process is called ordinary because it is instituted by the Ordinary of the place: He (the bishop) establishes a tribunal to interrogate witnesses and gather evidence which the Congregation of Rites will use in its ascertainment of whether or not there exists the "fame of sanctity" and/or "fame of martyrdom." This process is informative for it will provide the Holy See with information necessary to verify whether the servant of God exercised heroic virtue or whether the servant of God died for the faith (martyrdom). The bishop must have thoroughly searched all writings of the servant of God to ascertain its purity of doctrine (should such writings exist) and that no public cult has been accorded to the servant. The ordinary acts of this process are preserved in the archives of the diocese and a sealed copy "transumptum" is delivered to the Congregation of Rites in Rome. This ends the Ordinary Process.

Introduction of the Cause

The postulator, after studying the "Transumptum" has the duty of presenting and discussing the cause before competent judges of the Congregation. The advocate - procurator of the Congregation in turn prepares a brief based on the "Transumptum" aimed at proving the existence of a true reputation of sanctity and therefore the acceptability of introducing the cause. This brief must prove that the elements required to proceed in further inquiries on heroic virtue or martyrdom are contained in the cause. The advocates work, consisting of *information* and the *summarium depostionum*, then undergo a thorough examination by the Congregation. The general promoter (or better known as the devil's advocate), proposes his objections to the advocates defense *anima dversiones*. The postulator then demands from the advocate a counter defense to the objections raised by the general promoter.

All information and material so far defined are printed into a volume called *Positio*. This *Positio* is presented to all the Cardinals and official prelates of the Congregation for examination. They in turn will express their individual judgments in discussions held in the Vatican palace or the residence of the Cardinal *poners* or relator.

The Holy Father upon being informed of the outcome of the discussions, will, if he so deems it opportune, decree the so-called Introduction of the Cause.

Apostolic Process

By the Decree of Introduction of the Cause, the cause is transferred from the bishops to the jurisdiction of the Apostolic See. In the apostolic process, the Congregation of Rites decrees on whether the practice of virtue or martyrdom is to be instituted.

The Holy See delegates the judges for this process. The general promoter, represented by a subprompter before the tribunal, prepares the questions for the interrogation of witnesses. New witnesses may be presented and interrogated.

At the end of this process a new authenticated volume of the act is translated into an official language, if need be.

The postulator is consigned a copy and assumes the responsibility, along with the advocate, of a new study for further discussion on the heroic practice of virtue or martyrdom.

Decree on the Validity of the Process

Before authorizing a discussion on the heroic practice of virtue or martyrdom, the lawfulness and validity of all the acts on which the discussions were based, are first guaranteed. The Congregation, after close examination of the preceding processes, issues a decree on the validity of all the acts of the processes, thereby guaranteeing their legitimate use.

Heroic Practice of Virtues or Martyrdom

When the validity of both the ordinary and the apostolic processes have been assured, the postulator and the advocate prepare and present to the Congregation of Rites a summary of the following:

1.) A clear disclosure of the life of the servant of God and his virtues or martyrdom

2.) A summary of the material accumulated from the interrogation of witnesses on the above points during the preceding processes

The purpose of this summary is to demonstrate, in the case of a non-martyr, the servant of God's life, inspired by Christian charity toward God and men, and that he practiced daily Christian virtue in a truly exemplary, perfect and heroic manner.

In the case of a martyr, this summary intends to prove that the servant was killed in *odium fidei*, the supreme sacrifice of love for Christ and the Church.

This summary is then carefully examined by the Congregation of Rites. The general promoter of the faith, again, presents his doubts and objections to the conclusions so far drawn and he requests a reply from the postulator and advocate. Their answers along with the above materials, are printed and the volume is then distributed among the Congregation's officials and consultors. They in turn, after due examination of the contents, present their judgment at the Antepreparatory Congregation.

Difficulties and reservations are assembled by the prompter under the title of *novae animadversiones*. The postulator and advocate prepare their answers which are then the basis of the second discussion by the Preparatory Congregation with Cardinals, officials and consultors present.

After this second meeting further difficulties raised and answered, *novissimal animadversiones*, are discussed at the last General Congregation. This Congregation is sometimes called Congregation Corami Sanctissimo, because of the presence of the Holy Father.

Historical Section

If it is proven that a worthy cause has insufficient evidence by eyewitnesses or in the causes where there no longer are any witnesses, recourse is provided by research into documents of historical character. The preparation of these historical essays is directed by a general relator, assisted by a vice-relator and by consultors (ecclesiastic as well as lay), chosen from the historical sciences.

Miracles

The Church demands a confirmation in the form of miracles before proceeding to beatification, even if the practice of Christian virtue in heroic manner has been concluded. Our Lord announced that extraordinary intervention of divine omnipotence would be signs that would distinguish His Church and His faithful children who believed in and lived according to His gospel. Therefore, the Church deems it most important that signs of this intervention be present. Miracles are unequivocal proof of the approval given by God to the person and life of a future saint. Miracles performed during the life time of a servant of God and especially those miracles which occurred after death, where the servant's intercession is invoked, are a sign of God's confirmation.

Inquiries are made to determine 1) whether God truly performed the miracle and 2) whether the miracle is to be attributed to the intercession of the servant of God, who was invoked.

The procedural pattern and discussions are similar to the preparatory stage. Experts in the sciences related to the issues are also presented and interrogated. When discussions on the miracles are concluded and approved a final General Congregation is required. It is held, before the Holy Father, for the purpose of determining whether it is now possible to continue to the next step, beatification. If the Holy Father deems it opportune to continue he orders the publication of the decree called *de tuto*. A day is chosen for the solemn celebration and formal beatification in the Vatican Basilica. With the acceptance by the Congregation of Rites of the cause for beatification, the servant of God is allowed the title "venerable." No public cult is allowed, only private e.g. praising his virtue, praying to him.

Beatification

Beatification ceremonies commence with the proclamation of the Apostolic brief in which the Holy Father grants the venerable servant of God the title of "blessed." The blessed may now be venerated, however, the public cult is restricted to persons, places and or religious family. The newly beatified is unveiled, the *Te Deum* is sung and a solemn Pontifical Mass is celebrated as the first act of veneration of the blessed.

This most formal celebration declares the blessed as having practiced heroic virtue or true martyrdom, and that after death, when invoked in prayer, two first-class miracles have been attributed to the blessed's intercession.

The Holy Father does not exercise his infallibility, for he does not declare definitely that the blessed is in glory.

Canonization

When information is received regarding two further miracles obtained through the intercession of the blessed, the cause is reopened with the final step of canonization being the objective.

This new process then follows the procedures of "Miracles". When it has been proven that God performed these miracles through the intercession of the blessed, the Holy See proceeds with the solemn canonization.

The canonization ceremonies are extraordinarily solemn. While the *Litany of the Saints* is chanted, a procession, carrying a standard with the new saint's image, precedes the Holy Father into St. Peter's. After the procession arrives at the papal throne, the postulator asks *instantes* (urgently), then *instantius* (more urgently) and finally he begs *instantissime* (most urgently) for the canonization of the blessed, followed by the singing of *Veni Creator Spiritus*. The Holy Father reads the papal bull of canonization, declaring the servant of God a saint. This bull, the final and definitive sentence by which the universal Church may now venerate the new saint, declares, infallibly, that the saint's life was exemplary and praises the saint as a heavenly intercessor.

This part of the solemn canonization rite is concluded by the singing of *Te Deum*.

A pontifical Mass is celebrated and a solemn procession carries the symbolic gifts of candles, bread, wine, and doves to the Holy Father at the Offertory. This Pontifical Mass is the first act of veneration of the saint.

As already stated, the above is based on Benedict XIV Treatise, *De Servorum Dei Beatificatione et Beatorum Canonizatione*. However, *Novae Leges Pro Causis Sanctorum* (New Laws of Causes of Saints) was passed in 1983. The causes of canonization of the servants of God are now regulated by special pontifical law, but the procedure is basically the same format.

RESL'S BEATIFICATION PROCESS AS OF 1996

Bishop Manfred Mueller, of the Diocese of Regensburg in Germany, would be the bishop to initiate the "Ordinary Process," the first step in the Beatification Process. The purpose of the "Ordinary Process," as stated in the previous chapter, is to form a tribunal which gathers all information available regarding the candidate and then produce a sealed copy of the "Transumptum" to be delivered to the Congregation of Rites in Rome. The Ordinary Process does not pass judgment as to whether there actually exists heroic virtue or martyrdom. That decision is made by the Congregation of Rites.

There appears to be a confusion as to whether this process is indeed in progress. The Diocese of Regensburg is and indeed has in the past, accumulated information and has interviewed many witnesses. Though this would point to the Ordinary Process being in effect, the Bishop has not officially instituted the process, and has indeed stated that it is not in progress.

ARGUMENTS RAISED AGAINST BEATIFICATION AND THEIR COUNTER

By far the most frequent objections for the commencement of the Beatification Process in the case of Resl are: (1) her not submitting to another examination concerning her inedia, (2) her at times impatience, irritableness, and anger, (3) a fraudulent conspiracy in the family and village, and (4) her stigmata was produced by hysteria.

When the request from Bishop Henle, then the Bishop of Regensburg, to submit to an examination to substantiate the validity of her inedia was made, the Bishop did promise Resl and her family, that there will be need of only one such examination.

Cardinal Preysing of Berlin assured Resl and her father that since Resl was not of any religious order she need not obey the Cardinal's or Bishop's request for any examination at all. This last affirmation of the Cardinal is the assurance with which Mr. Neumann, Resl's father, staunchly reiterated, in his defense, his "no further examination" resolution.

Dr. Edward Aigner, a most ardent follower of Hitler, made known his great desire to examine Resl in his own clinic, for he wished to "gift" Hitler with the knowledge of how to exist without food or water. This must also have had much to do with Mr. Neumann's determination not to submit Resl to further examinations.

In a letter dated Jan. 4, 1937, to Countess Chiassi, Resl wrote of the following incident. Two gentlemen (priests?) from the Ordinate of Regensburg came to Resl and presented her a letter from Rome requesting another examination, one of four weeks, at a clinic to be determined by the Bishop. This request deeply troubled Resl. She did not wish to disobey the Church and at the same time did not wish to be disobedient to her father. The two gentlemen (?) proceeded to threaten her by saying that the Church would deny her Holy Communion if she did not co-operate with the investigation. This would be tantamount to excommunication! When Rome heard of this threat, Rome instantly withdrew its request.

Here are remarks from two Popes concerning further investigations: (1) When pressured that the Church conduct more medical experiments on Resl, Pope Pius XI said "Let the girl alone!" (2) Pope Pius XII said: "There would always be physicians who would find fault with the method of investigation and continue to demand one more investigation."

The objections because of her, at times, impatience, irritableness, and anger, certainty does *not* preclude beatification. When Our Lord cleared the Temple of the money changers, he did not do it in a calm, demure fashion.

Unfortunately, and to his great vexation, the following statement made by Ferdinand Neumann "She expresses her opinions
forcefully at times," has been distorted and construed to mean that
Resl was ill-tempered, impatient, rude, and undisciplined.

The Rev. Donald J. Murphy, the Catholic Chaplain with the
357 Regiment of the 90th Infantry Division, has written an account of his many visits to Konnersreuth during the immediate
occupation of that area after World War II. After his first visit he
wrote, "I asked myself what or how could I best describe Therese.
I decided that she reminded me most of a kindly and judicious
Superior in a religious community." He further comments on her
"fresh simplicity, unassuming manner, her smile and her usually
being the embodiment of good humor." At times Rev. Murphy
had between 100 to 200 soldiers with him to see Resl. "Even when
she was obviously tired she was charming to all the GIs and took
interest in everything and everybody."

Many writers, Gerlich, Witt, Teodorowitz, Scorpio, Von Lama,
von Aretin, O'Rahilly and many others, who knew her personally
or had studied her thoroughly, did not find her character to be
such that she could ever fall into the categories put forth by her
adversaries. On the contrary, they found her the opposite to the
accusations against her.

The Rev. Donald S. Murphy did observe that "She was not
cooperative with the many journalists and writers." Perhaps that is
why some journalists and writers gave her bad press.

ARGUMENTS FOR BEATIFICATION

As required by the process for beatification, Resl's life was a
continual submission to the Will of God. She had overcome
her own desires to such an extent that her every thought and action was for the Lord, for the Glory of God alone. Her only passion was to love and serve Him. She submitted to her sufferings
because God asked her if she would take onto herself this suffering. She certainly did not like to suffer. To live amidst constant
observation, ridicule, and under suspicious eyes, with continual

streams of onlookers parading through the house and even her bedroom, a life that could no longer be called her own, took an enormous amount of courage. Her life, for over thirty-six years, was heroic indeed.

The miracles also speak to her favor, those before her death and those after her death (as the plaques on her grave indicate.)

The many mystical phenomena she experienced, though not a requirement for beatification, did show, the many graces God had bestowed upon his servant Resl.

As for virtues, her continual interest in people, helping them whenever possible, with actual assistance and of course with prayers, gave an example to all that it is indeed possible to lead a life which is holy and dedicated to the Will of God and still live in our present secular world.

There were many Cardinals, Bishops, etc. who visited Konnersreuth. Even now, they continue to come to pay their respects to her at her grave and to pray in her bedroom where she underwent the passion so very many times.

The following is a brief note from Ferdinand Neumann plus a list of the dignitaries whom he has had personal knowledge of having come to Konnersreuth. This is by far not a complete list for many times Ferdinand Neumann was not present at Konnersreuth.

Translation:

The following is a summary of diverse Bishops and "High Dignitaries" of the Church, who had shown special interest for my sister Resl. I have listed the cases which were specially well-known to me.

F.N. Feb. 1996

Prelate Geiger of Bamberg has, as early as 1926 to his death in 1960, spoken for and defended Resl. He was frequently, and often for days at Konnersreuth. He published several defense papers against antagonists. Resl's first trip after her healing was to Bamberg at the invitation of Geiger, who then was Cathedral Pastor. I accompanied Resl. We stayed at the Cathedral house overnight where a special event took place which remained unforgettable for me. Geiger, together with Cardinal Preysing most energetically supported my father in his resistance against Regensburg, when Resl, in the late 30's was to be "admitted" into a clinic. There are numerous documents on this subject in the archives.

Bishop Sebastian of Speyer, together with prelate Molz, came to Konnersreuth in 1928 and 1931 to witness the Good Friday Passion. In 1929, Resl was at Speyer for a few days, when Bishop Sebastian christened the convert Rothshild. Resl was Godmother. Molz and his Bishop Sebastian later issued a brochure about Resl.

Cardinal Piffl, inspite of his age, came to Konnersreuth in 1929 and 1930 to witness the Good Friday Passion.

Cardinal Faulhaber, of Munich celebrated Holy Mass in Resl's room in 1930. In 1929, Faulhaber christened Dr. Gerlich in the diocesan Chapel. Resl resided in the Cardinal's palace for three days. At a symposium, he declared that he had obligated his servants to watch Resl day and night to see whether she took any nourishment. She took none.

All Bishops and prelates of Eichstaett, on the basis of her frequent visits from 1932 to 1962, were convinced of the extraordinary happenings with Resl and their truthfulness.

Bishop Graf Preysing, later Cardinal of Berlin. In two instances he dictated to my father the letters my father had to write to Regensburg on matters of further investigations of Resl.

Bishop Michael Rackl of Eichstaett (1935-1948) concerned himself intensively with the problem at Konnersreuth. Most importantly, he gave significant advice to Fr. Naber.

Bishop Joseph Schroeffer of Eichstaett garnered credit for acting on an issue which was actually the duty of the Bishop of Regensburg. In 1953, he officially deposed Resl and some of her siblings. Schroeffer received the red hat and in 1967 was called to Rome. Before leaving, he turned over these important documents to Bishop Graber.

Archbishop Dr. Sigismund Waitz, Bishop of Salzburg. He repeatedly visited Konnersreuth on Fridays in the years 1928 to 1939, accompanied by other dignitaries. In 1930, he published the brochure *The Message of Konnersreuth.*

Bishop Dr. Georgius Schmid of Chur (Switzerland,) visited Konnersreuth in 1930 and invited Resl to come to Chur. In 1931, Resl, in the company of Prof. Wutz, Dr. Gerlich, and F. Neumann, spent a few days with Schmid at Chur. The Bishop took her, on this occasion to Brother Klaus, Einsiedeln, and Disentis, where there was a meeting with the famous Fr. Maurus Carnot, who publicly supported Resl to his death in 1935 (he was Court Chaplain of Emperor Karl of Austria).

Archbishop Dr. Teodorowicz of Lemburg, Czeckoslovakia, an expert in mysticism and a critical scholar, repeatedly visited Resl with his *Bishop Coadjutor Lisowski*. His extensive work *"Konnersreuth in the Light of Mysticism and Psychology"* appeared in 1936. The American periodical *"Spousa Christi St. Paul,"* Nov. 1951 writes "with this book, the hateful statements of Hilda Graef have been well refuted."

Cardinal Dr. Karl Caspar of Prag (died 1946) came to Konnersreuth from 1928 to 1938 (occupation by the Nazis;) mostly accompanied by Dr. Hynek (who did scientific studies on the Shroud.) The Cardinal published a paper in 1932 "Impressions of Konnersreuth."

Cardinal Innitzer of Vienna visited Resl in 1934. He played a significant role, as Resl sent me (F.N.) to him in 1941 (directed by her in exalted repose,) to have him deliver to me, in his palace, the Jewish priest Fr. Schwarz, to save him from the Nazis. I (F.N.) prepared a special report on this matter.

Bishop Dr. Goellner of Linz (Austria) came to see Resl several times in 1932. He then maintained close letter contact with her. In this regard, there is one interesting connection: When the Marian Sisters of Carmel were driven from their home in the Sudetenland (Czechoslovakia), a few of them came to Konnersreuth: Resl was to help them find a new home. In her efforts to do so, she visited, among others, Bishop Goellner at Linz and begged him to help. Shortly thereafter, the sisters received a new home at Linz. This is the reason why Carmelites now take care of the Theresianum at Konnersreuth.

Archbishop "von Hauck", Bamberg, visitor, took a positive position toward Konnersreuth, probably influenced by prelate Geiger.

Bishop Augustin Kilian of Limberg declared of his visit to Konnersreuth: "Konnersreuth was my life's greatest event."

Bishop Schreiber of Meissen, began his visits to Resl in 1927 and repeated these visits on Fridays.

Cardinal Dr. Bertram of Breslau was in Konnersreuth in 1928 In a sermon, he declared "Resl is a living tool of the Will of God."

Bishop Dr. Mathias Ehrenfried, of Wuerzburg said, after his visit in 1936, "Resl is an immense tool of Divine Providence."

Dr. Friedrich Dircks, Bishop of Lienburg, spoke after his visit in 1946, "Resl is a sign of God for mankind in our days."

A Bishop from the Lombardy (Italy), name unknown, was an ailing man, who in the late 30s was repeatedly at Konnersreuth. Fr. Naber told me (F.N.), "This Bishop had entreaties (deep concerns,) but spoke not a word of German. He, Naber, could only converse with him in Latin." The reason this Bishop visited was that he could submit his entreaties to Resl, when she was in the state of exalted repose. But he could only do this in Italian, but Resl gave her reposes in good, clear Italian. The Bishop told Naber after these sessions that he received much good advice and consolation.

Archbishop Dr. Joseph Paracattil of Ernakulam, India, (Panzer report.) The Archbishop visited with Resl in 1958 and 1960. His particular interest in Resl was that the Aramaic language is to this day, the liturgical language of his diocese in the province of Kerala. There, they speak of "Thomas Christians." The apostle Thomas preached there. During his visits, he conversed much with Resl about the pronunciation of the Aramaic words. Resl corresponded with him. The last letter bears the date April 12, 1962.

In the holy year *1950, several Bishops* from Rome came to visit Resl.

The Mission Bishop of Windhoek (S.W. Africa) came to see Resl. He stayed at Konnersreuth for several days.

Rector of the University of Milano, Gemelli. A significant visit, 1928, Gemelli came to Konnersreuth at the official request of Rome, to examine Resl not only as a theologian but also in the capacity of a physician. His verdict, "Not a trace of sickness or hysteria. There are no natural explanations for the events here." Following his report, the Pope gave Resl his apostolic blessing. (Pius XI.)

Cardinal of the Curia, Bea. The meeting lasted three days at a friend's house in Ravensburg. At the farewell, Cardinal Bea asked of her prayer for a great entreaty. The Cardinal was responsible for the preparations for Vatican II. She gave her promise of her submission to the cause, she would give the Saviour her life for the success of the Council. Cardinal Bea later wrote to Fr. Naber from Rome (after Resl's death.) He was still deeply moved by Resl's promise at the farewell at Weingarten, that she would gladly give her life for the success of Vatican II. In a later letter he wrote: "Preparations should begin for the intitiation of a beatification process."

Fr. Kea, a Dutch Jesuit came with the Apostolic Nuncio of Norway, who later became pastor of St. Peter in Rome, to Konnersreuth for

Dignitaries of the Church Visiting Konnersreuth

Year 19...	From Rome	Cardinal	Archbishop
26-60			
28-31			Waitz
29-30	*Pius XI	Piffl	
27-48		Preysing	
	*Pius XII		
30			
30-36/46		Caspar Innitzer	Teodorowicz
			v.Hauck
28			
36			
46			
38			
58-60			Paracattil
50			
28	Gemelli		
62	Bea	Bea	
35			
35			
27-50			
65			
68			Conakry
95		Meissner	
			Zichy

Therese Neumann of Konnersreuth   *F.N.*
April 9, 1898 - September 19, 1962

1945 to 1951. The scene before the Neumann
house at Konnersreuth on Fridays

F.N.

Christmas Vision,
1947

F.N.

F.N.

Christmas Vision,
1947

F.N.

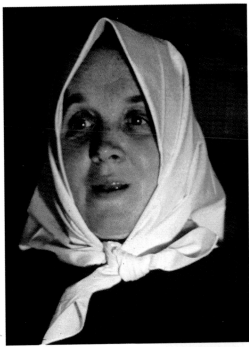

F.N.

Resl's Vision,
1947

F.N.

F.N.

Resl's Vision,
1947

F.N.

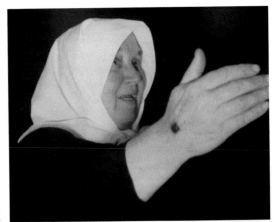

F.N.

The Stoning
of St. Steven,
Vision

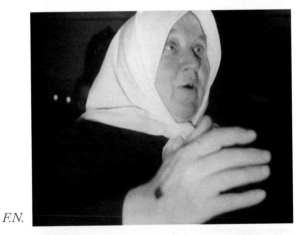

F.N.

F.N.

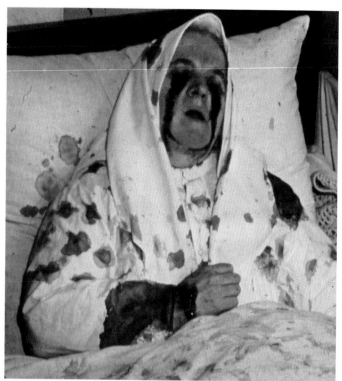

Good Friday Passion, approx. 1955   *F.N.*

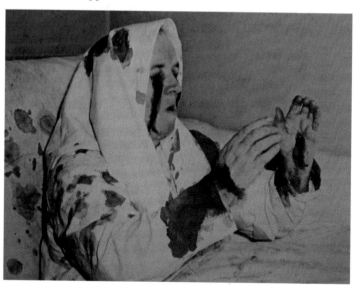

F.N.

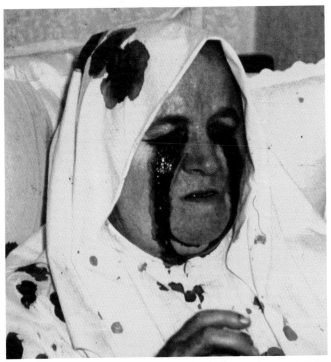

F.N.

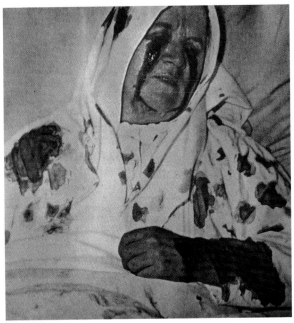

F.N.

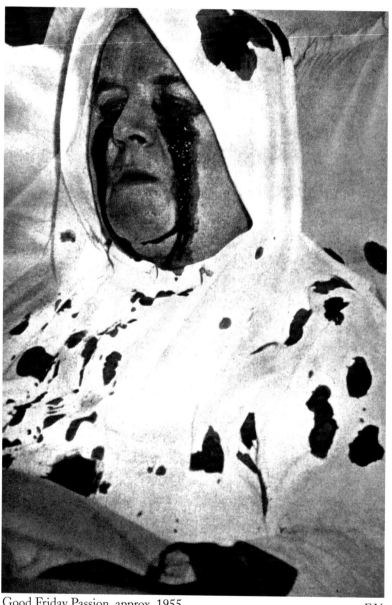

Good Friday Passion, approx. 1955   *F.N.*

Father Joseph Naber, 1870–1967
Benediction at end of Holy Mass in
Resl's Room

Resl laid out in the living room of the
Neumann house, September 19, 1962

F.N.

As remembered by Ferdinand Neumann.

Bishop	Abbott,Abbess Msgr., Special Emmissarie	Country
	Geiger	GE
Sebastian		GE
Buchberger		AU
v.Henle		GE
Graber		
Rackle		
Schroeffer		
Schmid		SW
Leitmeritz		CHE
Goellner		AU
Limberg		GE
Schreiber		GE
Bertram		GE
Ehrenfried		GE
Dircks		GE
Lombardy		IT
		IND
Several bishops from Rome		
Windhoeck		AFR
		IT
		IT
	Kia,Nuncio Norway	NOR
	Schweikelberg	GE
	Plankstretten	GE
Schmitt	Benedikta von Spiegel	GE
Fatima		Port
28 Bishops from Rome, Vatican II		IT
		AFR
Zaktaki		IT
Hoffman		GE
Malan		HUN

* Did not visit but were aware of Resl or had contact with her.

a few days. Both submitted a special report of their impressions of the Friday Passion, to the Officio of Rome.

Two Benedictine Abbots of Schweikelberg and Plankstetten made several visits to Konnersreuth in the thirties.

The Abbess Benedikta von Spiegel of the Abbey of Eichstaett remained in closest friendship with Resl from 1927 to the Abbess' death in 1950.

Bishop of Fatima and his secretary Fr. Condor came to visit on Resl's 10th anniversary of death in 1972, stayed several days.

28 Bishops from Rome (from several countries) came in 1965 during the Council. After a visit to Resl's grave and her room, they assembled at the Theresianum where Fr. Naber gave them a talk which was translated into several languages.

Bishop Granados of Toledo, Spain, 95 years of age, thanked Fr. Naber in a letter and declared for himself and his companions, "The visit has left all of us with a deep impression."

A large number of foreign Bishops should be named who came to Resl's grave to pay their respects. Examples:

1968 Archbishop of Conakory (Africa)

Bishop Willing from Indonesia

1980 Archbishop Cesare Zaktaki from Rome, President of the Papal School of Diplomats.

One can firmly state that *the Popes Pius XI and Pius XII* all held Resl in honor and esteem. Pius XI made the well-known statement, "Let us leave Konnersreuth to the Divine Providence."

Pius XI sent a relique of St. Frances of Assisi to Resl (through Countess Chiassi. He also invited her to visit Rome.)

Pius XII, still in the capacity of Vatican Secretary of State, a year before his election to the Papacy, sent several persons to Konnersreuth, bearing a written request to Resl's father that these people may please be treated well on the occasion of their visit.

Cardinal Dr. Meissner of Cologne, visited Konnersreuth in the spring of 1995. After his visit to her grave, he spent a long time in Resl's room. At the farewell he said, "In this place, the Savior wrought great things."

His Bishop's Coadjutor-Dr. Hoffman took part in one of my (F.N.) talks and also in the ensuing discussion.

Bishop of Leitmeritz (Czechoslovakia) 1928

Archbishop Graf Zichy of Kalocza (Hungary) was in Konnersreuth in 1928
Bishop Antonio Malan of Petrolina (Brazil) came to Konnersreuth in 1930
Bishop Dr. Schmitt of Fulda came in Nov. 1928.

The list on pp.112-113by Ferdinand Neumann does not include the Bishop of Cleveland Ohio, U.S.A., *Bishop Joseph Schrembs.* Bishop Schrembs visited Konnersreuth with his Chancellor *Msgr. McFadden* in December 1927. The Bishop gave a lecture on Resl and wrote an article called "Amazing Therese Neumann." He said, "We stood in the presence of the super-natural."

REGENSBURG'S STALEMATE

Resl died on Sept. 18th, 1962. In 1966, Bishop Graber of Regensburg appointed a Fransiscan, Fr. Maximillian, to proceed, as yet unofficially, with the call for and interviewing of witnesses and the collection of written and pictorial material; i.e. the basics of the first step for beatification, the informative process.

At this point in time, Fr. Hanauer, a diocesan priest and as yet close friend of Bishop Graber, was given special privileges by his Bishop to have access to the material collected by Fr. Maximillian. There were strict conditions, such as viewing only in the presence of a witness, no removal or copying. Hanauer ignored these conditions and freely removed files from the archives. The situation reached a point where Fr. Maximillian resigned and the job was passed on to a Dr. Straeter.

In 1973, Hanauer published his book *Miracles or Miracle Craving?* This book is discussed under "Adversaries," Chapter 5.) The press picked up the scent and at an official press conference at Konnersreuth, presided over by Bishop Graber, the press, relentlessly demanded the Bishop's comments to Hanauer's book. The Bishop most reluctantly said that Hanauer was (past tense) his friend and that he had allowed him access to the files of Resl. He also told the press that he had a copy of Hanauer's book on his desk, but needed to put on gloves to touch it. Hanauer had revealed his true face in the book by his opposition and ridicule of his Bishop.

Shortly thereafter, in 1974, Graber initiated the process of exhumation of Resl's remains and transferal into the parish church. Plans were drawn up to prepare a special cryptal space before the Theresian Altar.

At this point in time, Hanauer served the following threat to his Bishop: Should he (the Bishop) proceed with the step of exhumation, he (Hanauer) will do everything possible to stop the exhuming and any attempts at starting the beatification process. He will do everything possible to slander and discredit Resl and the Bishop.

The Bishop "backed down". Some time later, at the dedication of the Theresianum, Ferdinand Neumann asked him when he would open the process. Graber replied: "If I knew when Hanauer dies, I could give you an answer." Resl's beatification had come to a dead stop.

It is unbelievable that the Bishops of Regensburg cannot silence a priest of their diocese! Both Bishop Graber and now Bishop Mueller have continually shown to be intimidated by this diocesan priest, Father Hanauer. What possible "hold" could this man have to so strangle the Diocese of Regensburg?

Bishop Graber died in 1976 and was succeeded by Manfred Mueller, who, at this writing is the Ordinary of the See of Regensburg. More recently, Fr. Hanauer has further escalated his threats, virtually into the face of Bishop Mueller and the Catholic community at large. His book *Konnersreuth: Lie and Fraud with Ecclesiatical Blessing?* is an open declaration of war against Resl and any attempt toward beatification. (Chapter 5) In 1988, during a radio interview, Fr. Hanauer again made it absolutely clear that he will do everything in his power to prevent the beatification.

In the fall of 1992, the chairman of the present "Ring of Konnersreuth" Richard Daentler, officially inquired as to the status of beatification. Here is a translation of Bishop Mueller's reply:

Mr. Richard Daentler
Roemerstr. 27
8078 Eichstaett

Oct. 19, 1992

Dear Studiendirektor!

I would like to state my sincere thanks to you and all the other undersigned for your letter and faithful prayers. I recognize your efforts to assemble the documentation and would like to express a special may-God-repay-you.

I too am much impressed with the well researched address of editor Toni Siegert. The credibility of Therese Neumann has thus been much strengthened. Nonetheless, I do not see the present time to open the process of beatification on the Diocesan level as being opportune. Permit me also to mention that several significant preconditions are missing.

The presently existing internal situation in the Church makes the opening of a process inadvisable. I know this myself, and keep hearing it from my fellow priests, that this undertaking would precipitate a dangerous rift in the clergy and laity, even to far beyond the diocesan borders. Many are only waiting for internal disagreement in order to do damage to the Church. Most certainly, they would unleash a running cannonade, starting with the "Spiegel," down to the many regional publications, not only against Theresa Neumann but in particular against the Church itself. How should the phenomena of Konnersreuth be accepted by our present day secular world, when even the miracles of our Lord are being doubted? It would remain wholly unnoticed, thereby, that in the process of beatification the virtuous life plays a central role.

One must be fully aware that the expected public contentions would not only damage the Church itself, but also Therese Neumann. Apart from the ridicule and scorn, from which I hope to spare the deceased and her family, it would in no way be advantageous for the process to be drawn into the crossfire at the very outset. It could in fact lead to a polarization between supporters and antagonists. The unforeseeable consequences of such a development could lead to a exodus from the Church. My predecessor, Bishop Dr. Graber was aware of all these dangers and therefore did not risk to open the process, even though Therese Neumann was personally known to him and he felt a certain bond toward her.

Nor do I see the necessary precondition in place for the opening of the process. According to my official counsel, Fr. Ritter, in no way has the collection been completed, preventing the start of the document process. There still are writings by Theresa Neumann which are in private hands. These might yield conclusion as to her spiritual life and her world of thoughts. I therefore wish to continue with my plea to you to maintain your efforts, and, as much as possible for you, to submit all documents, at least in the form of verified photocopies.

I would like to tell you also, that Counsel Ritter has received my approval to begin, yet this year, with the written interviews of witnesses.

The virtue of wisdom out of love for the Church commands patience until the time is ripe and all preconditions exist. Until then let us pray and not let the objective go out of sight.

With greetings and blessings for today, and a may-God-reward-you for all you and your wife's endeavors,

Your Bishop

+Manfred
(Manfred Mueller, Ordinary of Regensburg)

Since this is the latest official word from the Roman Catholic Church, it is worthwhile to look closer at some of the statements made by Bishop Mueller.

Mueller's remarks about "Resl's credibility being strengthened by Siegert's speech," I ask, just where is Resl's credibility in the eyes of Regensburg? How many more Siegerts are needed to begin the process?

To open the process "would precipitate a dangerous rift in the clergy and laity, even far beyond the diocesan borders." What a perplexing statement! If Resl passes the thorough scrutiny of the

Congregation of Rites, then, according to the teaching of our Church, she is truly a saint and in Heaven and we must rejoice! If she fails the multitude of tests by the Congregation of Rites, then, so be it. That is what the Congregation of Rites is there for. In either case, why are these priests so vindictive? Why this rebellion? The Church has set the guidelines that are to be followed, and the process should be formally begun while there are still people who have known her, be they pro or con, and while material and information is still present, not lost. The priests who rebel should be counseled by their Bishop and reminded of their vow of obedience. It is difficult to understand what these rebellious priests fear?

John, Chapter 6:35-71, "I am the Bread of Life." can be applied, not only to the Holy Eucharist but to true belief in Jesus and His Church. We are his followers only if we believe in Him, the Son of the Living God, and in His Church. It is interesting that, not all that did not believe, left Him. In verse 70, Jesus says that even after being chosen by Him, some will be working against Him. "Have not I chosen you twelve, and one of you is a devil?" This is not to say that priests who are rebelling or are against Resl are devils. However, "by their fruits you shall know them."

It takes humility to become a true believer. Humility, which according to St. Augutine is the foundation of all virtues and is a moral virtue. Perhaps there is a lack of humility and thereby a lack of obedience.

His Excellency fears the *Spiegel,* a German tabloid which feeds solely on society's ills and spiritual cadavers. The Church is much too great to fear the judgments formed by reading such low-class publications. If Fr. Hanauer is going to make good on his threats, then indeed, the Bishop has reasons to be fearful. Our Lord was constantly at odds with the world and the establishment, so we, the Church, will always be at odds with the world, its "isms" etc.. Jesus did not compromise and neither can the Church.

About "acceptance of the phenomena of Konnersreuth by the secular world," here again, it is not the acceptance of the secular world but by the Church that we must be concerned about. After all, as children of God, we are not of this world, only in it.

Quote: "Public contentions would not only damage the Church itself, but also Therese Neumann." unquote. The Church has been attacked for 2000 years. I am sure the opening of the Informative

Process will not shake Her too much. What harm could the process do to Resl? The facts speak for themselves and are to be judged only under and by the rules and regulations as set forth for Beatification and Canonization.

"Bishop Graber was aware of all these dangers." Yes, Bishop Graber did know the problems, but these were of a very personal nature, and not of the Roman Catholic Church per se.

Quote; "could lead to an exodus from the Church." The Bishop's concern of this exodus at this time is perhaps unjustified. Again, from John 6, the exodus of His disciples did not prevent our Lord from presenting the "truth." I am sure He wept bitterly for them. However, the "truth" He did not compromise.

Because the Informative Process has been delayed for over thirty years, the Catholic laity all over the world has been denied the grace of a beatification which historically leads to conversions, returns to the Church, and the spiritual elevating and rejoicing of the faithful? Who could even guess at the numbers? To this date over 35,000 petitions for beatification were received by Regensburg!

The Bishop states "several significant preconditions are missing" also "Nor do I see the necessary preconditions in place for the opening of the process." The Bishop does not state what these preconditions are. However, if these preconditions are the gathering of information, be they interviews, writings, etc. regarding the candidate, then he is preempting the Informative Process itself! As previously stated, the purpose of the Ordinary Process (or Informative Process) is to establish a Tribunal to gather such information and produce the "Transumptum" which is a sealed copy of the information which is then delivered to the Congregation of Rites. The Postulator studies then submits the "Transumptum" to the Congregation of Rites.

In defense of Bishop Mueller, it could be said that he is in a most uncomfortable dilemma. On one hand he carries the burden of Hanauer's threats with all its potential implications, while on the other hand he must be aware of the consequence of withholding the beatification from the legions of faithful Catholics and Christians. His letter is a cautious tip-toe navigating between Scylla and Charybdis, with the classic escape into indefinite postponement.

Two days after Easter Sunday, 1996, the German television station ZDF, aired a 45 minute clip on Resl titled "The Suffering Bride". It was orchestrated by a certain Herr Uwe Beck and featured Father Hanauer plus a nondescript psychoanalyst, Herr Hoffmann from Vienna. The program was a most shameful piece of libel, defamation and infamy against Resl. Father Hanauer offered his usual line of perversions and lies. The psychoanalyst gave "authoritative testimony" that Resl was an hysteric, her stigmata self-inflicted, her inedia a figment of her imagination, but most of all her visions, especially those of the Passion of Our Lord, were the product of insatiable masochistic mental sex orgies. Hoffmann also purported that Saint Francis of Assisi had a father complex and therefore he self-inflicted the "supposed" stigmata. Herr Beck offers his own theology by referring to Our Savior as a "Cruel God", "the guilt must be redeemed no matter by whom", also "The Catholic Church preaches suffering to the youngest, the Savior demands suffering". The show closes with the words "Her (Resl's) charm, ability to connive and the miracle craving of people, created the cult of Konnersreuth." Father Hanauer directed a whole series of ridicule against both his former Bishop, Bishop Graber, and his present ordinary, Bishop Manfred Mueller. With its insidious makeup, solemn music, out acting and facade of objectivity, this show undoubtedly fell on the now most fertile ground of the "enlightened society of Germany." Thus far, Regensburg has remained silent.

Perhaps His Excellency should gird himself with courage and openly face his antagonists by officially declaring the opening of the Informative Process. Others before him have walked into the arena to face the predators!

LETTERS AND VISIONS

INTRODUCTION TO THE TRANSLATIONS

Resl had hundreds of visions, almost on a daily basis. Most often, the content of the visions coincided and paralleled the saint's days and all the religious holidays and functions of the annual liturgical calendar of the Church.

Although a small fraction of her visions, the Passion of the Lord Jesus are the most outstanding, heart-rending revelations. I have therefore chosen to include them in this book. To allow the reader to understand how the text of the visions in this book came to be, to submit his or her mind to narrations, recountals, and facial expressions (see pictures,) four short introductory notes precede the actual text.

The first is Ferdinand Neumann's story of the technological part of the recording (and its perils); the second is Resl's own reflections on the visions; the third is an eye-witness account of Erwein Freiherr von Aretin; the fourth and last is the translators comments as to vernacular, linguistic particularities, and some specific characteristics of Resl's narrative.

EXPLANATIONS BY FERDINAND NEUMANN

It seems important to me to explain why I, exclusively, through all those years recorded my sister Resl's visions, and produced photographs and 16mm films of her. It came about through a virtual mandate from the Bishop of Regensburg, the Ordinary of the

Diocese to which Konnersreuth belongs. The occasion was a visit of Resl, Fr. Naber, Prof. Wutz and myself with Bishop Buchberger. He took me aside and said the following: "You are a student and have a good comprehension of how one must document important events for the future. Surely you could find friends at Eichstaett who would be willing to assist you in photographic documentation. Significantly important would also be a record of the recountals of the various happenings and visions of your sister. You bear a great responsibility here. Later on it will be expected of you to have created this material."

Friends of mine at the Salesianum at Eichstaett, Fr. Reif and in particular Fr. Kaboeck were experts in photography. Not only did they introduce me to the world of photography, but to get started, loaned the necessary equipment to me. I could, however not help wondering though, why the Bishop would give me such a far reaching directive without offering at least some financial support! Neither photographs nor films were to be developed by customary labs; I myself developed and edited all pictorial material. To be able to do this, additional acquisitions were necessary. That this procedure, to develop films personally was necessary, became immediately clear through the following. Normally, one would send the exposed 16mm film material to the development labs of the manufacturer, such as Kodak or Agfa. Usually within days, the processed films were returned. On Good Friday 1936, I filmed, for the first time, in 16mm, Resl in the state of suffering. As usual, I then sent the films to the Kodak lab in Berlin for development. I waited a long time, but the films were not returned to me. Only after I hired an attorney who contacted the firm did I receive, many weeks later, my film. This was the signal for me that hereafter I could not let any outside lab do the development. From that day on, I developed and processed all films myself.

In 1937, I was eventually able to purchase equipment to record sound, a so called Newtone recording device, utilizing "Zelit" (soft plastic) disc records. The recording technology in those days was most complicated and expensive.

In connection with these first audio recordings in the Christmas days of 1938, an important event took place. Resl recounts, in the state of exalted elevation, the happenings of a vision; at that particular time the liberation of Joseph of Arimathea. In her condition of total reclusiveness, she was unable to determine what went on around her. As she was also unable to see, she accidentally touched my microphone. Resl demanded of Fr. Naber, who normally carried out the questioning about the contents of visions, that this equipment be destroyed. Fr. Naber rejected the demand and most emphatically explained to her that the Savior is in full agreement with the recordings. To illuminate the actual exchange of words, I am adding here the words of the original recording of the voices of Fr. Naber and Resl. (Translators note: This exchange of words is contained verbatim in the vision of the Passion, as well as the subsequent discussion between Fr. Naber and Ferdinand, and therefore not repeated here.) This discussion firmly encouraged me to continue and intensify further audio recording.

Two years later, in January 1940, something happened which was quite disconcerting to me. I planned to record Resl's visions of the HOLY MAGI. Late in the evening, on January 5, I left Eichstaett for Konnersreuth, the car loaded full of complex recording gear. It had snowed some, and I decided for a brief rest on the Autobahn somewhere near Bayreuth. About one kilometer later, there was a gunshot-like bang of such force that I had yanked the steering wheel off course, but managed to bring the car to a halt, positioned at right angles on the shoulder, right on the edge of a steep embankment. After I had checked all tires, which were O.K., I thought it could have been an explosion under the hood. But all was normal. After I turned the headlight back on, I noticed a strip of something across the entire windshield.

Looking at it, I remembered that it felt as though something had hit the windshield with great force. Therefore, I checked if I might have hit something as I came to a stop on the edge of the embankment. But there were no signs of any obstacle. I continued on and arrived at my parental home in Konnersreuth around 2:00 a.m. I quietly slipped into my room and at 7:00 a.m., the Feast of the HOLY MAGI, went over to the church without having talked to anyone. My place there was always behind the altar, next to Resl. After Resl received Holy Communion, a time when she was always in the state of exalted repose, she gave me a sign that she had something to tell me. Invariably with mixed emotions did I respond to these requests, because it happened at times that Resl, in this condition had reprimands for less glorious behavior of oneself.

Resl said to me the following: "About what happened last night, you don't have to have any anxieties; the evil one (Resl's expression of the devil) wanted to get you off the road and to have you plunge over the embankment. Take a look at your windshield and you will see he brushed across the car. It was not after you he was, but the destruction of the recording equipment. Stay in good graces with the Mother (the Holy Mother of God), for She is stronger than the evil one."

If this accident had actually happened, it would have had tragic consequences for me because I would not have been able to replace the equipment. It would have meant the end of any audio recordings of Resl.

Another clarification is necessary. Especially in more recent time, I keep hearing, not infrequently, that it was indeed strange that it was I who made most of Resl's photographs or was the only one who had her approval to do so. This opinion seems to have been generated or strengthened because of a movie with voice, produced by the fashion media some years ago. Since then, this movie has been widely distributed. At one point in the movie the statement is made: "She does not at all appreciate to be photographed. At the clicking sound of a camera she often turns away. Only and alone her brother Ferdinand is permitted to take pictures of her."

The statement in the movie is of course exaggerated. Many of the existing pictures were the work of my brother Hans. Of the two of us, he was surely the better amateur photographer. Of course, the majority of all pictures were mine as well as all audio recordings.

The opinion that I had special privileges in the presence of my sister Resl had also been furthered because of a written declaration by her and attested to by Fr. Naber. This declaration reads as follows:

Konnersreuth, 15-03-1955. Declaration:

My brother Ferdinand Neumann, presently County Supervisor of Kemnath, is irrevocably and exclusively authorized to take pictures, movies and audio recordings of me. He is obligated to pursue unlawful publications of any kind through legal means. He is furthermore authorized to use and dispose of this material and existing pictorial and aural documentation according to his own judgment.

Signed: Theres Neumann
Attested to: Father Joseph Naber

This declaration came about for the following reason. In the year 1955, pictures of Resl in the state of her Friday Passion began to appear in the area of the city of Konstance. The attorney I had engaged was unable to prevent this. Therefore, I had to produce this declaration with which it was then possible to attain a restraining order from the courts against these business practices.

For me, throughout all the years, Bishop Buchberger's mandate was indeed decisive for all pictorial and audio documentation.

−Ferdinand Neumann

RESL'S OWN REFLECTIONS ABOUT HER VISIONS

Recorded by L. Witt, and transposed from her Stiftlaender dialect into German.

I cannot help to have visions. I consider myself solely a tool which God can use as he sees fit. If, for myself, my unusual wounds would vanish this day and my visions would cease, that would be all right with me. I do not care whether I have visions or not.

During a vision, I look, observe. I am so totally engaged with the loving Savior that I have no time left for myself to in any way shape or form think of myself.

At the outset of a vision, I see the loving Savior, suddenly, flaming into existence like lightning. Every single event occupies me in its totality, not allowing me to think of what else there is to follow or that I might have seen it in a previous vision or might have learned all this in its main features from the Holy Scriptures.

Everything is new to me again, like the first time. My physical surrounding I neither see, hear nor feel in the slightest.

I don't see pictures, I see real objects. I see the Savior and other persons as clear and effortless as anything one would see, and like what goes on in a street. But I cannot reflect at the same time, that I would like to see this or that more accurately. I cannot select the objects of my interest according to my own desires, as one is used to do when viewing things. That which is most significant thrusts itself onto me. I have no time for idle curiosity. I do not watch like a spectator sees a stage play. Nor do I see what I observe as though it is somewhere in the distance. But I watch like one who is part of it. I am unaware that I am lying in bed though. Had I been part of it 2000 years ago, I could not have seen clearer, not have perceived it more closely then I see it now. To me, it is as though everything is happening for the first time, everything I see and watch.

THERESE NEUMANN DURING HER VISIONS, AS OBSERVED BY ERWEIN FREIHERR VON ARETIN

As far as it is possible to come to a conclusion from all the data, one thing is certain: that these visions constitute knowledge, knowledge which neither the visionary nor any witness present could possess. Resl appears here to be entirely the object of an external force, a force imperceivable to our senses.

This is also the visible picture of these visions. With a matchless brutality, often in the middle of a word, at times in the middle of functions which draw Resl far away from the spiritual world, do these visions crash down on her, like primeval thunderstorms, yank her from her pillows into positions which defy all physical laws of gravity, drawing her tensed arms forward; only her facial expressions, incredibly alive and reflective, tell us what she is seeing and experiencing.

The verbal recounting of the experiences, and with it the interpretation of facial expressions can only follow.

(On Good Friday's vision of the Passion:)

In unrelenting crescendo, mankind's most grave deed, passes before us, in precise sequence known to us in the Gospels.

A deeply gripping thought: to gaze into those bloody eyes which see the Savior, to look at these ears which hear words and sounds, which resounded in a distant land 2000 years ago. With frightening regularity, defying all natural, and, oh so fervently attempted explanation, do these events repeat, every Friday, accurate to the minutes, so that my guide (Prof. F.X. Wutz) could predict for me with unerring precision all that, down to the smallest detail, was to transpire.

TRANSLATOR'S NOTE

The original wax record recordings made in 1941 by Therese's brother Ferdinand, were transcribed by him from Resl's Stiftlaender dialect into German. Ferdinand told this translator that his transcription (into written records) is meticulously verbatim, even if the resulting sentences do not seem to make sense. After some deliberations between Ferdinand and the translator, the decision was made to maintain the English translations also verbatim with only the most minor adjustments where deemed absolutely essential.

All of Resl's recountals as recorded were told by her in the state of exalted repose. While there are several greatly divergent opinions as to Resl's age of "comprehension of abstract thought," anywhere from infantile incomprehension to that of a five year old, the translator could find no evidence to any claimed childlike comprehension. Resl's entire personality of most intense partaking speaks from every word she says. What may have caused some of the above opinions, is her not infrequent helter-skelter narration, simply due to excitement and the desire to tell it all at once. The fact that she uses character and event descriptions of people, such as I-DARE-NOT for Pontious Pilate, or the EARCUTTERER for the Apostle Peter, agrees with the fact that she never could in advance learn the actual names, since each and every time the visions came, they were new to her.

For the translation of the Aramaic words and phrases, the translater is indebted to Prof. Guenther Schwarz and his recent book *Das Zeichen von Konnersreuth* (The Sign of Konnersreuth).

Lastly, Resl, with her strong personality also possessed a definite form of thinking and speaking. Essentially uncomplicated, yet directly to the point, and with her natural wisdom uncovering the thoughts and intentions of persons she sees, her ability to grasp the meaning of foreign phrases while the academic verbiage remained hidden, all form a delightfully live narrative. The translator has therefore endeavored to give Resl the English she would have spoken, had she been American.

Concluding, the recountals are published here for the first time. The reader should be aware of this distinction. All other publication were, without exception, second or more often third hand. Here, for the first time, Resl speaks to all of us directly.

– Wendell E. Rossman

FROM THE VISIONS OF RESL; THE PASSION AND DEATH OF JESUS CHRIST

A verbatim translation from recordings and transcriptions by Ferdinand Neumann.

The Mount of Olives

Resl: Then the Savior walked away, you don't have time to think, you are simply there, it goes like lightning, you just can't even think, I think to be there and you are plain there.

Naber: There is no ship, no horseless carriage?

Resl: Yeah, I was simply there. But you know, there was the Savior, with the men, all of them except the one who got a little piece of bread and then went away. The vicious one, the fake-saint (Judas), not with him, but with all the others did the Savior walk down the hill, away from the town, nice and slow did they walk towards a hill, a garden. Yes, it was a beautiful garden. And the Savior often stopped and talked to the men ever so kindly. It was so hard on Him, so hard, and He said something to a few of the men. The garden was so beautiful there, with smaller and bigger houses. And it had beautiful trees. It was night and the moon was quite a ways up. The moon was not quite full, a little was still missing. It was a beautiful and bright night, but pretty cold it was.

And there we went up and I went with them and then the Savior said something to the men. You know only to some of them who stayed there, they did not go further, but the Earcutterer (Peter), the young man (John) and the other, who likes so much to be with the Savior (James.) These three liked to be with the Savior. They went with Him. Then the Savior went on by Himself. There, the garden became wild, the three went a little ways into the wild part, but the Savior went on to where it was even more wild.

There were such rocks sticking out, such shrubs hanging down, there was this cave into which the Savior slowly walked into and it was so hard for Him, you know the moon was so bright, it was gruesome and there the Savior got down on His knees.

He liked to do that in the night, praying in the mountains. Then He put His hands so together, you know so under His beard, the hands into each other. Then He prayed, looked up to heaven, then thought so, looked so, much did the Savior think about.

I went in with Him, The Savior did not see me as yet, did not look to me. Not there but later. Oh me; did it get ever so hard for the Savior, oh, and all that He must have thought about. And I think He thought of all His pain (coming,) you know the most terrible thing but not only that, but He must have also thought how the people did not want to know Him, how they did not love Him. I mean all that He thought about, like I felt it in me, it was so hard on the Savior.

Then for a while longer He kept kneeling there, then He got up and walked around. He was in such sad shape. It was so hard on the Savior, I can't say otherwise, so hard that He kept looking up to heaven and put His arms up toward heaven and then turned around and went to the men.

It was hard on them too, they had sort of propped them-selves up on the rocks - and were napping. That was for some time. He then said something to the men. For them this was hard too. They did not recognize the Savior like that. They got up and wanted to go with the Savior but He did not let them come along, He had said: You stay here. You know, not - our language, but one could see it was like that. The Savior then left again, He walked slowly, it was again hard on Him. It was not long and He again got down on His knees, prayed again and put His hand kind of in front and let His face down to the ground and prayed. And woe! It was so hard on Him. The Savior then started to sweat. The blood came from His forehead, from the nose and all around the mouth, from His hands the blood oozed out. Woe, it was so hard on Him. He kept wiping it off but it didn't help. Then He got up again, looked up to heaven and lifted His hands up again. Then He was leaning up against a boulder because He staggered some with His knees. He couldn't stay up properly any more. You know this made the Savior so weak. The fright, the fear was so hard on Him. One saw that. That He had for us, surely for us. Now He went back to the men.

As He went back, He talked again with the men. They again had fallen asleep, you see they could not quite take it any more.

Then the young man wanted to go with the Savior, but He wouldn't let him. Because the young man so much liked the Savior. The Savior tottered, one can say did not walk right any more, He was swaying. He went farther forward, and Oh! It felt gruesome for Him, so He was leaning up against the boulders in the cave, looked up to heaven, knelt down again and put His head to the ground, the hands bled sweating blood. The blood drops just pressed out of His hands. The blood ran down over His eyes, His face.

Then the Savior prayed again, He kept saying, "TE SEBUTACH - TE SEBUTACH," (Your Will - Your Will.)

Here, the Savior looked at me quite fully. As the Savior said, "TE SEBUTACH," I got a pain at my heart and something flowed from it. It was like if someone stabs into it, and like if something is ripped out and something cold ran down. And since then it never closed again. No, since then again and again blood comes out whenever it is hard for me because of the Savior.

I gladly bear it. I say, my Savior for whom ever You want it. Truly! Yeah, it was hard for our Savior also, so we can join Him a little ways. Has it no value I always say, Savior, I add my little bit to Yours. Then it has also value. Then You can give it to who you would want. Sometimes I do say and would think (for whom,) but I leave it to You Savior, for whom you want. I like saying it like that. Really, one self gets to feeling so hard. I get so cold all over, I felt so sorry for the Savior, you know, He so agonized, looked up to heaven, and how the blood kept coming, you know, so hard. I felt so sorry for the Savior, so very much; there I did have to weep. There my heart hurt so much too. And when it was quite so hard on the Savior, like He could not go on any further, all at once a lighted man (Angel) came. Yes, yes, a lighted man to the Savior and said something to Him, did He then sigh so relieved the Savior, and now He went back to the men. There He again said something reproaching to the men and the Savior was so restless. He then said something that made the Earcutterer come quite so much to life. And sleep left him right away.

In the meanwhile, what would you think happened? One could see that from down there, from town, some came with burning torches. The Savior knew about that already. There were some, some Wantobesmarter (Pharisees) ones and some wild people, there was one, and one and one and one. They were all furious and the Savior looked at them and the men (Apostles,) the Earcutterer (Peter) just like he is you know, right away eager. The Savior told him to calm down. And when the Savior saw them coming, He started to shiver, the Savior, yeah, one could see that the Savior shivered because He was quite so weakened. Thirsty

He was too, one could see that. The others (apostles,) the ones the Savior did not want to come out, they were restless and lay in waiting because when the others had arrived, the men got there too. They lay in waiting what was going to happen and why aren't we not allowed to come forth. They did after all hear and sense what is going to happen. They screamed over and over, "MA HA DA, MA HA DA" (What is this, what is this) when they saw them coming.

A long pole they had, and a fire was boiling on it. It smelled like pitch and torches they had, burning ones, when they came up they lit some more which was not needed because of the moonlight. Truly, they themselves were afraid, I think, then when the Savior saw them coming, the Savior walked towards them, and there He was forceful now. He went to them and said something, then they said "JESHUA NAZREA," I don't quite know it.

Then the Savior said, "ANNA" (I,I.) At that, some of them fell down. The Wantobesmarter and the furious ones did not fall down and the two-faced one (Judas) and the furious ones neither. But the ones who keep order in the house, (temple guards,) they fell down, yeah, but not the Wantobesmarters. No, and then the Savior said to them, "KUMO" (Get Up). Now, but in between, they lunged at the one (Judas), I have to tell you this first, the Earcutterer and the other one, the tall one (James), would you believe they grabbed the two-faced one.

No, I know what you want to ask, but that comes later, no they charged at the two-faced one, they knew he was the snake in the grass, but the Savior called them off and did, when they had gotten up again, then the Earcutterer tore loose again, went forward and pulled somebody's knife out, because he did not have one himself and he ripped out his knife and wanted to cut his head off, but only hit his ear.

(Resl touches my microphone) What is this! There is something. No, I want to tell it to you (Father Naber) only.

Now the blood ran down, the ear still hung by some skin, then the Savior went to him, touched the ear and right away it was right again. Yes, and He said to the Earcutterer "Put this back," you know, into the leather pouch he had to put it down, like they carried it. First he (Peter) took the other fellow's knife, but to cut off the ear he real fast pulled his own knife. First he had taken the other one's but the Savior had held him off because he was so very impulsive, ha - ha. So had to put it back into his leather, he kept it stuck under his garb, so that he had to rip out the other's knife and that the Savior did not allow at all.

Then he (Judas) went to the Savior afterwards, He (the Savior) was very grave, the one whom the Savior put his ear back, well, he sort of slunk to the back, yes he got the scare. But now, the two-faced came, and he liked (kissed) the Savior.

Naber: Only now?

Resl: Yeah, only now for sure, no not before, otherwise they would have grabbed the Savior right away, they did not grab Him at first, it indeed takes a short spell, no, only now. Then the Savior said something kind to him yet, then He said something serious. At first, before he liked (kissed) Him, the Savior said something kind, but then something grave, something very grave. Oh, the men looked on with big eyes, the ones who belonged to the Savior, and the other one who always fixed things, always had some water with him, (James) he was leaping over and yelled, "KANAPA MAGERA" (Thief, Traitor,) so did he yell, and grabbed him up front. At that, the Savior called it off. The Savior did not want that.

When the Savior said it is Him and pointed at Himself He talked for the others (apostles) that they should not be harmed, one could tell. They had nothing on them (apostles), they wanted only the Savior. Yeah, him on whom the Savior had put the ear back on, he slunk out of sight. Yeah, the Savior did nothing. When the one (Judas) liked (kissed) the Savior, and when all the others argued around, the others (temple guards) used the moment went forward and bound the Savior but horribly they bound Him; so much they tied Him from the elbows crosswise forward, over and around the elbows, the arm together at front, so that the Savior couldn't move any more. And this was such a blight for the Savior. Now He fell down easy and could not help Himself. If only His elbows would have been free. But the elbows were yanked and tied to the back. And they, the furious ones were raging, and the Wantobesmart ones. The ones who keep order in the house (temple) helped along.

Yes, they too helped. With the ropes, they made a belt around the Savior. There were many little iron hooks on it, which hurt the Savior very much, they were on the inside of the belt. Those were iron hooks, you know, that pressed in the Savior, you know, when they yanked on the ropes, so the Savior could much feel it, and the ropes went to one and one and one and one from the belt. More straps than ropes, and so they grabbed the Savior. He could not get away any more.

That way they went down, a long ways. The Savior kept looking up to heaven and prayed, always. Looking up and praying. Weak He was and thirsty too from when it was so hard on Him, you know. Well now, they went down along the wall, down from the mountain, they did not go into the town as yet. They could have, up there already. They went down, down towards the creek. They came down from the mountain which was a long ways until one gets down and then they went across the bridge. On the bridge they threw Him down, you know, He had such a hard time walking, He kept tripping, then on the bridge they pushed Him into the creek. And that was something.

As we came near town, some men stood there, not the straight men (Roman soldiers) but the ones who keep order in the house (temple guards). As though as they have been expecting us, they lay in wait, more and more were on the way. They did not go up into the garden, only when we came near town. We went past this place, to the creek. There, on the bridge stood some. They did know that the others came this way. Why? They most likely were afraid of the people, so that no uprising could happen. So it looked to me.

Oh woe, now they push the Savior into the creek. There was little water in it, pushed Him in, they did. It was quite a ways down. Oh the water was so dirty. The Savior was thirsty and He did drink from the water. Oh my, I felt so bad for Him. You know, the thirst. Then they pulled Him out again. He couldn't come out Himself. He was soaking wet, not able to help you know, on account of His arms which were tied so tough, you can't help yourself that way. You have to imagine the Savior. They pulled Him out that way. And you know, if they pull, the hooks hurt so much. At that, the Savior lamented, He called out loudly Ah Ah, the belt hurt so much around the soft chest part around the ribs where the hooks hurt where He had the belt around. And the Savior now had a very hard time walking. The wet attire slung itself around His legs. There, they walked down, there would have been smoother paths but they did not go there. They went through a rough area. There were rocks, and the Savior was barefoot, oh, soon His feet bled, He kept tripping and through thorn brush they walked. The furious went through but felt nothing.

Now I need to tell you this, oh my, now I remember something I should have told you before. Already further up, the young man (John) and the Earcutterer are there, they followed them and soon the Earcutterer made off quietly, and I saw him no more. But the young man followed and they recognized him, now they grabbed him by the shoulders, but he quickly reached out, let go of his coat and slipped away. Yes, he wanted to go to the Mother (Mary). The Mother was there in the big town in a house with the women and the young man went to surely tell all to the Mother. He then went. I didn't see the Earcutterer any more, I think he got himself lost and the others (apostles) I didn't see at all any more, they did not dare show themselves any more.

We then went in through a little gate, the Savior had been there often, they are very poor people. That is a whole quarter outside of town, all very poor people, they liked the Savior. The Savior often helped them, I think. There were a lot of people (guards) posted. They already knew of it all. They put a lot of these people there, to wait. And in spite of the simple people got news about it and they came out and lamented around the Savior, they got down on their knees on the street and clasped these hands and wailed and bemoaned the Savior, and the Savior looked at them, and it was good for the Savior that they had compassion. Oh so, I felt pitifully sorry for the Savior. The people sobbed and kept crying, "JESHUA, JESHUA BAR DAVIDAM," (Jesus, Son of David,) they kept repeating it. Do you know what that means? "JESHUA NAZAREA" (Jesus of Nazareth) they kept crying. And oh, "MALKA, JESHUA MALKA" (Jesus, King,) and woe, were they mad and mostly they were mad at these people (posted guards). They went through, and while they went through, through their quarter, one could see that all right, the people stuck together. Some followed, and they tried to push them back but the people would not let them. They simply followed. Right there, children once cried out, "SELAM - SELAM" (Hail, Hail) at Jesus' entry into Jerusalem. Yeah, here the Savior went through once. But oh, did these people have compassion with the Savior. They knelt across the road in front of them (temple guards), they tried to stop them. But nothing helped, they brought in more guards. You know, they already had assumed that.

Then they went on, there was sort of a corner, sort of upwards and then about we went into someone's place and meanwhile there there were bunches of people. You know, in the town we went up a little ways and into a big house, we went through a courtyard and everywhere big fires were burning. There were pots on poles, and torches crackled everywhere. We went through a courtyard and in the middle a big fire burned. On the sides there were kind of corners where the smoke went up, you know, drawn up, like chimneys they went up, and the smoke was drawn up that way so that they did not have it smoky. The Savior felt terrified. They already waited for the Savior to come. Men sat in kind of a semi-circle, there were all sorts of people, as many as had room went in.

The Earcutterer and the young man came in with the people, you know, with the people they came in because there were so many. There was pushing and shoving, good and evil, all went in. Then one of the guards hit the Savior in the face. Just think, one of them. He had iron on his hands. Iron you know, he was sort of a straight man. Not one of the straight men (Romans) who came later. They were not there yet. One just hit the Savior in the face. And sneering, you know, he wanted to make points with the old one (Annas.) The Savior did not respond. The one up there kept talking, he talked long. The Savior was in deep earnest and said nothing. Then the old one wrote something on a scroll and put it somewhere. You know, the Savior said something to the one who hit him. To the one up there He said nothing. You know, I felt why He did not want to talk to that one (Annas.) It had a meaning why He did not want to talk to him.

Because He, you know; no, I have to tell you something else first. The one up there had something rolled up and he wrote something yellow into it and put it onto a little stick and stuck the whole thing into the Savior's belt. The Savior then said something serious, something serious He said. Do you know why the Savior did not speak with him, because he was no good, yeah, not good, with him the Savior did not want to talk.

Then they led the Savior to one, out through the courtyard, through the fire. They belonged together, I think, to the one to whom they led Him now, a younger one, this one here was so old and haggard. To a younger (Kaiphas) one they led Him now. That one I think belonged to this one. And there they brought Him forward, past the fire, the Savior. And there the Earcutterer and the young man (John) slipped in. Oh, were there a lot of people. And all the others went in too. And up there, on a fine seat one was waiting already. A fine outfit he had on and on the head he had something, on the head something sparkling and in front on his chest he had something like little plates, in all colors. And a bit putting on it was, but really so very hollow.

And into there, they led the poor and dejected Savior. The Savior had to stand, down there. A lot of men sat on kind of steps, it was in tiers. There they again questioned the Savior. Then some talked against. A real confusion it was. Then the Savior spoke. Up there some jumped up. The one up there got into a rage. And the Savior spoke, decisive and mighty. And as the Savior spoke, the one up there (Kaiphas) took a knife and cut into his tunic, slit it all the way open and screamed AH, AH. Then he sat down up there. The others too sat down. Some talked against, but it too did not help. Of the people too some yelled, they were instructed to do so. And, how these goings on are. Then they did, this I tell you also.

It was cold. Now the Earcutterer came out and the young man also. A lot of people left when that one slit his clothes, a lot of people went away. The young man came out and he went to the Mother and the womenfolk. I went with him. Oh, it was hard for the Mother. He told her how the Savior was. Then they helped to get the Mother ready and lead her in to near where the Savior was. But the Mother left again, because she couldn't take it in this house. There were good womenfolk, but she couldn't take it.

Now, the young man guided her to close in, the Earcutterer did not come along, like he is! He had to stay there what is now going to happen, he was getting cold. Well, then he came out, went to the fire. But soon, some women found him out. Of the women some were quite impertinent. They started talking at him, but he fended them off. Oh, then again one talked at him but he fended her off. This went on for a while, but much came later.

In between I have to tell you something else. I want to tell you this right away, there it is easier on me, a man said something but he (Peter) again repulsed him. Now, you have to imagine how they had the Savior in there. Him, they lead out now, onto a square. Oh so, the others, those up there could look down on Him. But it was more outside, not with those in there. It was all open around. Oh how, what do you think.

Naber: What did they do there?

Resl: Took His clothes off and put an overcoat on Him. Oh, how did the Savior look. The coat put on, they put a stick in His hand, they put a hat on Him, of straw and a pointed cap on top, of straw. They spat on Him. A sort of tube He had in His hand. And screamed, "MALKA" (King), they kept screaming. Oh, why this? Oh, how horrible did they make it for the Savior, then they poked and pushed Him and kept spitting on Him. Oh, Oh my. I felt so awful for the Savior. On then, and in the meantime, the Earcutterer out there, had talked against the Savior, he denied that he knew the Savior, with the womenfolk. And I told this before, also to the man, who was an older man.

Now they led the Savior out. Now in this house there are kind of holes in the wall at the bottom, and into one of these holes they put the Savior. With the overcoat, they hung a heavy chain around His neck. It hung down and kept hitting against His knee. That way, they put the Savior into such a hole. The one up there (Kaiphas) had ordered it. And they were still staying together, the ones up there. Yes, into such a hole they locked Him up. He couldn't lean up against anything and He couldn't sit. So they chained the Savior up against the side.

Yeah, they had opened the ropes in there but now they re-tightened them, they did. You know, they loosened the ropes so they could strip him from his attire. Oh, during the night I went to visit the Savior several times. I felt so sorry for Him. And once, He looked long at me. A few stayed around, but He would not have run away, for certain. In one way I was happy that He no longer was in His wet attire, the Savior, on the other hand it was hard on me that He now only had a mere rag around Him. Why did they mock Him so, with an overcoat, it was sort of red, the coat, the one they put on him. Sort of reddish brown it was. Oh so!

Naber: Yes, and what about the Earcutterer?

Resl: Yeah, this I must tell you also. How they led the Savior out and put him into the hole. There, from above, a little bit of light came down. The moonlight came through. You know, the Earcutterer was there. There the Savior, well He had to be led past, before the fire, there he stood. There and then, the Savior looked at him (Peter) full of pain and love. And he (Peter) started to weep. Ah, indeed, it was hard on him, and beside himself he was, so beside himself.

I didn't see the Mother as yet. The young man took her down into town. Oh! and now. When it started to become daylight, they led the Savior out again. You want me to tell that right now?

Naber: Yes, Yes!

Resl: Because I am over it.

Naber: Indeed!

Resl: Much I will not tell you any more!

Naber: Do the best you can!

Resl: Inside it's getting so hard. You know, how one felt so sorry for the Savior. I had to weep this night. One thinks one can perhaps, one wants to help the Savior but one can't, can't help at all. Oh well, what do you think! It's not simple at all. Now, be patient and let me tell you.

So, as it was toward morning they were still together. Either they were still together or came back to be together again. You know...the one (Nicodemus) had protested, he did not accept what happened the night before. They should not have allowed to have the Savior so abused and not have finished with Him so early. The one, who once came to the Savior at night, he was after them. Then in the morning they were together again, all of them. Then they had the Savior brought in again. The one up there talked again, the one up there full of ridicule, oh, and sent the Savior away to one, a young one. They did not argue much more, but he wrote something. They sent this with Him. Oh so! He went along and also the old one. They got on horses.

The Negotiations with Pilate

It was pretty far to the mountain, to the young man there. To the I-Dare-Not (Pilate,) to him they went. And many went along and a whole bunch of Wantobesmarters (Pharisees) too. Oh my! It was a murderous train of people by now. Oh so! The old one could have stayed home, oh, he came along. Oh, and then the Savior. Oh my, and now to the one (Pilate). They did not dare go up all the way. There was a kind of a rise, they halted there and kept the Savior there also. A small piece further, and they stayed back. You know, you have to imagine, there is a large open square. And he was up there. He sort of slept. Not exactly sleeping but resting. You know, like a half a sofa, lazy he was laying there. Perhaps tired. He did not like the idea that they brought the Savior. Most likely, he had already heard about Him. Then they screamed all the while and put on a huge show, and the Savior stood there. And he (Pilate) talked with the Savior and the Savior did. He is the only one with whom the Savior talked serenely. Then, the Savior also talked, talked decisive, then he did again, yeah, he was the only one who was not malicious against the Savior. You know had no hatred. Only, he was afraid of the others, one could see it. They did not leave. Oh, if they had not come along, at the end it would have turned out all right for the Savior.

But they came on their own. No! They heaved the old one up on the horse. He was the last one we needed. Oh go! Then they talked some back and forth, and he didn't like that. He continued talking with the others. It was one big yacking, criss-cross wise.

The Savior stood alone there, you know. Oh my, go on, you know, in His coat. He looked heartbreaking. Then they talked again and talked with Him. And he did too, the one who didn't have much courage. Then he sent the Savior to another. They all went along. To an older one. I knew that one! I know him. Yes, he had, oh he is powerful.

Ah! To an older man. What is his name, the name of the one he sent him to?

Naber: Herod!

Resl: Yes, that be it. To him he sent the Savior. There he will have thought. He! They also fit together. He and the young one belonged together, just like the old one and the Robeslitter. In that way they also fit together. I think so, no? At the least, they understood each other, the young I-Dare-Not and this one. Did they belong together or did they just have the same ideas? Because he sent Him to that one. It was all right for that one. And they again came along.

Naber: (recording garbled)

Resl: But they did, even if they did not belong to each other, they did cooperate. Oh yeah, go! Why did he send the Savior to that one. There was something they had to say to one another. I had that impression.

   That one roared at the Savior. He too sat up there, high and mighty, he had a ruddy face. A red beard he had, and was pompous. The Savior did not talk with him. He let the Savior be mistreated and roughed up, terribly, terribly so. Oh, the way they kicked the Savior around. They, of course were there too, the old one and the Robeslitter. He (Herod) left things as they are. He then sent the Savior back to the I-Dare-Not.

   Oh! And in between something happened. He (Pilate) had a wife, she was not bad at all. And the wife, when the Savior was away, begged the man (Pilate) for the Savior. It was very obvious. Oh, and then the man gave his wife something, a beautiful, big flashing ring, he gave her. It had a meaning, it was so obvious. The wife left them, relieved. She had told the man much and he was restless. The wife left happy when she received the flashing thing.

   He sat high up and they led the Savior up. And there some mistreated him again.

(Return to Herod:)

Naber: What did that one (Herod) look like?

Resl: Awful wild. I felt so bad for the Savior. You know, they
        were such furious people. Why did the I-Dare-Not send
        the Savior to him? Because he himself had no courage,
        and because the wife talked so serious with him, because
        he gave his wife the flashing thing. I saw it. And Oh, they
        maltreated the Savior badly. But they didn't manage to
        handle the Savior. Then they led Him like He would es-
        cape and He was so tired.

        No, he (Herod) had something be done. Here, the face
        of the Savior was full of blood from all the blows and beat-
        ings and full of spit. He, when they brought the Savior in,
        pretended that he was repulsed. There, he had the Savior
        washed. Then they led the Savior up and they had some-
        thing hard and with it they rubbed the Savior down. He
        did this, I believe, only so he could maltreat the Savior. Oh
        so! But the Savior gave no answer. Now not, either. It lasted
        some time, quite some time.

Naber: When was it the Savior said nothing?

Resl: And there! You would like me to tell you?

Naber: Get started, go!

Resl: Oh, well the, wait, it was like this. Once before, they put a
        white robe on the Savior, then they put something on His
        head. And all the time they kicked Him around. There,
        the Savior did not say one word to him. First though, He
        spoke to the old one (Annas) and the Robeslitter (Kaiphas).
        But the other one not at all. He talked to the I-Dare-Not
        but to this one absolutely not. I think, it was because the
        Savior did not want to speak with him, I think I had that
        impression earlier, the Savior despised him. It was obvious.
        There, the Savior looked down so much. This made him
        (Herod) mad, that he didn't talk. He would have all along
        faked liking Him, faked liking the Savior. Yes, one could see
        all this. The Savior did not react. You know, the Savior did
        show His inner self a bit. They all looked so stupid when this
        one ridiculed Him and the Savior said nothing.

Then they again brought the Savior. Yeah, and that one had another robe put on Him, because the Savior at that time wore His own robe. They did not have the coat the Savior had on in front of the Robeslitter (Kaiphas). Then, this one (Herod), especially put yet another robe on the Savior and put a kind of pipe in His hand. Yeah, that one now, that one. It was a completely different robe, no more than a rag.

And then, Oh, the Savior had His own robe on again when they went, they had to walk through so many people. It was a long ways from the Robeslitter to this one (Pilate). Is true, I almost got it all confused, really, with all along this was put on, then that robe.

But, now let me tell you. Now they had the Savior again. And the I-Dare-Not sent one of the straight men (Roman soldier) to give him a message. Now, that one send someone ahead, this was well known. Yes, he to send someone, he was not pleased that the Savior said nothing.

Naber: Did you like that?

Resl: Yes, oh! You know, now I am pretty tired.

Naber: Then, let's quit.

Resl: No, because I tell you some more. Then when they brought the Savior back, he didn't like it at all, when they came back with Him. Yeah, did the I-Dare-Not dislike it. So they led the Savior up there. Oh my! They kept screaming, "SHALAPO, SHALAPO" (crucify, crucify!) That is what they yelled, but they did not dare go up.

I think they were not allowed to go up. Yeah! Did the Savior ever look dejected, when He saw all the people, fearful of the many of them. It was a pain for the Savior. And the young man had brought the Mother and the womenfolk to the place. Just think of it, I saw the Mother and the womenfolk there. It was hard on the Mother, they had to support her, there I felt so sorry for her. You know, she heard it all. It was on an open square, one could see a long ways, it was kind of a hill. And, oh! Then the I-Dare-Not had Him stand out there, and how horribly defaced and wounded was the Savior. No, before he had something else done, when they (mob) did not want to give in, he had the Savior beaten, and that comes first too. Oh, I won't tell you this any more, O go!

Naber: Then just tell it to me some other time!

Resl: Quite a bit more would come now. You want me to tell you that also?

Naber: Yes, all you had seen and heard.

Resl: Well so, they led Him back. Oh! In the meantime they were still at the I-Dare-Not, were still there. Go on, why? So they brought Him, back, the Savior. Oh!

Naber: Did the Savior wear His white robe?

Resl: Yes, when they brought Him first, this way yes, the other way no.

Naber: Did He still wear it?

Resl: Coming back, no.

Naber: How long did He then have it on?

Resl: Just wait now! There were the men, I saw this first, there was a marker in the cobblestones where they were not allowed beyond. Why, those Wantobesmart ones, why? They were down there. Oh! There it is now, there it was now bright daylight, you know day, bright day. A lot of people came together. Oh, some were for the Savior, the more of them against. Was it a chaos! You know, one could realize that they lied, up to the Savior, just plain lied, plain lied up to Him. Oh, go on! He (Pilate) didn't feel very agreeable that they brought the Savior back. It was so obvious. They kept yelling up to him (Pilate). They were not allowed up. They had led the Savior up. Now, they said something. I just don't understand the language. And them. Oh! Then he (Pilate) talked something with him. I just didn't understand. There was a lot of talking, a lot of talk. On they kept yelling, up.

Then they talked very serious with each other. And

there, the Savior talked very serious with him (Pilate) and
he too talked serious. Then he had the Savior again stood
in front and shouted something down to the people. And
they roared like the wild ones.

It took too long for them, much too long. Yes, the Savior was with him (Pilate) the longest. Then he said something, he, and gave an order. Oh woe, then they led the
Savior down. There were these large courtyards, no roof
over, you know cobblestoned. There are these columns,
several columns there. Then they tied the Savior to a column. That was what he (Pilate) had ordered. To tie to one
of these columns. On top, there was a kind of a ring. Go
on, I am not going to tell you this.

The Scourging at the Pillar

Naber: Go on, do tell it, so we too can have compassion for the
Savior.

Resl: Oh woe! First they, and the Savior had to help, took all
His clothes off. There He was so tired and His knees were
shaking.

Naber: Did they also take off His white robe?

Resl: Yes, everything off. His undergarments, they had not even
put on Him. Those they already took off at the Robeslitter.
Those they brought later. Then they put His arms up -
like, that the skin became tensioned. Those were ferocious
people, those were. They had placed them there. One of
them did the ordering. They beat only as he called it.

Naber: What was it they hit with?

Resl: Looks like small brooms, from brushwood, long rods, tied
into bundles. When they were done with that, they took
something-there were small spikes on it, it would bend
and on it were the spikes. Also blobs.

Naber: (recording garbled)

Resl: Go on, that's besides the point. And they beat the Savior, the skin was torn open. Those were iron spikes. Then they had yet something else. In the back it had a hole, and short chains were on it. I rather not tell you this.

Naber: Oh, go!

Resl: And on them there were kind of hooks fastened. Oh, I felt so sorry for the Savior. And they beat at him, the flesh was ripped out. Oh go! I am there again, alive.

Naber: Look here, so we do have compassion for the Savior.

Resl: Ah, Oh! My heart hurts at that. Then they turned the Savior around when they were done and did, they did tie a rope around over the knees also, or the Savior would have sunk down because He was at His end. And His arms backwards onto the column and they tightened it hard. And then beating again. Over the arms, the feet, no not the feet, but down to the knees. Oh, I felt so terrible for Him. Then, when they let go, when they opened the ropes, when they were done, then the Savior had collapsed. It was so terrible for Him. The Mother, for sure, was not far away, together with the womenfolk. I saw them today.

Naber: Did she see the Savior?

Resl: No, she was far enough away, but she heard everything. There, the young man was with her and the other women. I saw them several times during the night. All along, they were not very far distant, but not there where one could not see them. Oh go! And then the Savior tried to reach for His attire. But there was one, a young hooligan who kicked it away. A hoodlum, you know. They had, you know, and I found that out all right, they agitated, you know, the Wantobesmarterers, they bought something for them to drink so they were stone drunk. This, one could see clearly, this didn't pass by me.
        (Unclear). There was kind of a corridor to the back, and a stone was there. On it they stood Him. Then they draped a kind of rag over Him. His attire not put on Him. The rag they just draped over, shreds of a cape. His hands

bound together, then a tall grown stalk they put in His hands and then the Savior had to sit. He was so done for. Oh then! They put the thorns on His head. They didn't touch them. It was like a complete cap, only a little open on top.

Naber: How long were the thorns?

Resl: Oh so, there was one that had come out at the eye. Oh so, know they were pierced there into the forehead, they went in there. Mainly there they pushed them in. On the head. Oh come! Did I feel so sorry for the Savior. And all along they yelled and mocked. Oh, there were a lot of people present.

Naber: What did they yell?

Resl: "CHELA MALKA, CHELA MALKA DE JUDEA SHELA SABODACH MESHECH," (Hail King of Jews, Hail Your Grace) continually kept screaming.

And the Savior shivered so, you know His hands were roped together and He shivered. You know, He was freezing and He was thirsty. There, He all along opened His mouth, the Savior, and they went and just spit on Him, talked mockingly, all along it brought Him such pain. Then they lead the Savior again up to that one (Pilate). That one had the Savior being brought again. And there, one could almost hope, but it did not help. And there was one, a fierce one, one could see that, a real fierce one. And this fierce one talked first, they brought him in first. Then they (mob) screamed even louder. First though, is true, I should have told this first. Yeah! I had forgotten. I should have told this before. This one (Pilate), had the fierce one stand next to the Savior. And they kept screaming "BARABA - BARABA," before they beat the Savior, yes before they beat Him.

Now, he had the Savior brought forward. He led Him out alone. The Savior walked crooked. So fully bent over did he walk there. He couldn't quite stand up straight.

Then he talked something downwards. And now as the Savior was here, did the wife send the flashing thing to the man. And at that he (Pilate) became very excited. Got to be so restless. And there he led the Savior out so all could see Him. With the stick in His arm, so tied up. The rag over him. Some tassels hung down from it. You know, shreds, ripped off. Pieces ripped out. But oh so, now I am not going to tell you any more.

Naber: Oh, come on. Look, we didn't see how it happened for the Savior. Go on, so we too can feel compassion.

Resl: Yeah, then I will tell you some. Oh, they had no compassion with the Savior when they saw Him like this. They screamed like mad. Oh, you know the old one (Annas) and the Robeslitter (Kaiphas) were still there. That they didn't get restive? It did take long, quite long. Then they led the Savior back again. And again, he (Pilate) talked with privately, with the Savior. And with great might and power did the Savior answer. Then He said something this one didn't like. No, then he went outside and talked with separately, with the people.

They yelled, "CHALAPO, CHALAPO" (CRUCIFY, CRUCIFY.) Powerful they screamed. Louder! They yelled this at first, but now much worse. Oh, Oh, and then, when this one talked to the other, they brought something where they poured water into, over the hands. Then he yelled something down. On that, they screamed even more like mad. Oh, then this one sat in there for a while by himself. And the Savior stood there to the side in the corridor that led into this one's place, stood before those who held Him, ferocious ones, you know.

Condemnation

Then, this one raised himself up to grandness. The ones down there still did not quiet down. Then they brought his (Pilate's) attire, a kind of coat, the I-Dare-Not, then he put something on top of his head, something that sparkled and he yelled something down to them.

And that suited them. Yes, this he then wrote down. Then he wrote something else too and this was sent to somewhere. Then they brought him something else, a kind of brown wood, and he scrawled something in white on it. On line and another line and another line, every line in different writing. Onto the wood. This he read to them down there. He sort of pointed it downward. It did not suit them. But he did not let himself be talked into changing it.

Naber: What was the writing like?

Resl: Like in church so. Then another one was (garbled) and another one was sort of frilled, you know, like the other Father (Prof. Wutz) could do it.

Naber: (recording garbled)

Resl: I can't tell you that, I don't know the language. Oh so! There were some people who were favorable for the Savior. It was not agreeable to them. But the others roared like mad men. And then, it all turned into one confusion.

They then went away, went away, you know the ones, many of the Wantobesmarters, they all of a sudden were in a hurry, they went toward the big house (temple). Tell me, why were they in a hurry?

Then, he (Pilate) ordered some, many straight men (Roman soldiers) many and many went ahead, took some trumpets, and then put the Savior, you know what they brought, horrifying!

But oh, I must be ahead of it. They pulled off the coat and took down the thorns and put on the Savior's own brown robe, they had brought.

Naber: (recording garbled....) the belt He had on before?

Resl: They had tied it around Him earlier. And then first, after they pulled off the thorns, it (the belt) over the head because it did not properly untie, it was closed up so much. Oh How!

Naber: What did they do with the thorns?

Resl: Put them back on. And, oh, the robe was by then already glued to His back. When they ripped off the robe that had already glued on, the blood started to flow anew. When they pulled away the old robe, the shreds had glued on. Then they brought a piece of wood, a large chunk.

Naber: What did it look like?

Resl: Oh, in the meantime they brought two, real wild, men, they brought. They then tied a hunk of wood onto their backs. They could not get away from the wood.

Naber: And what did that look like?

Resl: There was a long one and on top something else was tied.

Naber: On their backs it was tied?

Resl: On their shoulders, one complained and screamed. The other one was quieter. They waited there. Then they brought some wood to the Savior, one, a long one, a short chunk and another short chunk. It was all hard roped together and they threw it onto the Savior. Onto the shoulder. Oh so, it hurt Him terribly.

Naber: What did the long one look like?

Resl: Not trimmed, but the smaller ones were. They had been trimmed for some time. Yeah, it was obvious. They had already weathered some. Then they did. Oh so. They had put the Saviors belt back on him. Where they, one and one on the back and one and one had ropes tied to the belt. More like leather straps from the belt, from there on like ropes.

Naber: (recording garbled)

Resl: Haven't I told you this today. Oh go on! And they had some small, wild, people, had brown faces, unkempt, sort of a beard, and had nothing on. Only below, something around. No sleeves. They then led the Savior ....unclear - there were enough of them.

The Way of the Cross

Yes! They went down the stairs, they had tied ropes on the back end of the wood. Yeah, some of them held on, or it would have fallen forward. You know, they pulled, so it (the wood) would go forward. Some others took ladders and other stuff along.

(unclear)

Then the Savior came. No, first came horses where some Wantobesmarters were on top. They then went away, they were in a hurry. The Robeslitter and the old one, they were in a hurry. First, some of the Wantobesmarters were gone, but they now waited yet, where the road turned, and after, they too went toward the house (temple). They didn't all go out. The others did though, they went out with the ones who stirred up against the Savior.

Those who had come out by then went into the garden, not many of them though.

(recording garbled)

And then comes the Savior. And behind came those, the two wild ones and then came more people. Oh so, they came down, from up there, they walked like down. And hardly were they down there where the road turned, did the Savior trip and fall. You know He could not properly walk any more, the Savior. He was so worn out from the night. Oh no, go. You know, now I won't tell you any more.

Naber: Please tell a little bit more!

Resl: You know. Because they prepared just for that. That is why they tied the leather strap with the ropes around, you know, to pull back up. Oh so! And they just pulled the Savior up again. Then we went a little stretch further. In the meanwhile from the upper gate, one is, the Mother came in. The young man (John) stopped under the gate and the Mother went over to the Savior. Yes, and then the Savior.....(noise), "AVE BARACH," Oh so! And they right away pushed Him away again. Oh! This was still in town, the cobbles were so rough . . . and the Mother wept. The young man took her outside again. They went on again. (Noise...)

And then, when we had walked a ways, now a man came, he had a brown skin. Two boys were with him, they were going to bring something into town they wanted to sell, a shrub, cut off and already started to leaf out. Yeah, he looked at, kind of curious, what was coming. And while he was still thinking about, they didn't give in until he came over. You know, they were afraid they wouldn't be able to get up there with the Savior on account the Savior was so worn down. Yes, but this man did not want to cooperate, he was in a hurry. But they didn't let him go, then he was forced. He was not one of them. Then he looked at the Savior, wildly, he was mad at him. He then picked up on the wood, from back though. That way it loaded down in front and it became even heavier in the front. Oh, and the little kids ran away. Are they going to find him again? I felt sorry for them.

Naber: What happened to the shrubs they brought along?

Resl:　They had to throw them on the ground.

Naber: (recording garbled)

Resl:　Yes, they didn't let up. They kept going a while. It was so hard for the Savior, since he picked up the wood so far back. Then once, the Savior looked him in the face, straight. At that he (the man) saw Him so different. And when He looked at him, the blood run from His eyes, ran down from the Savior, down so, from the forehead.

(Noise)

And he sure changed when he saw this.

Naber: How did he carry the wood, did he walk behind the Savior?

Resl:　Now he did, to the other side of the Savior. On this side was the Savior, on that side he walked.

(Noise)

And we kept walking some further. Then, from the other side, high up down from a house, a woman (Veronica) came. I knew her.

Naber: Indeed!

Resl: Yes, she over, when the Savior was down there, She was a sick woman. She was all crippled and did .... she didn't dare to come closer. At that, the Savior turned around. He had His white robe on then, because He had been speaking. There were sort of tassels on it. And she kind of touched from behind. And the Savior looked at her. She was afraid. But He didn't mean to frighten her. Oh, I had seen the woman often with the womenfolk and the Mother. Yeah, and with the tall black one (Martha.)

Oh so, and she came down with a little girl. And the little girl had a cup. She wanted to give the Savior something to drink. But it was not possible for her. Then she wept. And the woman quickly took her kerchief and leaped over. The Savior was pleased to take it, He nodded to her, that He was grateful, then with one hand, He could not let go with the other, He wiped His face. Sort of blotted. Kind of pressed up against. Then he gave it back to her, nodded, satisfied. And she grabbed it and quickly hid it in her coat. And they started to roar like mad again. And the little girl, had opened her cup and held it up to her mother. They did not let her any more. She wanted to give the Savior something to drink. The Savior was so thirsty. Oh so!

Now it is turning around a corner. Oh, I won't tell you any further.

Naber: Oh, do tell some more.

Resl: There is, in the big town first a wall, then a wide open square, then another wall. Now, we went in front of the wall, where it turns a corner, crossed over and went out. And there was now, you know the Savior could not look much down to His feet, there came different cobbles, outside the wall. Then there were puddles, because it was wet, because it was rainy. Now they went along, just kept walking along and suddenly the Savior tripped and fell down.

Why, because the other did not into the water, the Savior went on ahead. The Savior went on ahead, He did not see the wet stuff.

The man behind, he watched it, he went past it, on the Savior's side he carried, just before, he had changed sides. Oh, the wood went down, all down. The Savior fell down pretty hard, he tripped several times before, but they always quickly yanked Him up again. They let go with a yell. Just then they blow the horns. Oh so! They kept on walking further, further they walked, up and between the walls. Oh, Oh so! then, by a tall gate it went outside and there, the straight men (Roman soldiers) changed contingent. They sounded the other ones first, then they changed. The others were there already. Oh, and the many women were there with their kiddies and they all wept. Then the Savior said...?....Oh, it was so hard on the Savior, he was badly worn. Oh so?

F.N. - At the following Passion Friday, in the afternoon, after both visions, my sister Resl speaks of her own troubles and pain she had to suffer during the vision of the Passion; toward the end of the vision on this particular Friday, her condition had become so critical, one feared her end.

Resl: Oh, I am so tired, my back hurts so much. Then here in the front. The feet, the knees, that's another pain. The shoulder, is the big hurt. The hands hurt especially. The heart hurts especially. Pain, only pain!

Naber: One pain - Resl!

Resl: Yeah, almost I was not going to make it. It was so hard.

F.N. - After her condition had improved, she continued to relate:

Resl: Oh go! There was no end to it. All along I had thought it would quiet down, it will be easier on the Savior. Then they did something new to Him. Truly, it was terribly hard.

Naber: Listen Resl, you told us once (previous Friday Passion) how it was so hard on the Savior! How they tied Him up and brought Him in. First to the old one (Annas) to the Robeslitter (Kaiphas) and where they mocked him so.

Resl: Then to the I–Dare–Not where they beat Him so.

Naber: How they put Him into that hole. How they led Him out again in the morning.

Resl: Just say what you want me to tell you, don't keep beating around! I am already so sleepy.

Naber: How they beat the Savior so, put the thorns on, how they led Him up, we arrived there, until the Savior fell down flat out, there.

Resl: You know, when the Savior tripped and fell down, this night. I think I didn't tell you about every time.

         First, He fell down, then again, and again. He tripped, and again He tripped, and again He tripped, and once more. As often, once and once and once really hard and once and once and once and once not quite so hard.

Naber: And then at ......

Naber: Yes, when He so totally, totally fell down.

Resl: I know that, we just went out from town. Oh so! What I meant, when we came to the gate, where all the women were, the ones that wept so much, that's also where the straight men (Roman soldiers) changed. Oh, say, they had, when they came in, they had locked the gates. Why did they lock them, this night? They had locked the gates!

         And, when they went out with the Savior, they opened the inner gate, there were two walls, and they had to unlock that one also. They made such a racket, so the ones there heard it and opened the locks. Why did they lock them? Yes, like them, they were afraid of the Savior.

         Oh so! I felt so sorry for the Savior. There, the Savior, when we went out, couldn't go on any more. No, no, he couldn't. Now, I tell you. His knees kept kind of buckling forward, but he did keep on going. Once, the man (Simon) bawled the wild ones out. Yes, that's what happened, they carried on awfully, the Savior couldn't go on any more. These wild ones wanted to press forward, and there he bawled them out. He had compassion with the Savior. He saw that the Savior was at His end. Yeah, then they kept like going on. He then really picked up on the wood. The Savior also carried some, but he carried the bigger load. You know, the Savior just had no more strength. Finally until they reached the top of a hill, on top of a hill up we came up. Something had been going on on this hill before.

Now, I don't know whether I told you this before. They went into the big house. Now I know what they did. They didn't go out, the I-Dare-Not and the Robeslitter, a little ways they went all right, but then they turned around again. You know, I know, when the Savior died, between the big house, what they did there. They butchered little animals, there came a lot of blood which they put everywhere. They burned it. Ugh! There was much feasting, they did. They were all dressed in festive outfits, I saw this sort before, but when the big earthquake came they ran in all directions when everything crashed down, the pillars, then the people vanished fast.

But we are not there yet, I told you this so you can follow along.

See now, we went up there, they took the wood off the Savior and the man. Then, the Savior was so weak He had to sit down. There were horsemen, wild ones, and Wantobesmarterers and the wild ones. The wild ones didn't ride, but the Wantobesmarterers rode, they positioned themselves around. Then the others went out too, the ones who beat the Savior. Nosy they were and had plenty of time. Those who led Him, they took off the leather belt with the ropes, they left His belt on Him, left it on Him because the Savior had also His belt on. Yes, then He had to, on the wood, they sort of placed it together, it was so hard on Him, He looked up into heaven, there He had lay down on the wood, the Savior, sort of had to sit on it, then they pushed Him down.

Oh! It was not good at all.

Naber: How did they join the wood together?

Resl: So, one lone one and one and one acrossed, kind of sloping. I will tell you how they did it. They used small wedges, they marked with little stones, but they were not real stones. They gave a chalk color. Yes, at the Savior's hands and feet they made markings, then at His back, there, they made a marking. I know this, because they hollowed it out later, I saw that, everywhere they marked up, then they pulled the Savior up. He could not raise Himself up an more, He was too exhausted. Then they led Him back there.

Naber: Did they say anything then?

Resl: Yes, (KUPF CHOOM ...Get to work), yes, then they led Him towards the back. And oh, He was so unsteady! Oh, cannot even say walked! I felt terribly sorry, I had to weep, all along, wept. And when I wept, it was like fire in my eyes, inside my eyes they are full of pus, it hurts so much, you know deep inside, and hot it flowed out, hotter than water, it flowed out.

Naber: It looked like blood, bright red blood at first, then it turned darker.

Resl: Oh so, I think so too, because it was so sticky, water does not make eyes sticky. Oh, whenever I wept, then always the eyes got sticky, and when I stopped weeping for a while, they were stuck together hard, and when I did not weep for longer, then it was not so sticky and more? Oh and, Oh, then they put the Savior into a hole, it once was a grave, now it had become a ruin, they just lead Him back there, and just pushed Him into it. There were some stone blocks, where there was a little wall, there He had to sit down, then they positioned themselves in front of, there He put His hands together, sort of clasped and laid them on His knees. Oh, and how he shivered, it was like fever.

Naber: About the stone he sat on?

Resl: The dead were laid on it, like they always did, it was some-what hollowed out. I knew that, on account....(garbled).
        In the meanwhile they got the wood ready, and ten-oned up, the big piece laid down, then the side piece ten-oned in, and below the other tenoned in and then drove wedges in, so one's arms couldn't pull it out, you know, wedges were driven in.

Naber: How did they put these pieces in?

Resl: Yes, slantwise, sort of sloping up or it would not have held, to go in straight it would not hold, slantwise it had a resistance.

Naber: How long was the piece that projected out above?

Resl: Not very far, they did..... there they hollowed it out a ways, so the Savior could lean up against it, and down at the feet they hollowed out a lot, a lot they cut, and they fixed something there. There, with all the hollowing it would have come out too far, they then nailed a piece to it. Yes, I saw it.

Naber: I suppose, the Savior was to stand on that?

Resl: Could stand, Yes! Otherwise He would have torn loose. Then, when they were finished, then they took the others (the two insurgents). The others who had also been along, one and another one. They loosened them, the wood pieces to be free, they did not have them tied below. Then, they drove pegs into the wood, then they tied ropes on them (insurgents) there they took a ladder, from behind, then they climbed up from behind, pulled on the ropes and they had to clamber up over the rungs. Yes, and then, when they were up there, no, you know clamber up, clamber backwards, not right side, you know with the backs toward the wood, they had a different kind of cross. A long wooden pole that went straight up, and on top one across, then they grabbed their arms one could think they would break, bent them outwards, behind the wood, pulled down and then tied hard with ropes. Yes, not tied straight but wound around.

Naber: (not clear)

Resl: Ah, there were pegs driven into the pole, there were holes drilled into.

Naber: Into the pole itself?

Resl: Yes, into the pole, holes were drilled and in these they stuck the pegs and there they had to climb up backwards. It can be done! You don't think so.

Naber: Did they have them tied up already, from above?

Resl: For sure! They had the ladders set up and had pulled some
         on the ropes, but they (insurgents) had to help for them-
         selves by stepping up with their heels on the pegs.

Naber: Left to themselves they would not have climbed up? There-
         fore they had them tied up.

Resl: Yes, they could not have freed themselves, they were in
         ropes. They did loosen the ropes somewhat, but then tied
         them up strong. Yes, one went mad, the other one was
         quieter.

Naber: How were they towards the Savior?

Resl: Sort of sideways, they could look towards the Savior, not
         directly straight on, somewhat from the side, somewhat
         looking this way to the Savior.

Naber: Where they in front or back of the Savior?

Resl: No, no, to the side.
            And now, when they hung there, they led the Savior
         out from the hole, then they did to Him, should I tell you
         this, does the Savior want it?

The Crucifixion of the Savior

Naber: Yes, the Savior does want it!

Resl: Yes, but the Savior knows very well that I am so sleepy, so
         tired. Well, then, if He wants it, yes.

Naber: The night.

Resl: Yes, the night is long indeed, yes, the Savior gives me new
         strength, indeed He can do everything. Yes, I like to
         talk..(unclear)..only, how it is with His back, it burns like
         fire.

Naber: Think of it what befell on the Savior.

Resl: Ugh, woe, this is awful, terrifying not awful; terrifying. I don't even know how you can, can't even talk, awful, it is terrifying. Oh so! Then they had led Him forward, then they wanted to, then they had His robe, He had it kind of rolled around, He had it around Him, twisted like a sausage, over Him, they liked it that way when they traveled, well they took it off of Him.

Naber: Did the Savior have it on when they led Him up?

Resl: Yes, it was wrapped around.

Naber: What kind of a robe did He have?

Resl: No, this was twisted around, not in the middle, but from the shoulder down, rolled together, yes.

Naber: Tied together down below, in the front (garbled).

Resl: Well, all around.

Naber: Tied together, or the like.

Resl: No, it was arranged that way. They are good at it. Oh then, they wanted to take off His robe, the brown one, now they could not get it off. It had only one small cut opening. There it was tied, laced with a small leather band. Yes, it was laced with a small leather band.

 Then they did, Oh, they took the thorns down from the Savior. Just think of it! They did not come off very clean, down over the head. Then, where it was tied together. And it was stuck to the back. Like if you were to rip off my shirt, I would scream. The Savior did not scream. You know, I would be fussier, I would scream like mad. No, I would not let them touch me. I am fussy, to be sure. Now, and the Savior! Yes, Oh. Then the blood started to flow out again. He sighed though, and then they pulled down the other one. There, He had something around His chest. They pulled that down, left nothing. They pulled down everything, left nothing on Him.

 Yes, and something else. Would you believe who else was up there also? The Mother and womenfolk and the men who were good with the Savior, they were all nearby. Yes, I saw them. Yes, the Came-To-Life-Again (Lazarus) and those who are not so often with the Savior (disciples). Oh so! Now the Savior put His hands together because He was embarrassed, on account He was completely naked, down to his feet, absolutely nothing. Like this morning, when they beat him so.

And suddenly, one, leaping out from the crowd, yelled at the wild ones and held a cloth before the Savior, and the Savior grabbed it and nodded, and the one, as fast as he came was gone again. A long piece of cloth which the Savior tied around His middle.

Naber: How did he tie it?

Resl: This way and so, together. Yes, the Savior was pleased. Ah, so! I mean it was something like the women have, when they sweat, to wipe off the sweat.

Naber: What color?

Resl: Yellow like wool, wool - yellow. They like natural colors.

Oh, now comes something not nice at all. They wanted to, Him something to drink, which the Savior did not take, no He touched it with His tongue and He pushed it away.

Then they took Him to the wood they had put together, as I told you. Then they gave Him one shove. No, He had sat down at first, then they gave Him one shove that He went on the wood with His head, Oh so, then they put the thorns back on Him. When they tried to give Him something to drink, no, where He wanted nothing, they put the thorns back on Him. Did it hurt though! They pressed them down on. And I had to weep. Oh, water came out of my eyes, it burned. Ugh, not like water what came, much thicker.

Naber: How did they handle the thorns?

Resl: They handled them all right, but then they took rods to press it down, or they would have stung into their fingers. It was like a cap, made of thorns.....

Oh so, then they put the thorns on the Savior. Then one of them knelt on it. No something is coming I don't like to tell.

Naber: Now see, the Savior wants it. Oh, so! It is hard sure, we too feel sorry. When we do learn everything, how it was, we feel even more compassion for the Savior, and that will please Him.

Resl: Yes, He likes it, when we feel compassion for Him. Yes, then I will tell it to you, but tell it fast to get it over with.

Naber: Yes, but you must tell it all!

Resl: Well, you think it's easy?
         Yeah, then they stretched the right arm outwards, rope-tied it hard, then one of them knelt on it (the arm), it hurt the Savior so, then He put out the arm, then they began to pull. They had looped a rope around His wrist, and so, no not - this came later. With my telling so fast, I must tell it slowly.

Naber: Slowly, slowly!

Resl: When they had the Savior so tied up, they, right into, through the middle of His hand drove a nail, it made a crunching sound. Yes, there was a bore hole there. They, while the Savior was in that hole (the abandoned grave), checked to see that the nail fit. Otherwise, it would not have gone into the wood. The blood squirted into the face of the wild one. Oh, the blood come out so much. Oh, the Savior whimpered.

Naber: Did the people, the Mother see it also?

Resl: Yes, sure. You could hear a long ways.

Naber: Who was with the Mother?

Resl: Yes, the tall, dark one (Martha) and the one........ . Then, the arm did not reach to the hole, to where it was supposed to go. No, they looped a rope around the wrist. Then the one who knelt up there, and some behaved so stupid there, Oh did it hurt Him. The Savior pulled up His legs, He tried to release it into Himself, you know, then they tied up the other arm, tied it hard, and then they drove a nail into it.

Naber: Did you feel that in your hands too?

Resl: Yes, felt it also and afterwards they did not wait long, they pulled down His legs.

Naber: Did they also ....

Resl: Also, tied ropes on it, they pulled down the feet, then they had, over ..... tied up. Not hard as yet, they tied it up hard later on, or it would not give any more. And then yanked the feet downward and there they also had holes drilled.

It went through (the nail) very poorly. Oh, it hurt the Savior so much, a lot of blood flowed out, flowed down. Oh so, did I feel sorry for the Savior, down through the bones. You know, over the bones, I think so, into the drilled holes into which they drove the nails, I think so, some flesh went down into them, it sounded like it, when they drove them down.

Naber: How did they nail the feet down?

Resl: They had also, as I have it, if one touches it, I have them tangled.....

One can't see it now, my wounds fit nicely one on top of the other, crosswise, slanted. Not like so, but like this. When I put my wounds together like that they do not fit, the lower goes on the upper one this way, not the other, like that it fits.

Naber: And that way they nailed the Savior?

Resl: Yes, that's the way they nailed him. In the back, the heels went into the hollow, and on the slope. They yanked until they (feet) were on it. One thought they were going to pull the Savior's guts out the way He was stretched. Oh so!

Naber: How did they have it, did they have one or two nails? Did they put the feet one on top of the first?

Resl: One only.

No, no, this is the way they did it. First, they took the Savior's foot, they they drove a nail through, a weak one, they pulled out again, then they put the other foot on top, then they went through that one, then one looked and held the foot, then the other foot with a much longer one, it was much longer than the first nail, then it went through the lower one much easier....... .

Naber: What did they do with the first, the small nail?

Resl: Pulled out again, otherwise, if they had not pulled it out, they only drove it in to make a hole, because it would not have gone through both feet with one blow, no, no.

Naber: How were they able to pull out the nail?

Resl: They had to hold Him, it was so cruel.

Naber: Did they throw the nail away?

Resl: They most likely picked it up again. You know, the weak nail out, the foot on top, then the nail in. One of them watched very close that everything went smooth.

Naber: Haven't we seen the nail somewhere?

Resl: Oh so, we were in a place, but they had beaten around on the nail, so stupid, beat it crooked, that was not necessary. Oh, I fainted there. There was also the high Father (Prof. Wutz) with us, for sure, and another one and another one. Then they carried me to the sacristy (was most probably at Trier 1933's. F.N.)

Oh, so! Then they put around the body and pulled tighter.

Naber: Then, they had only one rope around?

Resl: They had one around at the body, and of the knees, one and another one.

Naber: At the knees one also?

Resl: Yes.

Naber: They tied the Savior up twice?

Resl: Yes.

Naber: On the knees once, and then each arm?

The Raising of the Cross and Death of Jesus

Resl: Yes, each arm. Oh so! Then they, now listen carefully, how they uprighted the Savior, that is remarkable.

They had driven stakes into the ground and tied a beam to it, yes, and onto the beam they tied ropes and the ropes they did, no, on the Savior's wood, it was like that, on the back there were iron rings, up there. That's when they tied the ropes, then they had poles and stuff to lift with and strong things, and then these ropes, as the Savior came up, looped around the beam so they could pull on them to keep the Savior from falling forward.

Naber: These ropes?

Resl: There were little rings on it. One and one. And there was a stake, and further down a stake and a beam tied across, that was on it, they used it when they were pulling up, the Savior, so they could stop, they looped it around, around the cross beam. Then they left it so, tied up. Why this? Why were they worried it would fall over, since it was tight? They probably thought that if the hole in the ground wouldn't hold it, they had wedged a lot of little pebbles into it when they had uprighted the Savior. Then they let go. It shook the Savior. You know, they carried on so brutally. They couldn't care less whether it hurt Him. Oh, then, I am supposed to tell you everything (sobbing) I don't want to any more.

Naber: But the Savior wants you to!

Resl: Yes, but I again feel so terrible for the Savior.

Naber: Yes, now , we also have compassion for the Savior.

Resl: And I don't really want to tell you so accurately.

Naber: Oh go on, the Savior would like to have it this way, indeed!

Resl: Then, when they had hung the Savior on it, had uprighted Him, I want to say, then His head fell down onto his chest, then the Savior was like unconscious. He looked like a corpse. Just like a corpse, could not see.....see any more.

You know, the jolting (dropping the cross into the hole), they pounded pebbles down so it would hold. You know, it went far back into the rocks with the ropes that were tied to the back, were supposed to hold it some. You know, so it couldn't go backwards, no, I wanted to say forward. You know, the Savior's weight was up front, and the ropes were supposed to hold it back. Oh so!

Naber: How high up was the Savior?

Resl: Not awfully high, well, how should I say it, I cannot measure it.

Naber: Look, you said the young man (John) was there?

Resl: Yes, the young man stood there, he had his head at about the Saviors side wound.

Naber: His chest?

Resl: Yes.....Oh, and then were the Mother and the men, the people who were there. She wept, indeed they had to support Her, they held Her up.

Naber: When did the Mother come closer?

Resl: Now, as the Savior hung there, first She was afraid, all came closer now.

Naber: Did someone lead the Mother?

Resl: Yes, the womenfolk, they are, when they came up from town they hung something over Her face, so one could not see the face.

You know, now I know what it was with the nails, I didn't know last night what they were intending with them. This morning though, when they, the Mother, when the young man brought Her in through the upper gate, now some knew the Mother. There were some young hoodlums, in a small box they had the nails. But I couldn't understand their language. They held them in front of the Mother and said something, yes one and another one, one of them had in his hands. He held them up to the Mother and said something mocking. Oh, it was bad for the Mother, they knew her, I believe. Yes, because there was some noisy chattering when they saw Her. Now I know what was with the nails.

Naber: How many nails did they hold up to Her, all three?

Resl: No, just one and one. They pulled them out of the little box. Ah go! And then, when the Savior hung up there, the torturer sat down and pulled His clothes apart. They plain stole it away from the Savior, they were His.

There they could not divvy them up. His Robe was laced together, kind of laced. There they had such things, there they did, one to the others, I don't know the meaning of this.

Naber: Did they have kind of little stones?

Resl: No, it was of wood, cube like, such large ones they tossed back and forth. I think this was to mean something.

There is this man, it was later on, I need to tell you. They then came in, in attire, there the old man (Nicodemus) showed up, the one who once came to the Savior at night, he had another one with him, and surely, this one took all from them and gave them some money, they laughed, they were pleased, and he was even more pleased. Inside he was, but he didn't let it show. Oh, now one could see it well he was satisfied on account he held the Savior in great reverence. Yes, he thought, indeed they will not have them (the Savior's clothes). I would not let them to have it, these wild ones, it's not theirs, so much blood was on the brown robe. Yes, we saw it once, you know we saw it indeed, one could still see the blood stains (Trier 1933).

Naber: What did they do with the robe?

Resl: They cut it up with a knife. And while they messed around with the attire. Now they (the two insurgents) began to fight, the good one and the not so good one, you know. I think I hit something

F.N. – Resl touched my microphone which I had placed too close, Resl could not see in her condition.

Naber: No problem.

Resl: But I will have to take a look, I thought I hit something.
          Now they argued with each other, one could see. They
          argued all along. They talked the same language. Then sud-
          denly the one over there said something to the Savior, at
          Him, you know kind of up to Him. He was so impressed
          when the Savior, for those who mocked Him and who tore
          apart His attire and who ridiculed, prayed for them to the
          Father, for, He had looked upward, the Savior did. There,
          this one got up some courage and said something. The one
          over there, he kept mocking all along.

Naber: The one over here did not?

Resl: No, not even in the least.

Naber: At the beginning neither?

Resl: At the beginning he was upset, but he had nothing against
          the Savior, like, that he would have said something to ridi-
          cule, only they then got at each other, they were against.
          The one would not have talked like the ones below. He did
          not like that at all, he was also older and not so wild, it was
          obvious, and then just think, then the Savior said some-
          thing to him........there, were he said something the Savior
          said something compassioned to him.
          Like something begging, like begging, he had figured
          out that the Savior was no common people. Then the Sav-
          ior said something decisive to him, with a firm, strong voice.
          Then the one over there got stupid again and started to do
          some more ridiculing.

Naber: Where they placed somewhat in front of the Savior?

Resl: To the side, the side, I already told you.

Naber: A little bit forward?

Resl: It didn't make much difference from below, but it did up
          there at the arms. At the sides, a little bit this way. Why
          surely, on account the Savior hung here, and they hung

there, had it been in a straight row then I would have had look this way, like it was I could look across.

Naber: I thought so.

Resl: When it would have been in a straight row, I would have had to look like so, or so, they were hanging to the side, the Savior could easily kept them in His view. Oh so! And then the Savior hung like this for a while, and another while. He could not hold His head up, could not bend back on account of the thorns, He could not put His head back, the Savior. There He hung, heavy, and there He set down, it.........and with His hands, He always went like this.

Naber: Curled up His fingers?

Resl: Yes, when they nailed Him on, I forgot, they had held the fingers straight, straight outwards.

Naber: Did they nail into the Savior where you have your wounds?

Resl: Yes, where else would they?

Naber: Well because, some thought back there where the hand starts.

Resl: No, I saw it exactly, right into here.
     Oh so, and the people came ever nearer, when the Savior talked to them, and the Mother stood there, the young man was over there with the other men.
     Now, all at once the Savior talked down, to the Mother, then He said something to the young man.

Naber: Did you understand any of it?

Resl: ....to the young man, to the Mother "AVE BARACH" He went over behind the Savior.

Naber: Behind the Savior he crossed over?

Resl: Yeah, and there were the womenfolk and the Mother, and the young man supported the Mother, it was so hard on the Mother, one could not recognize Her any more if one had not known the Mother.

Naber: Did anyone else help support the Mother?

Resl: The tall one, the one I don't know who she was, Yes!
        (Martha)

Naber: Probably on to the right of the Mother because She went
        around that way, though.

Resl: And right away came closer. Oh so! And then the Mother
        looked up to the Savior, it was very hard on Him then, and
        to the Mother as well.

Naber: To you also.

Resl: Yes, there were quite of few good people along, they were
        scared to come forward, but one saw it now, they came in
        closer. And then the Savior hung there for a while, and
        they mocked up to Him, it hurt Him so much. He again
        hung there for a while, it took long, so long you know.
        Yew! Then it got to be so hard on Him, the Savior
        had.......Oh go on so! Then suddenly He said, "AY ELOR"
        (My God), there He moved His head the other way and
        back again, then He looked upwards with His eyes, breath-
        ing heavy, one saw it was hard on Him.

        And suddenly He said, "AYLOI, AYLOI, LAMA
        SABACHTANI" (My God, My God, why have you aban-
        doned me) Oh so!

Naber: Was it hard on you too, what did you feel?

Resl: Oh there, like when. I felt like that often before, also dur-
        ing night. To the Savior it was as though the Father didn't
        want to have anything to do with Him any more and I felt
        like the Savior didn't want to have anything to do with me
        any more. Indeed, that is hard. Surely, when you think it
        can't go on any more and you can't bear it any more, that's
        hard indeed. Oh, it was awful for me today.

        Oh, they, down there kept ridiculing, the
        Wantobesmarterers. That too was something, they yelled
        they did not understand the Savior, what He meant.

Naber: Did you understand what they yelled?

Resl: I don't know, I didn't understand, they kept yelling in
        confusion.

Naber: Did they also say Aloi, Ayloi?

Resl: No, a little different, but it sounded similar. Oh so! It was so hard on the Mother, the Savior was breathing so heavy. The lips turned blue, the Savior's, no fresh blood had come at all, no, no, it became all black.

Naber: Who was still at the cross?

Resl: Oh, the girl (Mary of Magdala), she had her arm around, I think they could have beat her, oh, they ridiculed her bad, also the Savior, because she did not go away.

Naber: She was there!

Resl: Knelt, sort of sat on her knees. Then and now she raised herself up to fully on her knees, at that she almost reached up to the Saviors feet.......

Naber: The blood must have come down on her?

Resl: Yes, she was full of blood but didn't care. The Mother is......Oh, go! The Savior was not like a human! The flesh so crushed, the arms, and then, when the Savior was so dehydrated, one could see this, and the nose turned black. The lips blue and then the fingers turned blue too, and He was breathing so very heavy, then He was so thirsty and He went like this with His tongue. He put His tongue out not straight but always upward between the lips, then He said, "AYSHEM" (I thirst), oh, slowly, "AYSHEM" then they ridiculed Him on that.

One of them went there and then put something on a pole. They had that fixed up, they were going to give Him something to drink.

But they had something else, not exactly different, but one kind, they first had one kind, then another kind. That they poured together. Before they had nailed the Savior down, they were going to give the Savior something to drink, and now they put only one kind into it, but more had come together, on account the Savior did wet His tongue some. He did not get much, just enough to wet the lips, and it was gruesome, gruesome to the Savior. Oh, it was bad!

Naber: How did he give it to the Savior?

Resl: Well oh, he had on a pole, something grown (sponge) and
        he held it up to the Savior, yes, it was no good, had it been
        water, it would have been smarter, because this knocked
        the Savior around and, then He looked at me with great
        passion. Oh, at that, I walked up really close.

        Say Father, did I tell you, when the Savior had hung
        on the cross only shortly, when He was in this terribly bad
        shape, the sun started getting murky. This morning it was
        hazy or when we soon went up on the mountain, before
        we got there, it turned brighter, one could even see the
        sun, and now it turned murky, gruesomely, foreboding, dark.
        Uh, uh, gruesomely dark.

Resl: Could one see one another?

Resl: One could see others all right, not dark like night but murky
        it was, black murky. All of a sudden, one could not hear
        anything anymore, when it turned so dark. The birds, they
        behaved so like in terror, they screamed horrifying, then
        one could hear nothing, no animals nothing any more.
        Everything was completely quiet.

        Then, some of these Wantobesmarterers, it's true, I
        should have told you this, they made themselves thin, they
        did not feel good about it, they sort of vanished.

Naber: When it got so dark what did the Savior?

Resl: When He was, got into this terrible shape, when He had
        barely been on the cross, soon thereafter.

Naber: When He said, "AYLOI, AYLOI," or right away?

Resl: No, earlier.

Naber: Oh so!

Resl: When the Savior hung.

Naber: Yes, when He fainted.

Resl: On account He had been hanging on it for quite some
        time already. When He was on it, and when He much talked
        good and all along kept praying, then, the one who was the

top man jumped down from the horse (Centurion) and yelled something.

Naber: When did he jump down?

Resl: Still then, when the Savior hadn't been dead. Now at the end, he jumped down and just let the horse run free, and then he went, went into the big town, and, would you know where I saw him - at the I-Dare-Not. That's where I saw him. He let his horse, he went down from it, then he threw his stuff down on the ground, he had a spear which he also threw away, but then picked it up again and gave it to the one who pierced the Savior into the side.

Yes, and he didn't, didn't any more properly look after his horse. You know, they have to, if the horse is supposed to stay put and collected, they have to have it reigned in somewhat, this he did not do because the horse was also so tired, out and down with his head. He did not pay any attention, you know.

Naber: When this one left, where he jumped down from the horse, had the earth already started to break open (quaked?)

Resl: Yes, it heaved already.

Naber: Was the Savior dead by then?

Resl: It all sort of happened together, it was hard to say, the Savior was breathing heavy, the earth, the rocks had not as yet begun to crack, as the Savior did not breath any more, it all happened together. And when this one.....

Naber: When the Savior so uprighted Himself on the cross and then collapsed, had the earth started to quake?

Resl: It all happened together, it was not possible to say which came first. You have to understand it went on for a while, the shaking. Yes, it had started while the Savior was still alive, yes, indeed. And they blew into their trumpets when the Savior was still alive.

Naber: And, about then he jumped down?

Resl: And while it, the earthquake wasn't over yet, while the Savior was still hanging a while.

Then, after, when the Savior had already said, "ABA" (Father), this one yelled, this one cared about no one, and just left and then another one, other one pushed the spear into the Savior's side, is true!

And he went into the town, yes, I saw him then, he was with the I-Dare-Not (Pilate). Was that one ever frightened!

I was in the big house (Temple). Oh no, did it ever look awful, there were the high feast days, but the people were all frightened and beside themselves. Oh, and where one comes in, they again had the gates locked. Why did always lock the gates so fiercely?

Naber: Around the wall?

Resl: Yes why? When the straight men (Roman soldiers) came, they stirred them up, because they couldn't get in. Yes, and others came in with the straight men that way, out there were fewer people when the Savior died, only some straight men. Some good people, some blasphemers and some of the wild ones still. Those, who tormented the Savior, they all left. They had done their job, then they left. Oh so!

And then, when He was barely gasping, then the Savior's knees sort of went sideways, you know, because the ropes were not all that tight. Yes, they had loosened up a bit, there the knees fell sideways, and the hands stayed curled up, then at the end the fingers straightened again.

Naber: As He died.

Resl: Yes, He couldn't raise His head any more, it just hung down, down on His chest. Then He turned gray, kind of yellow gray.

Oh, and then He said the last. No, maybe I told this though. "SOLOM COLUCHI" (Paid is the debt). Yes, He said this not so firm but this He said firm, this He said strong once more:

"ABA BEATACH AF KETRUCHI" (Father into your hands I commend my Spirit.)

With His last bit of strength He said it so clear, He had moved His head just so much to the side. Oh, oh, then He gasped for air once more, stretched His body and again

He collapsed. Why didn't He get any more air, the nose moved and He was suffocating. Why, you know, suffocating, like the Savior.

Naber: Did you feel that too?

Resl: Yes, I got chilled inside of me and frightened when the Savior, when He died now. Ugh, and just then the trumpets sounded from the great house. One could see into it.

By now, it became a little brighter, but it, the earth really quaked. A little earlier, a crack appeared, coming in on the bias. There were then two big cracks, one could put something into one, so big. Yes, this one came aways, on the bias, the other one right across and another crack stopped right there. Just think, if you looked into it you could have seen a long ways down.

Naber: Where were the trumpets?

Resl: From the big house, it came. Smoke, came out, something awful. And at that, I was in the big house. Guess what went on in there? They butchered the little animals, and then incinerated them. The blood, incinerated. They stoked it some, it smoked and then people went in all directions. What it was like when the Savior went dead! When the Savior had looked me in the eye, when the dead ones came walking around, all bandaged. Only the heads stuck out, they came to the Robeslitter, was he then terrified!

Naber: What was the condition of the big house?

Resl: You know, you walk up a series of steps, then there is this large, tall gate. There are two tall stone pillars. The earthquake blew out the two pillars, and then this gate became "unglued" so to say. Was a beautiful gate! Then, behind the gate was a curtain. It was beautiful also, sort of furled, but now ripped apart, all this on account of the earthquake. It could never have happened by itself.

Naber: (recording garbled)

Resl: It collapsed inward, inwardly it fell, they went out. The upper side came down, everything was chaos.

Then, also the dead floated around. Yes, and where the Savior once sat, up there on the large chairs, they had fallen over, thrown into a jumble. It looked gruesome, for sure. But you know, with the old one (Annas) I felt good when he got so frightened when the dead floated around.

Naber: What did they in fact look like?

Resl: They were still wrapped up, you know, but the head bare, just what a dead would look like. No flesh, only bones......

Naber: They had no more body?

Resl: No, with a few one could think, the way it looked, just bones, you know....The head was free, all else was wrapped. One could not recognize them. The one, who once couldn't talk and....I meant that one. I mean he had a kind of a thing.
And the I-Dare-Not. Did he ever get terrified. First, the one who had jumped from the horse, had come. Then the dead ones!

Naber: To the I-Dare-Not, did others come?

Resl: I had not seen the woman any more. I believe she had left. She, I think had gone. I do believe. You know, she was very distressed when he gave in. You know, she sent the thing back, the flashing thing with the big gem. It was wide, very wide where one can wrap it around the finger. It was a whole sleeve, all sparkling. Oh go on! I am so tired, Father. I believe I told you the worst. But no, I will not tell more, but there is still much more.

Naber: Yeah, we are satisfied, indeed. You tell it to us some other time.

Resl: Oh, since I am so sleepy.

Naber: You tell it some other time

Resl: But, when I get lively again I let you all know, now my back aches badly.

Naber: The Savior does not ask to have it all at once.

Resl: The Savior would leave me in peace all right, but you!

Naber: (recording garbled)

Resl: The Savior would have let me sleep, I didn't wake up properly. You understand?

Naber: If the Savior hadn't awoken you fully, you couldn't have told all to us.

Resl: But I am so tired though, and now again.

Naber: Go on, sleep some

Resl: Then if someone wants to know more, just wake me up.

One half hour later

Naber: Well, I was pleased.

Resl: Go on, but no, not true, then let me quickly tell you this.

Naber: Well now, I think it was all correct.

Resl: You know, I was right sleepy when this one jumped from the horse, when the Savior talked so firm and when the earth started to quake, and when he got down from the horse. Did I tell you that some more of the straight men turned good, that they too then turned good?

Naber: No. Any others?

Resl: Yes.

Naber: How many of the straight men where out there?

Resl: Many, when it got to be so dark, many of the Wantobesmarterers, they the Wantobesmarterers got lost. Then, other people came by, but the majority had left by then. Then many of them were straight ones (Roman soldiers) and there, where one leaves through the gate, there stood a troop, I saw, when we went in.

Naber: How many were out there, approximately, how were they positioned? In a circle or how?

Resl: In a half circle, yes, towards the Savior, and then how the

Savior, when there was the earth quake, how He spoke once more so mighty, He spoke firmly, with all His strength, and then sunk into Himself.

Naber: Had the earthquake already started when the Savior said "ABA"?

Resl: Yes, yes, then abouts, I can't remember exactly, but it was pretty much, I did tell you already today, pretty much at the same time.

Naber: Yes, therefore, there were a pretty large number of straight men present?

Resl: Yes, there were, a large troop.

Naber: Resl, listen. How was the Savior positioned, did He face the town?

Resl: No, no, its like "women and children", Father. Nothing new though. I really don't know now (excitedly). Indeed, I look at the Savior like this (let me sit up though).

Naber: Now its better. I am very happy that you are more revived.

Resl: Oh so, Father. I look at the Savior from here. Not like this, like so. Here the Savior hangs, and where one looks toward further away, there I can look into the town, or, the Savior has His back towards the town.

Naber: That is what I wanted to know, yeah.

Resl: Oh, this is important too! (slightly mocking)

Naber: That's good, don't you think that's good, that the Savior turned His back at the town that rejected Him?

Resl: Yes, I could in fact look at it, especially there at the big house....the big house (temple).

Naber: Yes, surely, as though the Savior wanted to have nothing to do with it, and then Resl, listen, you said, of the ropes that went out aways, were they only in the back or also in front?

Resl: No, no, they were not needed there, in front was the Savior, every time when He moved a little, the cross wasn't anchored all that well, the cross shook slightly, moved slightly. Where the Savior moved it was more pulled forward.

Naber: When they uprighted the wood, did they have to pull it out again?

Resl: Yes, as the Savior fainted, you know, He fainted on account of that, they had to stop and chisel out some more. It didn't go down deep enough, the Savior was heavy after all, they lifted it out once more and took out the stones, and chipped out some more, and then they let it go back down......

Naber: So they let it down twice?

Resl: No, so, once not as awful, once they let it drop in, the first time. Now they were more careful and lifted it in, mind you the Savior was still unconscious. He did not experience much there, maybe nothing. Oh, so!

Naber: Resl, pay attention, the boy (Ferdinand Neumann) would like to know how the wood pieces were fastened on each side?

Resl: Didn't I tell you already?

Naber: Ferdl (nickname of Ferdinand) wants to know more exactly.

Resl: Oh, he is not getting smart. Oh, now listen, I tell it once more.

The long piece was laid down, on the side on which the Savior is, the bark was chopped off, then they, had measured when they had the Savior lay down, where the heel was, chopped out, did, where the head is and the thorns, chopped out some, did where the Savior hips are, thighs, chopped there also so He could lean up a bit so He wouldn't tear loose. Did nail a piece to it where they chopped for the heels so the feet could get some support on it. Had a bunch of wood which was the stem, another one, the wedges and another one. Then cut into the stem at an angle and inserted a piece, and below, on the other side inserted the other, because, if side-by-side, the stem would have broken off.

Naber: Below?

Resl: Below, then to fix it put wedges in, nailed through, drilled through, drove in wooden nails, not iron, then drove in wedges, so that nothing would give when they nailed the Savior, nothing could give. Now, from above it went on a slope, when one looked straight on, one could see through between the wood and the Saviors arms.

Naber: Was the arm higher up than the tip of the wood?

Resl: The tip was below the Savior's arm, on account they had drilled too far apart and had to stretch the Savior....Well though, even if it have been loose somewhat, but not so much, now you could see through underneath, at one tip a lot, the other not so much, because one (side piece of the cross) longer and jointed lower.

Naber: Deeper on the right side?

Resl: I don't know whether the right side, let me look, yes, I have to see it, on this side (right) was the shorter piece and that side (left) went down further, and it went higher up.

Naber: Therefore, as to the Savior, it was higher up to the left?

Resl: Yes, at left it was higher, this (shown by hand pointing) was higher at the Savior and the other was further down.

Naber: So it went further down at the Savior's right side?

Resl: Yes. The beams were quite weathered, they had been trimmed some time ago, they were weathered.

Now there, you know I would like to say something, once, the other Father (Prof. Wutz) asked of me, how I saw the Savior, I said: look at the Savior, not at the stone (this is from the vision of the Ascension of Jesus). Him, who is called Ferdl, should think of it as well.

Naber: The cross, of how the Savior hung on it, the boy (Ferdl) probably thinks, there was one who made a cross exactly like the one of the Savior.

Resl: Oh, they did make one like that, over there, a high Father (Bishop) had it made, he was here quite often (Bishop Schrembs of Cleveland). There, for a large church he had it made, there, where he put me into the window (stained glass), where I got so irritated across the water (Atlantic).

He had that kind of cross made, the people really liked it on account it was so natural, the other is artistic more, though.

Naber: It would be beautiful if one could make the Savior's cross like that.

Resl: Yes. In the back was still bark. What kind of wood? It was a hardwood, not soft, no, no, because where the bark had been peeled, it was like treated, like varnished.

Naber: The thing they nailed to it, below the feet, was it a just a chunk of wood?

Resl: Just a chunk, it was different, it was wood like the wedges, where they had the wedges.

Naber: Resl, now listen. You already told us some of how it was at the big house when all the dead came. Did you tell also....

Resl: Of the Robeslitter. Did I tell you that the old one (Annas), where the Savior was last night, that the dead came to him also, to the tall gaunt one, not at his home, not in his parlor, but in the big house, yes the big house, also the Robeslitter, him too. I didn't see the other one (Herod) though. Nor did I see any dead with him. You know, the one to whom the Savior did not answer. The other one is not in the big house, the I-Dare-Not, he is not there, he is at his home.

Naber: They don't let these people into their house.

Resl: Exactly.

Naber: Now Resl, listen, I thought you should tell us now what you saw this afternoon, still.

Resl: Yes, I will tell you. I know what happened next, in order.

Naber: I am not interfering.

Resl: I'd rather have it that way.

Naber: I am indeed silent.

Resl: But when I am sleepy you will say to stop.

Naber: Then I will wake you up.

Resl: Don't you think the Savior would let me have a bit of sleep?

Naber: You can sleep all you want, later, can sleep until tomorrow morning, noon, tomorrow evening, clear to the next day, in the morning.

Resl: That's better.

The Taking Down from the Cross

Resl: Yes, wait, wait. Where do I start? How they - no no, now I will begin. When the Savior was dead and the other one ran off, you know I was then in the big house and then at the I-Dare-Not, he who went to him and told him, the one who jumped off his horse. He (Pilate) then got very frightened, to be sure, he was awfully frightened. Then something else, there is this man, not the one who came to the Savior at night, but the other, the shorter one (Joseph of Arimathea)

Naber: An old one?

Resl: Well now, not a one of them was young, well, he went to the I-Dare-Not and told him something. At that, he (Pilate) got restless. Then he, and he was somewhat satisfied, he wrote something for this man (J. of A.). Then the I-Dare-Not gave this writing to the man. Yes, he had written something and gave it to him.
        I knew what it meant, namely that they may have the Savior, that was in the writing he gave him, and that the others weren't allowed to interfere. Then he sent for someone and left.

Naber: Who sent for someone?

Resl: Just wait! The I-Dare-Not sent a few up there. Now you know who was still out there, was the one who pushed the spear into the Saviors' side, and some other straight men.

Most of the others had gone back into town by then, they were not there any more, for the Savior had been dead for some time and this is evening, what I tell you now, that did not happen right away. He sent some up there, not straight men, who keep order, but the kind who could be hired for money, who were somewhat wild, they took some implements along. Iron implements and stuff made of iron and when they came up, what do you think happened, the two criminals were still alive, and they just clubbed them to death with the iron rods, just so, crashing, they beat in their chests, beat like crazy. The one over there screamed, the other one was quieter but also whimpered, it hurt so much. The one behaved stupid, said bad things; the Mother was still out there, yes and the womenfolk. When they were done with these two, right next to the Savior, I believe that.....he went near, rode his horse close in, of the other one who had it first, took down the spear.

Naber: Was he on the horse?

Resl: Yes, surely, and he plain ran the spear into the Savior's side, it went right through, where I have my wound, so much that it pushed the skin together and one could see the spear tip, didn't come out but was somewhat visible. Then he pulled back, then reddish blood-water came out, with a hiss, as it came out that fast. He then jumped down from the horse, and put on a hook.

Naber: The tip, could one see it from the outside?

Resl: Yes, it was visible. Had put the spear on a hook and jumped down, down from his horse. The blood sprayed all over this one's face, he was like washed down by it, he could not see properly. He was not very old, pretty young. He then, he wiped it off, he was not against the Savior from the beginning, then he looked very solemn and could see again properly.

Then he looked up to the Savior and also said something which I did not understand. The other straight men too were very solemn, only the wild ones cared for nobody.

But it was hard on the Mother, but she would have preferred it this way rather than the beating with the iron clubs. But this one (straight man with spear) stayed on regardless. Yes, now he couldn't leave because they, I believe were not allowed to leave, because the straight ones remained there, I believe. Now I went away, I was somewhere else. Then I was with the man, the one who got something in writing from the I-Dare-Not, you know where he went. He went to an old man, the one who once came to the Savior at night, they then went to the women and purchased all sorts of things, cloth, tasty herbs and dried herbs, sort of tea, they also tasted fresh but slightly hot.

Several men came along, there was one more well to do one, they went to him and he had some to whom he could give orders. They then took some water skins, pots and all this they took up there, and ladders.

Naber: Skins to get water?

Resl: They went for water several times, two skins they had. There was a water well and trough towards the valley, near the hill, towards the valley, where they all along went to get water.

They had a pile of things, you know, kind of tools. They went up and the others would not let them out, the gates were locked. What's the matter with them? Some straight men stood there, they just changed guards, they went home and others came, they change often though, and outside stood a few of them. He and the others (all Roman soldiers) were good toward the Savior, the straight men who stood there. They were there for some time now - as the others (Joseph of A. and Nicodemus group) went out.

Naber: The two who were clubbed to death, were they still hanging on their crosses?

Resl: No, no, they worked on them, they took them down, yes they were taken down.

Naber: After they clubbed them to death?

Resl: They tied ropes to them and pulled them down the hill, like animals they drug them. You know tied they were to several others.

Naber: What happened to the wood?

Resl: I don't know, they put it somewhere.

      When the other came up, they put a ladder up against and prepared it, they placed a carpet before the Mother, you know, she could lean up against a rock then they rolled a few blankets together they had brought.

      Then the Mother sat down. Then the Mother had to pull up her knees, they asked Her to, for the Savior. Just wait now!

      Now they tied two poles to the ladder and two spears, they held it like a fire ladder; Oh then, they pulled out the nails.

      Guess who came also? When they were there already? You know who came, the one who jumped from the horse (Centurion), he came running up, he was in a hurry but good, he came out all by himself, himself, alone and for sure they let him through the gate easy, they knew him, who guarded the gate. He, indeed, pulled out the bottom nail from the feet.

Naber: ....is repeating several questions regarding the nailing of the feet.

Resl: I've told you already, they pulled out the nail because, as one can say, pre-drilled the foot.

Naber: Then they nailed the right foot separately?

Resl: No, through the right foot and then through the hole in the left foot.

Naber: Did they place the right foot on the left right then?

Resl: Put it on top, of course.

Naber: And drove the nail only then?

Resl: Drove in the nail while one held the feet and saw to it that the nail went straight through, where he had pulled out the first nail.

Naber: And, the one who jumped down, pulled out this nail?

Resl: Pulled it out. Yes, he had the strength. The two old men would have had a hard time, at that, the servants helped, he had brought servants along.

Naber: They had that kind of servant come along?

Resl: Yes, of course, a bunch of them. One went to get water, several worked together and brought all these tools, lugged them up, it was heavy.

Then, only those others were allowed to touch the Savior, the servants were not, but the young man (John). Yes, when they pulled out the nails.

Naber: Who pulled out the upper nails?

Resl: Just wait! They pulled up, from behind the Savior, a long beautiful, linen, cloth.

Naber: What did they do with the ropes?

Resl: Taken away first. The one who begged for the Savior was the one who took off the ropes.

Naber: That would have had to be the older one (Joseph of A.)

Resl: Well now, the other one was old too, who came at night to the Savior.

Naber: Then, held the Savior, otherwise His hands would have torn out?

Resl: Sure, the young man was there, they stood on the ladder.

Naber: And they were the ones who held Him up there?

Resl: Yes. The old man was up there and the one other, a pious one also, he was one of those who are not always with the Savior (disciple). They had a good grip on the Savior, from behind, the ladders stood firmly, and they could fold over the long linen cloth, he (Joseph of A.) gave all the orders.

They, by the way, were not allowed to touch the Savior with their bare hands, they had a real, what's it called?

Naber: Reverence?

Resl: Yes, I surely liked that, surely liked it. It was good for the Mother also. Yes, She wept bitterly, the Mother. Oh so. I won't tell you any more.

Naber: Go on, Resl. It would please the Savior if we too were compassionate.

Resl: There. They pulled the linen cloth up. Then They pulled the nail out from one hand, then placed the arm carefully into the cloth, and then held in position on the ladder, so that the Savior could not slip down, you know..

Then, he had come down a little ways from the ladder, he then held the shoulder (Jesus') back and then laid the arm into it (the cloth), then they pulled the other nail out, and placed this arm into the cloth also, then they threw the cloth over His head. Oh so! And do you know where they put the Savior - to the Mother.

There they worked, prepared everything, the others brought water by then from down there, they brought a kind of pallet with them, and they had, for the Mother also .....

Naber: The pallet had legs?

Resl: Yes, and leather straps around. Like in a litter, there was leather laced through, or it would not have worked. Then they brought the water and washed the Savior's face. Yes, the Mother did that, especially, first washed out His hair, entire bunches came out, by the way. She thoroughly washed His eyes, they were full of blood, stuck together, washed them thoroughly. Also His mouth. Why were the Savior's teeth so full of blood, in between, and the whole mouth?

The blood was completely black, She pulled out the tongue to wash, they had smaller pieces cloth, no sponge you know, pieces from the linen and then, She did, on the neck the blood had much clotted and the shoulder; oh, did the Mother ever weep, it was so hard on her, and the young man (John) helped and the....

Naber: On the shoulder where you have your wound?

Resl: Yes, it was so deep, really terrible, and the one who jumped from the horse, he really helped, and the other who ran the spear into the Savior's side. And the other men stood by, they were most serious, they all along remained. Yes, remained; but do something? No!

Then the Mother washed the arms and hands. You known, they held them up to the Mother and the Mother washed them.

Naber: Listen now, did they leave the Savior laying on the same cloth they had to take Him down?

Resl: No, at first they had Him covered over at the Mother, then they brought something, something to keep the Mother from getting wet, in what She had on she would have gotten wet, the cloth they took off, rolled up and put another one down. And they covered the Savior with some sort of veil-like cloth.

Naber: Then they washed Him, but what about the other cloth?

Resl: They had rolled it up.

Naber: Once more, the cloth was pulled up behind the Savior?

Resl: Already told you, and then over the Savior and down.

Naber: Down in front?

Resl: Of course so, and that was the one they then took away.

Naber: From the sides, they wrapped the arms?

Resl: Yes.

Naber: Now, just be nice and patient.

Resl: Yeah, when you keep asking all that stuff, I am so sleepy.

Naber: Now, now.

Resl: And then all of a sudden I fall asleep and you get nothing.

Naber: No, no, the Savior will see to it that you will then get a good sleep.

Resl: And I lost track where we were.

Naber: Now, the Mother washed the Savior.

Resl: Then, they turned Him sideways, they washed His back vigorously and then...

Naber: What did it look like?

Resl: Oh, don't ask, totally torn up in shreds, they were black, the shreds were, entire skin shreds stuck out, they were brown, bloodshot, horrifying, yet one could see it well, the Savior even though He was defaced like this, but one would not have recognized Him, no, on account He was so swollen. And then, when the Mother had finished the upper part, the men prepared themselves, now the men helped. Now, the Mother could rest some. I was glad that the Mother could rest now, now the men finished up. The feet, the Mother could no more, it would be too far down, the men were to do that. The one who jumped from the horse, he did, and then the young man and the two old ones, did then. And oh yes, when the Mother was finished, she put something around His head, yes, and also, something to anoint, they gave Her, it smelled good, yes and then when the men were done,

Naber: Did She anoint?

Resl: The face. Yes, we are not finished though. That was after, when the men were done, with the washing down, you know, the legs the men washed down, the feet and everything.
        Then they anointed right away, onto His feet, the armpits and everywhere they put herbs were they had anointed. They worked together, they knew what they were doing. The one who jumped from the horse you know, he was clumsy all right, the two old ones much more handy than the younger ones.
        And how was it, the young man, kept weeping again and again, he couldn't help himself.
        Oh so, the men were in a hurry. First I saw them when they were in the big house (temple) where there was chaos only, they had to be there I guess, don't you think? You know, when it was like the earthquake.
        Then they anointed with some other, it was a white creme.

Naber: Had they put away the cloth by then?

Resl: Sure, or it would have gotten wet.
        Since the other cloth did not reach far enough, they once more anointed the Savior, all over, filled the armpits with stuff and the feet, filled them fully and wrapped, tightly wrapped, the young man wrapped.

Naber: How did they wrap?

Resl: The arms separate, then all around, then the feet separate and again all around, so it was all together.
        Yes, and the head. The Mother covered it again, then she put aside to keep the little pieces of cloth, then She put something fragrant into His hair, She squashed it, then She put something good into it, She also squashed that, She was able to squash it, She poured it out over His hair, and into the neck to put some ointment and closed up. And the Mother wept so much, His eyes wouldn't stay closed, so She had to push down all along. Yes, and it was: Oh so, the girl, she was always at His feet and all along wept, yes, how she had so much water to weep, really, I felt sorry for her too.

Naber: Did she dry His feet too?

Entombment

Naber: Did she also dry the feet?

Resl: They had washed them, no and when they were done, they laid Him on the pallet, on the pallet, and then the men, they helped indeed, the women who stood there; would you know who helped carry? The two old men then the one who jumped from the horse and the young man, they carried Him. The womenfolk walked behind and the straight men (Roman soldiers) some of them, on account it was evening and one couldn't see into the tomb anymore, they had wooden torches and lighted into the tomb.

Naber: Did they also go into the tomb?

Resl: No, they stayed outside, also because they had the horses with them, they had the horses.

Naber: Did all the others go along?

Resl: Nearly. Then the womenfolk and the men, the ones who were good to the Savior, they, you know, didn't sing but lamented, it went on a rhythm as they carried the Savior. Then first, they looked into the tomb once more, yes, indeed. They also cleaned up the garden, picked up stuff and twigs, the ones who had brought the ladders and tools. Then they, in the inside, on the stone, on which the Savior was going to be put, the laid down a brown blanket, then the Savior on top, then the blanket over Him, yes, a dark brown one.

Naber: What did the tomb look like?

Resl: Well, it was hewn out of the rock.

Naber: Where one entered?

Resl: First there was a space, no, first there was a hole.

Naber: Was it square?

Resl: Yes, it was square, then there was a chamber.

Naber: Sort of square, taller than wide?

Resl: Yes, sure. There was an open space and then a small door, looked like copper, one could open.

Naber: Slide open?

Resl: Yes, there was a bar in front of it that had to be removed first; they already had that opened. I saw all this only as it was being closed.

Naber: Could one slide the door?

Resl: Yes, for sure, could be slid easily. Yes, then put in front again and closed again so no one could get in. There is where they laid the Savior. Then, the last, the Mother went in, then the womenfolk but the men watched that it was enough, you know, they wanted to leave, wanted to close up. Then they did close and put the stone in front; it was indeed heavy, there the straight men helped. Yes, and then they went home.

Naber: Did they fix the stone?

Resl: It was in a groove, it held fast

Naber: Did they tie it down with ropes?

Resl: No, did nothing more, on account it was closed solid on the inside, yes, the interior door. There was a door inside, and then the men went into the town.

Naber: And the straight men?

Resl: They too left, everybody left, it got to be quite empty outside. They pretty much left together on account of the gate. For this reason, the Mother took care that She came in with the men because they would be let in, they always lock right away again, they keep it always locked, they were plain scared. Yes, surely, first they were so cheeky, now they are running scared. Yes, now they lock themselves in.

Naber: What did they do with the wood on which the Savior hung?

Resl: No, I didn't see that. You know, there in town, at the I-Dare-Not, men came, they were not two-faced. One could see that he (Pilate) was frightened, was so scared; you know where he was when that one came to see him, the one who asked to have the Savior; I surely saw what went on there, he (Pilate) stoked a small fire in front of a cattlehead (idol). There were two others with him, they and he kept putting something into the little fire, was he ever scared, he looked awful, in front of the cattlehead.

Oh go! Why then was he so scared? But he did get with the one and gave him something written. Now, this I must tell you. Now they argued, he (Pilate) wasn't comfortable with it, but the others were two-faced and impertinent. Yes, then he said something, he agreed to it, the others pressed him, he had something to say. Then some went out, in fact a whole troop went out, and the one the short one was with them, the one who ran the spear into the Savior, he went along.

Naber: Were they on horses?

Resl: No, they walked, they had sort of poles, two of them, two pots and some split wood they took along, and some food-stuff they had in leather pouches. And then they had yet something else to put over the stone; several went along, a whole troop. Then, as they came up, they took away the stone, the men helped at that.

Naber: Others; no straight men?

Resl: Some went along, straight men also. They took away the stone, the one the others had put there, others who laid the Savior in there, did and and then opened the door, then looked into it and felt to make sure the Savior was really there you know, looked into it, the others too, and touched Him.

Naber: Was the door lockable?

Resl: No, I did not see a lock, there was an iron bar in front of it, it was sort of hooked in, then they closed the door again, drew the door shut, there was some noise. Drew the door shut and replaced the stone. Then they sort of half, it was not quite round, they smeared something on top and bot-tom in a half-round mold, there was a manhead, a bald one, he was bald, he was, they pressed on the stone and pulled a ribbon across, and on top of the ribbon they pressed this half-round. There, one could see the head, somewhat like a sickle, but big you know, like a half-moon, like a half-moon. There, somewhat sideways, there was a head on it. Yes, this was a mold with a head on it. When it was pushed into the soft stuff one could see the head.

Naber: But the head was round?

Resl: Yes, it (the head) was complete, the mold was round.

Resl: Yes, it was indeed complete, the mold was completely round.

Naber: Now I see, the mold was.

Resl: Oh, Father, indeed; it's all so simple.

Naber: Well, you know, I did not see it though.

Resl: And then the majority of them went away, and the one who ran the spear into the Savior, and one more and one more and one more and one more and one more and one more and one more (seven) stayed on.

Naber: Therefore then, the one who pierced the Savior's side and then (in unison: Naber and Resl) one and one and one and one and one and one and one more stayed on.

Resl: I don't know what they were doing out there now. I went away and the others had turned around again. These others went home. Oh so!

Naber   You too went away?

Resl: I went also. Oh, I'm glad they can't mistreat the Savior any more, even if He is dead. Really, today I had such frightful pity for the Savior, I had such terrible compassion. I have some real pain now....but it goes away completely compared to the Savior, no piece was torn out of my body. They ripped whole pieces out of the Savior. And they really got Him on His sides. Whole flakes of skin were torn loose from the flesh. The flesh looked all black.

F.N. - This recounting on Good Friday 1941, late in the evening, was suddenly interrupted by a new vision. For this reason, Fr. Naber's exclamation of "Ui - Ai" (wow). Resl sees the happenings of the arrest of Joseph of Arimathea. Now follows her recountal of this vision in the state of exalted repose.

Naber: Wow!

Resl: All kinds of little branches and twigs were on the ground. He (J.of A.) had them picked up and removed so that the garden would look beautiful for the Savior. Then he went to him, and this was a risk for sure, to the I-Dare-Not (Pilate), you know the one who stoked the small fire. Now, just imagine this, he walked now, it is already night, pitch black night, but he really liked the Savior, it seems. He went around all by himself, there he came upon men who were looking for him, you know, ones who are more often with the Savior (disciples) and he told them, they were curious it was obvious. They had no light though, one could only recognize them by the pots and poles, you know there are these poles and and pots on them on the streets, only in the reflection one could see them, you know and they were vigorously discussing. All of a sudden some came; you know, they went around in the town, they all were from the house (temple).

Yes, and you know, they wanted to get them (disciples)- they were infuriated. Now they had the Savior, and they were thinking let's finish the job. Now let's look for all the others, the ones who go with the Savior, all of them they wanted to catch, I feel. You know, most were young men though and they saw those coming they guessed already, while the other (J.of A.) was busy telling and talking and they saw them coming, when they saw them - and I would have to lie - where they went; they were leaping, you know, racing away one should say, not a one did they catch, they were so fast you know, the others did not go after them because they quickly grabbed him, him they caught, the old man (J. of A.).

He is going to get it now: him they caught. Everyone jumped on top of him, you know they were terribly mad at him, they had no more time for the others.

In the meantime, the others went goodness knows where. You know where they put him? Into the big house (temple). There are, where the evil ones put the Savior, in a tower, into one of these towers, one can enter at the base, well, that is where they locked him up. He could not get out any more, I tell you.

Naber: How many towers are there?

Resl: Down below is one, then one is back there, I don't know if there are any up above, yes, but down below there are two, this I know. Father, he won't get out of there any more, he is going to perish in there.

Naber: Was there perhaps an entry from the inside?

Resl: From the side there, they drug him in from the house, from the gate. From the outside, the town, you can't get to it. No, no, they came in through the gate and then they went back there along the side, they had the things to get in, it was closed but now they closed it again. They put one in front to watch.

I felt sorry, indeed sorry for him. He surely is frightened. He's got to be hungry, had no time to eat or sleep. Well, now sleep he could.

They are so cruel though, believe me. The Earcutterer and the young man, where might they be? The Mother went down into the house, in the end the others will be there too so they at least be together some. That should be indeed ......not, but they were in the right, they in there.

Naber: Surely this (place) belongs to the good ones where they will not be able to find them.

Resl: The good one, that they can't get in there, but should not let themselves be seen much. See, for sure they would do this to all of them, or catch the Mother, that would be horrible. That the Savior will not allow!

Where? But he (J. of A.) didn't deserve this either, that they would rather have caught one of the others who weren't there. Really, I am so mad again. If they had caught one of the others who weren't along like it happened to the Savior, but he (J. of A.) always cared for all. Oh go; I feel so sorry, but that's how things go. Do you feel sorry too?

Naber: For sure.

Resl: You know, it got to the I-Dare-Not, because he (J. of A.) was a higher-up man, it was clear, in the way of his bearing and his whole get-up. How he pleaded for the Savior.....You know it was so obvious that he was not stupid. Oh my, say, why though, did he keep stoking the little fire?

Resl was usually in a deep sleep throughout Holy Saturday until up to the beginning of the vision of the Resurrection, during which time she recovered from her traumatic experiences of Good Friday. On Holy Saturday, she had a vision of the liberation of Joseph of Arimethea.

In response to questions by Fr. Naber, she describes the configuration of the tomb and the departure of the women from the tomb, followed by the liberation of J. of A.

Resl: You know, there is this man who yesterday, one could say yesterday, was at the I-Dare-Not, when he begged for the Savior, you know the one who owns the beautiful garden where they laid the Savior, the one who also has the beautiful tomb where the beautiful white stone lies, the shiny one.

Naber: Where is this?

Resl: So, in the tomb there is a white stone with yellow veins, brownish veins, this is a special stone, it is not a stone that was grown there. It is clad with something, the tomb where the Savior lies, with a beautiful stone, it is beautiful white, yes.

Naber: You hadn't told of this.

Resl: Do I have to tell everything?

Naber: Yes, of course.

Resl: There were brown veins in it, like inlaid it is.

Naber: The whole thing.

Resl: Yes, ceiling and the side, everything.

Naber: The room outside the burial chamber also?

Resl: No, not that one, that one is darker.

Naber: But also clad?

Resl: Yes, but darker, it is not clad as beautiful, actually, not really clad, no, it's more like the natural stone, but one sees it is cut into it. But there the stone would not be as shiny, no, no.

Naber: The whole tomb inside like that?

Resl: Now, let me just tell you.

Naber: Is it equally high?

Resl: Sort of sloping into the rock. Now let me just talk. The outside room is bigger, bigger than the burial room.

Naber: Now something just came to me, I have got to inject.

Resl: What?

Naber: You didn't tell that yesterday, you said you hadn't told it.

Resl: Well, now, do I have to tell all?

Naber: When the Mother liked (kissed) the Savior.

Resl: Yes, when the Mother of the Savior, oh, you know all along the eyes wouldn't keep closed. When they washed Him down and when they wrapped Him, and before they carried Him into the tomb, in the tomb they also liked Him. The young man, and the men were anxious, should come out now but kept wanting to go back in. The girl walked around, picked some flowers, which she, I think wanted to put in there also, but they wouldn't let her go back in. But the Mother did go in and liked the Savior, through the brown blanket.

Naber: Didn't they open up?

Resl: No, they were not allowed to open up again, because they had Him arranged and tidied, covered with the brown blanket, but the Mother liked Him. They did not hurt Him as they washed Him, and the eyes wouldn't hold shut. So all along She shut them and liked Him then, and the young man, he, the sides of the Savior, he liked, yes, but the others didn't have the courage, the men, only the Mother and the young man.

Naber: So, the Mother liked the Savior on His eyes?

Resl: Yes, on the forehead, and on the mouth, yes on the cheeks, on the lips, were so blue and the face gray yellowish.

Naber: Did the good man like Him also?

Resl: Yes, the good man could get close enough, he did the big injury, oh, there was the big injury where he was run into, stabbed in the side.
          Now, I tell you how the man came out.

Naber: What else did they like (kiss)? Yesterday you said you had forgotten it.

Resl: Yesterday, I forgot to tell this. The nails of the Savior, I forgot to tell yesterday, indeed I forgot, the nails they nailed the Savior with, everybody liked.

Naber: All the people who were there?

Resl: Yes, not all of the straight men, some though. Yes, I forgot that, I am sure I forgot some, you know I forget easily, but that is not the main issue. The main point I did not forget.

    Now, what do you want me to tell you?

The Deliverance of Joseph of Arimathea

Naber: The man.

Resl: The man they had locked up, he prayed in there, but you know, they (Gestapo) locked one of our boys (Hans), he too is praying. You know, when one is locked up one can't work, can't do anything, now one has more time to pray. The boy of ours, the young one, him who is the youngest, oh, he likes to pray indeed, in the past he didn't like to pray that much, you know, then he always was too busy, you know, now he has time to think.

    Why, he says to himself, do I think only now why I am on earth. Yes, yes and you know, the Savior is going to get him out all right, even if he doesn't send a light-man.

    Now, I remember something. The other one, what's his name now, Ferd (Ferdinand), the young girl (Terese of Lisieux), you know the one who helped me, if she hadn't protected him, he wouldn't have been let out, like it was decided (by Nazi courts) one year later, that he too had to stay locked. It would have been some time until he would have been let out. Listen now, he would have been finished in his nerves, he could not have taken it like the other (Hans). The other had strong nerves, he knows it that Savior will help him that his nerves are still strong. But the other (Ferdinand) would not have lasted through more Gestapo torture with his nerves, there he wrote me a note,

I went to the girl and begged for him (meaning: Resl went before the altar of St. Terese).

Now what should I tell you?

Naber: About the man. (J. of A.)

Resl: There he reached out, up to heaven, like these people like to pray.

Naber: Did he stand, sit or kneel?

Resl: He was standing, it was dark. It was in the middle of the night, then it was pitch dark. The moon was in fact......

Naber: Was there no window there?

Resl: No, no, just wait, we are going to be outside where we can see. All of a sudden a light man came and let a piece of cloth down and called something down, his name, "Ahther, Ahther," I can't quite recall, "Ahreuther," I don't know how, "Ahreuther," this I forget I don't know it; then he said something else, the last thing he said, "Ahrether, Ahremether," like that: I can't remember, then he looked around and said once more, said something, then he let a large, long piece of linen down, then he (J. of A.) clawed himself into the cloth; there, the wall was not smooth, like with brick, this was a stone wall, and then with both hands, it was strenuous for sure. The light man pulled up and he had to claw himself solidly into the cloth, was an old man after all, looked just about like you (Naber), not as tall, and you know like, ...and on he was concerned for everybody, just about like you, and then he helped push with his feet. It went slowly but of a sudden he was on top.

There is this wall, the tower is connected to a wall, it continues with a wall. From there, there is this wall toward the big town wall, this wall continues to the wall near the mount, where the Savior once did this (Last Supper), where houses are, there is a wall around.

When he (J. of A.) was up there, the light man had simply disappeared, but did look sheepish, he (J. of A.) did.

Naber: Did he get out of the tower on top?

Resl: For sure, and now he is there all by himself.

Naber: Isn't the tower taller than the wall?

Resl: No, no, no! Absolutely no!

Naber: Was it possible to get out from the tower, at the top?

Resl: Well so, for those who knew; then he sort of crawled along, slowly he looked around, in the end he got frightened. Across, across and across he clambered, looked somewhat to where he had to go, this, the light man did not tell him. Then he took the side wall, clambered across, that was possible, you know, to the right, there, where the Savior once did this (Last Supper), near there; quite soon it leads downwards from the outer ones, the house itself does not connect to the wall, not that you think the wall connects to the house, but in this vicinity is the outer Town wall, in that area, you understand! The inner one actually, there is a second one outside.

    That is where he came down, down on the wall, you know, here he knew his way, he knew it, it was here abouts he could easily see, the house where the Savior did this.

Naber: The breads.

Resl: Yes, breads and where He washed their feet, the Savior. By then, he guessed all right that here, the men and the Mother and all had locked themselves in. Now he came running up from the back, looked around and around so that no one could catch him, did he ever run, then he knocked and they wouldn't let him in, I was scared to death.

    But think though, then they did in fact let him come in, and they were overjoyed. Oh yes, I don't begrudge him this joy, he really deserved it, for all he did for the Savior. I felt so sorry they caught him.

    Oh, they had every right to lock themselves in. They would catch bunches of them. You know, they are dangerous, they are mad. But so, it went well. Go on, I get sleepy again, I can't fall asleep that way, something else crops up all along. But yes, this was so beautiful just now, again so beautiful. Oh, go on, was it beautiful, I don't begrudge it.

Naber: What happened to the cloth?

Resl: Oh, the light man probably put it away. Ha, ha, probably took it from somewhere...Ha, ha, (full of mirth.)

Interlude

F.N.- the following discourse, in the state of exalted repose:

After Resl's recountal of the deliverance of Joseph of Arimathea, Resl accidentally touched my microphone. She was appalled and demanded of Father Naber that this apparatus be destroyed. Father Naber declined.

Father Naber's statement was of importance to me! To quote him: "The Savior agrees with it" (namely the recordings).

Afterwards, I queried Father Naber regarding the statement of "The Savior agrees with it." He gave the following answer: "As I some time back, requested his (Naber's) assistance in recording the visions, he, in Resl's state of exalted repose (a condition following immediately after receiving the Holy Eucharist) asked whether this should be done. He received a clear, affirmative answer, in fact a mandate, to assist me in the recordings."

Resl: Now what is this, I got onto something.

Naber: Doesn't matter.

Resl: Indeed, well, let me see what this is.

Naber: Nothing important.

Resl: Now I thought I hit something.

Naber: So what?

Resl: Give it to me! Don't say later you gave it to me, you don't need to lie, just say.

Naber: It was very expensive!

Resl: That is not important, let me touch it.

Naber: No, no!

Resl: Let me touch it, I won't grab it. No, if I say so, I won't grab it.

Naber: No, it does not belong to me!

Resl: Oh, Father, my good Father, I too will give you something.

Naber: What is it you would give me?

Resl: Just like you! Oh, I've got something. Something carved, like it was of the Savior (A short while ago Resl received a carved Last Supper from Ober-Ammergau), that I will give to you. Now let me have this!

Naber: I have one of those myself.

Resl: Oh, just like you are, tell me what you'd like. But let's smash this thing. Easy for you. You hold it in front of me and I talk into it. So the others will hear it too.

Naber: Now, you try to talk your way out of it beautifully, yes, beautifully.

Resl: No, no, that would be horrible, I don't like that.

Naber: No, no, this is all right with the Savior, listen now, it is indeed all right with the Savior.

Resl: How would you know that?

Naber: I do know that, indeed, I do!

Resl: All of you just do with me as you please, don't you! I am just told to say yes and then, then you say I'm impatient. You know, this gets my goat.

Naber: Now listen, the Savior is taking part in this. You understand, He is part of this, does not ask for your O.K.

Resl: But then you say I am not patient, you know, then you keep saying I am not patient, I am being difficult and everything is supposed to be just fine with me.

Naber: Why, of course everything the Savior desires of you must be all right with you.

Resl: But then you can't say any more I am not patient.

Naber: What the Savior desires has got to be all right with you.

Resl: What again?

Naber: What the Savior desires has got to be all right with you.

Resl: But then I don't want to hear again I am not patient.

FN - *In view of the fact that Resl's condition on this morning of Holy Saturday 1941, as compared to the previous days, was unusually good, and the state of exalted repose continued on, Fr. Naber took advantage of the situation and went on with further questions for Resl.*
   As to the question whether her wounds (stigmata) still hurt, in the days just past, her stigmata caused her great pain. Her responses about the stigmata per se appears to me to be of significance.

Naber: Do the wounds hurt you?

Resl: No.

Naber: Your wounds do not hurt any more?

Resl: No.

Naber: I am going to give them a good whack. (Naber hits the back of her hands).

Resl: Yeah, just hit real good.

Naber: Yes, you don't feel anything?

Resl: No, not even here. (Resl reaches out with the other hand.)

Naber: You don't feel this?

Resl: No.

Naber: Go on, that neither?

Resl: No.

Naber: Well, now what have we here? Look, in the end the Savior is going to take your wounds away?

Resl: Wow, that would be beautiful!

Naber: You don't like them?

Resl: No, that would be beautiful!

Naber: Now, let me hit again, does this hurt?

Resl: No

Naber: Not at all? Well, what gives?

Resl: I am happy.

Naber: You slept over this! This would please you?

Resl: Yes, now I need to sleep a little so it will go away.

Naber: Your heart wound doesn't hurt either?

Resl: No.

Naber: Go on! Feet neither?

Resl: No.

Naber: None of the wounds hurt?

Resl: No, except I am sleepy.

Naber: In the end, the Savior is going to take them away?

Resl: Oh, would I ever like that!

Naber: Why so?

Resl: Because, I'd then work like I want to. So, I am always hindered.

Naber: You'd like to work?

Resl: Yes.

Naber: Go on now!

Resl: I keep working all sorts of things with my wounds, but not well.

Naber: But, if the Savior wants you to have wounds rather than be able to work?

Resl: Then that is all right with me. But the other I would like better. To like, or it being all right, those are, are two different things.

         I can be pleased with something and can say yes to something because the Savior wants it so, can agree to it, but I don't need to like it.

Naber: But you find joy in the Savior?

Resl: Yes! Indeed!

Naber: And in His desires? His wishes?

Resl: Find joy in it too, so! so!

Naber: One must indeed differentiate.

Resl: Well so .... just so I won't talk silly.

F.N. - *Concluding the description of her attitude toward her stigmata, Resl tells the story of an injury to her feet she received when she tried to warm them on a hot stove. Significant is that the burns were healed through Lourdes water.*

Resl: Oh, you know, for some time I have not been feeling too well. And, my feet were freezing cold. So I sat in my little living room and warmed my feet on the stove. Then I began to feel faint. As I came back I found I burned my foot. It sure hurt, I felt it. Oh....(garbled).

Naber: How many blisters did you have?

Resl: All this side and here. Then the butcherer (Physician Dr. Mittendorfer) was here. He looked at it but couldn't do any good either. Probably thought it will eventually go away.
        No, then, our boy went to somewhere, I told him to get something for me. When he got back he'd forgotten. Then another went, he brought a burn bandage. I put it on but it didn't help. It was some sort of flour stuff. It did no good. And I wanted to work something. Now, there is some water here after all. The one from the Mother...... .

Naber: Yes, water from Lourdes.

Resl: (recording garbled)
        Now, our young assistant pastor went someplace, where the Mother, I was there once .... is here the Mother came to a girl, where she said, "Immaculate Conception Immaculate," you know there, where the girl, the one who didn't know where the water was. Where the Mother said

something, she should work. There she then ran down to the water because down there a water flowed past. There, she didn't understand the Mother. Then the Mother had waved her back and pointed. Then there, with the hand, she scratched, took the dirt away, and would you believe, water came. Then, surely, she had to drink this dirty water, the Mother had told her so. She was repulsed. When she scratched there, the water just came. The Savior took me there once. Not to the lower water which flows past. When she scratched into the dirt, water flowed out and it keeps flowing.

And here, the young pastor brought me some of this water. Yeah, now you think it's funny, but this is serious.

Naber: No, now, I didn't laugh about that water because it is called that (Lourdes water.)

Resl: This is absolutely real, nothing to laugh at. I surely do not laugh, this is serious.

And he gave me of this water. Now I said: "Mother, I don't object to this burn......you know, Mother," I said, "Mother, I dip it into the water." She let it come out for this purpose after all, you told me....helped a lot of people already. I said this, because it did hurt something awful. Just so that I can sleep a little bit, this night. To get it closed I didn't even think of . Only, a little sleep I would have liked.

So, I put it into the water, bandage and all, you know, the floury stuff. It's there in the attic still, still wet and stuck together, like mush.......(garbled)......Now I felt nothing any more.....

Now I touched it, could feel nothing. Oh, so, has not hurt, can't even see where it blistered, and nothing there any more. Completely healed over. It was not the water that did it, it was the Mother Herself Who had helped. That much I did not expect. I just hoped I could sleep a little.

That is the way it is: if one begs the Mother for something, She gives far more then one thinks. Gets to where one does not dare to beg.

The Resurrection of Christ

Resl: Oh so, I am still tired and was so dazed, and suddenly the Savior rushed me away.

Naber: So, you thought of nothing special, like what is going to happen, or?

Resl: I didn't have time for that, I thought of nothing in particular.

Naber: Well, what did you think of then?

Resl: Oh, I want to sleep, I feel faint, I thought. Yeah, that about is all I thought.

Naber: And in between?

Resl: The Savior came, but so fast! It was like this: There I was in front of the tomb, no one was there, in front of the tomb, you know, where they laid the Savior, was nobody around and then it started to earthquake.

Naber: Nobody?

Resl: Well, now, I don't mean the Savior, and not the women-folk, you know I should, you know it yourself that they hadn't left, or don't you know; then I have to tell you this first, because you say nobody was there.

Naber: You said nobody!

Resl: Oh, I don't count these among people.

Naber: You already told us that some straight men went out there, now I thought if you said nobody is there, they too weren't there.

Resl: But yes, they were there, still are, ah, were very tired, indeed, you know, there was one, well, there were several of them all right.

Naber: How many were there?

Resl: Yes, yes, that's not important at all, I rather tell you about the beautiful.

Naber: You must tell all! Everything! In the right sequence.

Resl: Oh then, the beautiful first. Well, so. They were just there, the straight men, you know, like they were yesterday or whenever it was, went there; and then suddenly it, you know I can't tell you just like that, just wait, I can't tell it so fast how it happened, an earthquake and the Savior through the stone out and a light man down, all at the same time.

Naber: A light man

Resl: One and another one, he went into afterwards. Just wait now, I have to say it once more. Earthquake, the Savior out through the stone and the light man came, all at once, you know how it is, the Savior did not wait for the light man to move the stone and sit on it, He came out right through the upper middle of the stone.

Naber: Out up there?

Resl: Where then, possibly up front through the stone? Out on top!

Naber: Not right through the stone?

Resl: Not through the forward stone, out up there where the tomb is closed.

Naber: Then, through the stone that closes the tomb?

Resl: No, no, no, not through that one, just directly straight out, or the Savior would have had to bend over. He came out forward, He went straight upwards and went over; you know if you ask like that I won't tell you anything any more.

Naber: No, no, be sensible and tell. I just could not imagine this, I always thought the Savior came out through the stone.

Resl: He came straight out!

Naber: Then, you would have to have looked up.

Resl: Well, I did indeed; yes, came out and then, you know where He went, He floated, floated onward to the hill to the Mother, there was the Mother, out there all alone.

Naber: You once......first you have to tell us what the Savior looked like.

Resl: Yes, and how the men got terrified.

Naber: Of course.

Resl: Oh, I'd rather tell the beautiful.

Naber: Obey now!

Resl: We are going to get into a fight yet!

Naber: How the Savior looked, you must obey, the Savior wants you to tell all properly!

Resl: Well, then, one after the other, this comes. Then I will tell you how the Savior came out.

Naber: Why, certainly.

Resl: Well, the most beautiful was, surely His garments, they were white, like frozen snow when the sun shines on it and His wounds beaming light from His hands, His feet and through, through the heart.

Naber: The heart was beaming also?

Resl: You know, through, shone right through everything.

Naber: Could one see the heart?

Resl: The heart itself, no. But as He floated away, it radiated through, visibly, from the heart, the light went out through the heart, like from the other wounds the light came out, but no rays from the heart.

Naber: It came out different from the heart wound?

Resl: The hands and feet wounds had their own brightness and so had the heart wound. You must realize that the garments weren't crude, like something our father would sew together, you know, that was something so light, could not be from this world where light can't get through a garment, one can't explain it, one has to see it.

Naber: Have you ever seen the Savior with His heart?

Resl: Not so, oh, go on, no, no, when He had the thorns and the
        cross. No, no, not like this, I knew where its own bright-
        ness was, it starts from the heart wound. It so simple.
        Did you get any sleep, Father?

Naber: I was interested to know, what happened to the men. You
        are in such a good mood today, seems.

Resl: You know, it was such a joy and you keep asking always the
        same. And I though perhaps you were tired.

Naber: Well, now, you were the one who saw it.

Resl: It is not so easy to tell what one saw, I am just so full of joy,
        I would like best to tell it all at once. But you won't let me,
        you keep holding me back - that's not so nice.

Naber: Indeed. What happened to the men?

Resl: Now, I will tell you quickly, but you have to listen quickly
        too. The men were like dazed, they were frightened, full of
        fear and staggered, some fell down, one remained stand-
        ing, he did not fall, it was him who pierced the Savior's
        side, he staggered on his spear, he was back right away.

Naber: Were they all standing?

Resl: At first they were, then they fell, fell on their faces, then
        the Savior - and now comes the wonderful, I all along have
        to hold back, which is not easy (garbled). This I can't spill
        to you, how He looked at me so good. Really good He
        looked at me, the Savior!

Naber: (Joyous agreement). Did that make you happy?

Resl: Yes, I thought this I keep to myself. Yes, I didn't want to
        tell.

Naber: But, it is so wonderful when the Savior looks good at one!

Resl: Why sure, it's beautiful. And then the Savior went across.
        Further across He floated, this way He floated. Was it glo-
        rious. The garment flowed behind, like mist. Flowed after.
        It was solemn. So, toward the Mother.

Naber: What was the garment He wore, I mean the shape?

Resl: In the shape indeed. Tied in the middle, not straight down. And there was the Mother, on the hill, all by Herself, the Mother. Do you think She got any sleep this night? I am sure She did not sleep.

Naber: Was there any indication where the cross stood?

Resl: No, all was cleared away.
          But the Mother was where the Savior had died. But then, She could not sleep at home and so went all by Herself, alone. You know, I believe the Mother, when the Savior was still little, wasn't used to sleeping at night. Because the Savior prayed at night, the Mother too prayed at night.

Naber: Oh.

Resl: Yes, it's easier to pray at night. I too pray much at night. I pray much more at night than by day. This one can do, it simply is that way. One has peace. The Savior prayed through entire nights.
          So, the Mother was out here alone. When the womenfolk were gone, She most likely said, please leave Me alone. I didn't see any womenfolk, they were somewheres else. Some other place, they were.

Naber: I thought She went with them.

Resl: Yes, but then she likely said, leave Me alone, for a little while. They came later, I will tell you about.
          And then, the Savior and the Mother talked some, then the Savior vanished again. And the Mother was full of joy, one great joy.

Naber: Suppose you too were full of joy.

Resl: Yes, and just as the Savior came so fast, He also vanished fast. I then came back into the garden.
          Now, you have to imagine, all of a sudden the Savior is gone. And there, in the garden, they were still lying there, the men. But the one who pierced the Savior's side, he already walked some.
          And there was another, a light man, he looked like a straight man.

At the garden gate, some women kept milling around, the girl (Mary of Magdala), a woman and another one and another one. They shuffled around and would not get up the courage to come in, you know why they didn't dare come is, they didn't dare on account of the spears that hung lopsided and the men were lying on the ground still.......(noise).

I did not see him sit there any more, he didn't sit there any more, he first sat on top, like this was his place, the stone. So after, not to the side of, and now the girl and another one dared come in and the other two still did not dare, they just went right through and past the men and went in, and the girl, she knew her way all right, simply opened the door, the smaller door, the inner door. It was heavy but one could slide it open, she just slid it aside and looked into the tomb, she was in a real hurry, and horrified you know, on account the Savior wasn't lying in there any more; I don't know myself, I keep thinking, a light man talked but she did not hear him. When she saw the Savior wasn't there, she, in one rush was gone and ran and ran and not back the way she came in, that gate, but a smaller gate further up, which is closer to town, from the upper gate, down, through the town up the hill and with a crash into the men, there where the men had locked themselves in, and then the Earcutterer and the young man, they came, she said something exciting, you know she didn't know where the Savior. I could have told, you know, I could have said, I would know where the Savior might be....(noise).....

Yes, then she ran back up and the hair kept falling into her face all along and she kept pushing it back, you know she wore a veil, they don't like bare heads, these people, they all have something on their heads. Yes, and then the Earcutterer and the young man came out fast, you know though, the young man was faster because he was younger that the Earcutterer.

Naber: What were the other women doing?

Resl: Just wait now. And now they came out, but this comes first. Now, they came out, the Earcutterer walked slower and the young man ran faster, now I, I let them pass by me. And now, the Savior packed me back into the garden. Now in the garden, while the girl was gone and you know how, now the straight man who pierced the Savior's side, went up and reached there into the linen. He didn't see the light men at all, no, no, there were, in fact, two sitting there, one at the other end.

Naber: Two indeed? You just told us of one.

Resl: Because I myself didn't see the other one either. The girl, she was in such a hurry, just reached down and out she was again, said something to the womenfolk, then the women-folk went in.

Naber: How many were there?

Resl: One and one and another one and the young girl was not there at that moment, then went in, then the light men, one said something to them, was leaning against like, said something to them, "Ghalilahm," (Galilea) I understood.

Naber: He was leaning on?

Resl: On the stone, and one sat at the head.

Naber: What did he look like?

Resl: Him, I think, this the Savior can do, he (angel) only changed His garment, you know, as he came down, it was like a straight man and but he wore a long dress.

Naber: Well, did he come alone?

Resl: No, another one came with him. He went straight into the tomb up above the stone.

Naber: How?

Resl: Were two in there, at the front one was leaning, the other sat by the back, I told you.

Naber: Now, what did he look like?

Resl: Somewhat like a straight man but had a long garment.

Naber: Did they have a helmet like the straight men?

Resl: Yes, like the straight men.

Naber: (recording garbled)

Resl: Sort of like the straight men, that's why they were so frightened when they saw them looking like that.

Now these women came out again. You know, while the light man talked, did they come out again. All of a sudden, the young man came rushing also in, he went to the side of the little door, he was afraid to go in, he, I think he waited until the Earcutterer got there. Then the Earcutterer came, said something to him, then went in through the front and the young man right behind him also. Then he took something, some linen the Savior was wrapped into, took with him and stuffed under his overcoat.

Naber: What was the cloth like?

Resl: Yeah, this was to the side, the brown cloth was to the side.

Naber   Was it away?

Resl: Yes, somewhat away, to the side.

Naber: A little while ago you said ... (garbled).

Resl: That's such a trifle. Father, when the most important is so beautiful and you are after all that small stuff. Oh, go on.

Naber: Well, I just like to know what it looked like.

Resl: No, something beautiful comes, and then when, I have to all along think about the small things, I get so tired, then I do not tell the other things, because I am too tired, from the heat, I am perspiring, I am all wet, don't have a dry thread on me, so then I have to tell fast, 'cause I am tired, worn out.

My heart hurts!

Now, the Earcutterer and the young man went home again, of course the young man ahead and the Earcutterer behind. Now, the Savior floated towards.......he (Peter) recognized him, sort of, I think he did all right, but.....he was scared, he was embarrassed. Yes, I sort of felt what he thought, I know what he will have thought, in the end - in the end there, in the night once, where he betrayed the Savior. Oh yes, and he had put on such a big show over the Savior before; really put on, you know.

Now, something beautiful comes. The girl, when she returned, also went in. You know the girl was gone a while, went in, she had to go some place in between - don't know where ..... and at that the light men said something to the girl. She came out and wept and was sad.

Naber: Did they say something?

Resl: One said something, the other didn't talk at all; and sad she was, so sad, went around in the garden and wept, she did, and totally beside herself she was, so she went up around the trees.

No, someone was walking among the trees.....like any-body, and would you know the Savior disguised Himself to look like any people, like any man, not the Savior.

Naber: What did the Savior look like?

Resl: Like a common man.

Naber Just how?

Resl: Well, just like any man. Then He said something and she went like crazy, clasped her hands together, wrung them, bent over, and carried on like beside herself because she thought they hurt the Savior. Then suddenly, while she was lamenting quite so, the Savior lifted off the ground a little, was again so beautiful like when He came out of the tomb and said; at that she fell to the ground and said "RABBOUNI" (My beloved), and then the Savior looked good at her and was gone again and He had said something else also, something longer and then vanished.

I am happy for her. And then, I have yet something, I had forgotten; when the Earcutterer and the young man were gone, He was still around speculating, and the men had since gotten up, they left, yes they now left and He also went, you know where He went (noises...) He went to the....... No, first He said something to the women, and at that the women went into, you know they had gotten up some courage now that the men were gone, they were always afraid, some; the women walked around, very sad, did not want to go home, you know, the light men said something to them, for them to go home, even pointed which way to go, but they didn't obey, didn't leave, kept walking around and around, but not the girl, she was going to find the Mother because they surely took the Mother with them but the Mother probably said let Me go by Myself.

As they walked around, sad, who do you think came ah, who would you believe, would you think. Yes, how you might have known, suddenly the Savior stands before them. He was full of joy and the women were overjoyed, they immediately fell to the ground with their faces down..... .

Oh, they threw their stuff down, I wonder where the girl flung her lamp, she had a lamp with her.... She surely let it drop somewhere. She had forgotten about it when she ran to the men. She so carefully carried it. Now it is bright, the day started. It was beautiful and the women left by then also. Oh so, it was all so beautiful. It got to be so beautiful. The Savior, I am so glad now, it was so terrible for Him. Oh, when He was on the cross, now everything had healed and closed, except the wounds on His hands, His feet and the side, all healed back together, the torn, the bloodshot, and that in His face, that from the thorns, one came through at the eye, hung deeply into the eye, all is gone away, and as terrible as the Savior was mutilated, as glorious He was now.

At that we too wouldn't mind having wounds when we then are with the Savior, and had wounds we would be that closer with Him, surely?

Naber: Higher in heaven!

Resl: Oh, I don't like to hear that, one should say nearer to the Savior, because the nearer you are, the more beautiful you will be, because you have more of the Savior. One would have it so good.... . We could not go through the terrible harm the Savior went through.

Naber: How they took the Savior down from the wood; you had told us yesterday.

Resl: Yes, horrible entire shreds hung down, but still the Savior was good, yes, for sure one has to like pain, I had a lot of pain already in this world, one has to say "For you Savior, gladly, for whomever you want." Today my wounds don't hurt at all. It's possible I don't feel anything on account of my joy, I don't feel anything, only I am so touchy, everywhere it stings me. I had some wounds on my back and they are like healed again. I could rip myself apart. Oh, you know what happened to me?

Naber: What happened to you?

Resl: Oh, long time ago, something frightful, yes, I would not want to be in this way very long. The Savior left me! Oh, it was during the night, early into the night, I mean as night began.

Naber: Today is Sunday!

Resl: Sunday we have already? Oh, the Savior picked a beautiful day, to rise, especially a Sunday and a morning; indeed at dawn it was so beautiful ..... (garbled.) But, Father, tell you what to do. Now you are going to bring me the Savior, then I can help better, be in good shape, will be fully obedient, good.

Naber: Fully good!

Resl: (very quietly) I will be fully good. That's none of the peoples' business, they don't all have to hear that, I do not tell the people everything, only to you, with you I have nothing to hide.

Naber: I will bring you the Savior right away if you promise to be good, always!

Resl: Yes. But rather not promise too much, you know, in general, if one keeps promising and promising, I always keep promising so much.

I promised something for the boys, again, and then you have to be so anxious to be able to keep it you know. If one promises too much, one can't always keep it. Oh so, now go and bring me the Savior, don't take too long!

Naber: Meanwhile, what are you going to do?

Resl: Think of the Savior, wait in joyful hope!

Easter Sunday, at the Papal Blessings "URBI ET ORBI"

Resl: Now, it was at the highest Father (Pius XI), I recognized him right away, from when I was there a few times already, then when he became highest Father, I was there then, oh the many people, hot-humid it is there. It's much colder here, the sun was out, beautiful and the people screamed like mad.

Naber: What did they scream?

Resl: I don't quite, since it was such chaos. Papa, they always, I understood Papa, but can't finish it, and then the Father prayed first, then looked up to heaven ....

        Then he made a big cross, like through to all sides, I did the same, I was standing with the people, sort of at the side, one can get there from the side and I was there by them; then the highest Father did something.

Naber: What did you see?

Resl: They put a little stool there, and then they had several things there; the thing the women (Veronica) pushed onto the Savior, in a beautiful case, was fully dark inside, black, then something with which they beat the Savior, and something He had on His head and something they drove into His hands, then there was something I didn't know. What was it? I believe, but do not know, it was some blood of the Savior, so I thought, but can't say for certain.

        With all that, the highest Father was thankful, placed everything before, was most serious at it, I had to weep when I saw it, but all this was not just now, earlier, earlier, because I was away once and once more. Oh, when the Savior was Risen this morning, it was so beautiful, I am still so part of it, it was the most glorious.

Naber: (recording garbled)

Resl: That is not as important, no.
    In my thoughts I am back to this morning, early, when the sun rose, it was so beautiful, the Savior picked a beautiful time, indeed, what a glorious beginning and this night....., how He first came to the Mother, you know, how the young man ran, and the Earcutterer who could not quite keep up, and how he then waited for him I was so happy for the girl, and the women too.

Naber: To whom else did the Savior appear?

Resl: To the Earcutterer.

Naber: Sort of in passing?

Resl: Well, now, no; He looked at him really good, he (Peter) knew very well what it was all about, he did some thinking to himself. I had some thoughts, too.
    (recording garbled for a time)
    I am now so tired.

End of Passion and Resurrection Recordings

FATHER JOSEPH NABER'S LETTER
TO HIS BISHOP

The first report (account) about events at Konnersreuth by Pastor Joseph Naber to Bishop Antonius von Henle of Regensburg.

Konnersreuth, May 4, 1926

Excellency! Most Reverend Bishop! Your Grace!
Concerning: Therese Neumann of Konnersreuth

Remarkable events have taken place here at Konnersreuth in the last few years with Therese Neumann. She was born on April 9, 1898 as the oldest of the 10 still living children, of the tailor couple Ferdinand and Anna Neumann. I have known them now since 1909. The girl was very pious, industrious, sensible and also cheerful. Not a trace of sanctimoneousness or other anomalies. As proof of how serious she took virtues and piousness already in Sunday school, I would like to note that all subject matter of the sermon and religious education she liked in particular, she put down in writing on Sunday afternoons for herself; when, at the age of 15, as a servant girl, a man was after her she decided: rather loose my life than my virginity. As the only escape she jumped from a catwalk in the barn down 13 feet to the ground.

In the spring of 1918, on the occasion of a fire, while lifting heavy buckets of water up a ladder, she injured her spine. Something suddenly snapped and she could no longer help. In the Fall of the same year, serious problems with cramps, paralysis, and muscle contractions began. In addition, at the beginning of 1919, she became completely blind. On the day of the beatification of the venerable Theresia of the Child of Jesus, on April 29, 1923, she suddenly regained the sense of seeing. She had gotten to know about the beatified in 1914, and because of Theresia's childlike simplicity, she had begun to love and honor her especially.

All other ailments remained until May 17, 1925, the day of Theresia's canonization. On this day, shortly after the afternoon devotions I was called to see the sick girl: "We don't know what she has" said the sister who called me. With the thought, that St. Theresia was allowed to bring her into heaven this very day, I took along stola and chrism and went to see her.

But I did not find a dying person. She lay there, with transfigured countenance, eyes open and gazing in front of her, her hands slightly extended, nodding and shaking her head as though in congenial and most devoted conversation, which let all else be ignored. Suddenly, she sat up by herself, something which seemed to cause her great pain. The transfigured condition continued for some time yet, then suddenly she began to sob bitterly. Finally, she dried her tears and began to pound for her family members with her stick.

I asked then where she had been. But rather than answer my question she declared with astounding assuredness that she could now rise and walk. Her mother then looked at her left foot, which she had pulled up under her right leg for the last 3/4 of a year, and found it perfectly normally positioned beside the right leg. The patient then dressed, and stood up. Through my urging and still somewhat supported by her father and a nurse (I could not conceive this to be real that she, who could not even sit up in bed for the last 6 1/2 years was able to now walk) she walked halfway across the living room and back. I asked her once more what she experienced just before. After submitting to her wish that all others leave the room, she told me (I had specifically requested that she should tell me, her spiritual shepherd, everything and all which I would disclose only to those whom I felt worthy) as follows:

During Marian devotion, as I meditated on the mystery - "He who has ascended into heaven," I became aware of a great brightness before my eye; indescribably beautiful and comforting for the eyes was this light. Then a voice began to speak. First, I became frightened, but because the voice was quite so comforting and friendly and trusting I soon was at peace. It (the voice) said: "Resl, wouldn't you like to be well again?" I answered "Everything is agreeable to me what my loving God desires, to become well, to remain sick, to die." The voice: "Wouldn't it make you glad if you could rise and walk?" I: "Everything that comes from loving God makes me happy, my flowers, my birds, new suffering, but most of all my beloved Savior." The voice: "The Savior is pleased with your unquestioning acceptance. Therefore you too shall experience a little joy; you are to rise and be able to walk; but you may suffer yet much and more and no doctor will be able to cure you. But be not afraid, I have always been at your side and will continue to help you. Through suffering you can best manifest your devotional conviction and calling to be a victim soul, you can thus save souls and support priests." Then I had the feeling as though someone took me by my right hand and helped me up. I sat up but felt severe pains in the injured part of my back. Soon I laid back again. Then, without being shy about it, I said: "I did not think that I could sit up again. But I would like better yet if I would not insult my loving Savior any more, but bring him only joy." Thereupon the voice:

"The Savior is pleased with you, you are his good child." I: "Oh, if I only never insulted him again." The voice: "You have not so far angered God seriously; but that is not your achievement but solely comes from the grace of God." I: " Oh, but I do insult the Savior so often, every day, every day." The voice: "These little faults do not insult the Savior. It is great progress if one recognizes one's own insufficiency and helplessness; With such souls the Savior likes to sojourn, with them he converses intimately. You must ever more say no to your own I." Then the voice continued on: "Try once more, you will be able to rise."

And again it seemed like someone took me by the hand and helped me up; I sat up - and again felt great pain in my spine (this was her second rising which I witnessed, I was not present at the first - Naber.)

I then said "Everything the good Lord wishes to do is fine with me, I only desire that I do not insult him any more but be of great joy to Him. In fact, I have no other wish but being the source of joy for Him, and that ever more souls would like Him." The voice: "And precisely through suffering will souls be saved...I had written already: More souls will be saved through suffering than through the most illustrious homilies. Fear nothing, only suffering; if the worth of suffering were only recognized more." Then the light left and I felt most desolate because all became so murky, so I wept.

The two vertebrae, which before were punched in as well as laterally dislocated and which were the cause of great pain in the sitting position, had returned into their proper location. Since that time, even any trace of cramps or paralysis had vanished. With the aid of a cane, and slight support by another person, she could walk. That she, who in earlier days could carry 150 lb. of grain up 5 flights of stairs, could do no better at this stage was due to her overall weakness.

For a full year, blood flowed from both her eyes and one ear as the result of a head abscess. Around Christmas 1922, she could not eat or drink for a full 12 days. From that time to this date she had not been able to take solid food; she only takes one small cup of liquid daily; she could not accept milk or consommé.

The 15 days before Easter 1925 she could not take anything, not even one drop of water. She does not appear gaunt at all, and is, when not with a particular state of suffering, quite alive and awake. She only sleeps briefly towards morning.

On Sept. 30, 1925 - the anniversary of St. Theresia's death - at 11:30 at night while Neumann prayed a litany in honor of the saints, the miraculous light returned and the same amicable voice of May 17 said: "It is good you are thankful. The Lord wishes now that the more visible suffering cease. You will now walk without aid. Instead, however, heavy burdens are coming. Offer these sufferings for the lukewarm souls! But it is not good of you that you reject people and do not answer their letters; you should encourage them to trust in God!" There upon Neumann: "But, do I know that I am on the right path myself." Then the voice: "Follow your father confessor in complete obedience and entrust him in everything! Always remain childlike simple!" From then on, Neumann was able to walk without any help.

On Nov. 7, 1925, Neumann again had to return to the sick bed. As of the 10th, she had terrible pain and became so weak that she could no longer sit up or open her eyes. On the 13th, it worsened by the minute. Finally, a teacher who came to visit called the doctor (Dr. Otto Seidl of nearby Waldsassen.) After examining the sick most carefully, he diagnosed acute appendicitis, and declared she would have to be admitted to the hospital at Waldsassen for surgery. He could not accept any responsibility if surgery were delayed to the next morning. At that point the parents called me in the hope I would advise against any hospital. After conferring with the doctor, I explained to the parents to see and hear God's will in the recommendation of the doctor. The father then went to get a carriage and the mother prepared bed and linen.

The sick herself called for the Pastor. Before I came, she said in presence of the doctor: "You know, if I tell it to the Little Saint, she could help without the cutting." Whereupon the doctor: "Do you really think St. Theresia does nothing but work miracles for you?"

She told me she herself would gladly submit to be operated on, that all of God's will is fine with her, but she feels so sorry for her mother who is bitterly lamenting; whether she could not beg St. Theresia to help without operation, if it were all right with God?!

With my affirmative reply to let a relique of the Saint be placed on the afflicted area, I requested all present to pray to St. Theresia.

At that point, the sick became seized by most terrible pain and contorted like a worm. Most suddenly though, she sat up, opened her eyes, appeared quite transfigured, raised her hands, said "yes" three times, sat up completely and pressed her hands against the afflicted area with the question "Really?" Since I stood directly in front of her during these happenings, I posed the question: "Resl, has perhaps the Saint Theresia been here again and helped you?"

Answer: "Yes, she was here and said I did not have to be cut; that I should go over to church this instant and thank God. Mother, bring me a dress."

Then the sick dressed, I had the church unlocked (it was about 7 P.M.) and we, about 10 persons went there to give thanks before the picture of St. Theresia. Much to our embarrassment it was only the sick who first thanked the Savior in the tabernacle. She genuflected twice and fully without support. Fever and pain had gone totally. During the night, the pus was expelled through the bowels. The next morning Neumann came to church for Holy Communion and toward noon we drove to Waldsassen to see the doctor. For the next 8 days, Neumann had scabbed lips as a result of the previous fever.

The very same light and voice had come again, this time accompanied by a hand. The voice spoke: "Your complete dedication and joyful willingness to suffer pleases us. So that the world shall see that there is higher authority, it shall not be necessary that you need to be cut. Get up right away, go to the church and thank the Lord. But you may still suffer much, much, and thus be a co-redeemer. And, be not afraid. Even your internal suffering you need not fear. But ever more you must deny your inner self. And always remain childlike simple!"

At Mardi Gras 1926, Neumann had to return to bed again. Her eyes began to bleed and her condition worsened rapidly. As I visited her on Good Friday, I found her in mortal pain. Her eyes were full of blood which flowed down her cheeks; she contorted apparently not only in physical but also spiritual pain. I went to get the chrism since I feared a sudden collapse, but could not decide for Extreme Unction with the thought that 3 o'clock, the hour of death of our Lord could bring about a change.

And indeed, at 3 p.m. the mortal pain ceased. The next day, blood and pus flowed from her right ear, she slept well during the night to Easter Sunday and she appeared to have entered a new life. But, on the upper side of both hands and feet round sores appeared, not infected, with pure blood issuing; and of the same kind but elongated, near the heart.

The wound at the heart had suddenly opened three to four weeks before Easter, during meditation on the Agony in the Garden, the wound on the left hand appeared on Passion Week Friday, all others on Good Friday. On that Friday, the sick witnessed the entire Passion of the Savior, from the Agony in the Garden to Mount Calvary, as though walking behind, co-suffering, even His abandonment by God the Father.

A good many days after Easter, Dr. Seidl came and examined the wounds. Even before that, attempts were made to heal the wounds through home remedies, but the sick could not stand the pain. An ointment prescribed by the doctor was applied twice but to no avail.

I now ordered the sick to once more apply the prescribed ointment so that no one could later accuse us of not having given natural medication a chance. The result was swelling of hands and feet and the side, together with great pain.

Only after 10 hours, and not a minute earlier and upon the fervent pleas of the parents to the contrary, did I permit the removal of the ointment. On April 16, the physician came and redressed the wounds himself. But soon, the pain and swelling returned and I permitted the sick to do what she herself thought best. The doctor's bandages were removed and simple linen applied. The wounds continued to bleed but the pain abated. Because of disobedience of doctor's orders, Neumann was in an embarrassed quandary and turned to St. Theresia for advice. Shortly after the appeal to the Saint, she felt the linen patches to loosen and the wounds to dry up. From Saturday, April 17 to Thursday, April 22, the wounds remained closed. On that day, the sick read to others until 10 p.m.

Soon thereafter, the living pictures of Good Friday reappeared before her eyes, she suffered with the Savior, like in the past, but not quite as severe. Eyes, heart, hands and feet bled again. On Friday I found her pale and weak. On Saturday, like Thursday, her wounds were dry again. Friday, April 30, the same thing repeated itself. Now, the wounds are closed up again.

These, your Excellency, are the "remarkable happenings" at Konnersreuth. In most instances, I have been eyewitness. Everything else originated from trustworthy eyewitnesses, mainly however from the sick herself. She is, to put it into few words, a big child, but in the perception of the Savior and St. Theresia of the Child Jesus, a Francis of Assisi type. A very soul-industrious priest, who spent some time with her recently told me: "His Excellency would very much enjoy this simple, natural, uncomplicated and innocent child."

Any thought of fraud, hysteria, autosuggestion could arise only with someone who does not know the sick one. I would like to cite one event, which most decisively speaks against autosuggestion, a behavior which can be expected to be proposed. In the presence of Prof. Dr. Scherer of Passau, I asked the sick last Saturday, what had taken place in the night between last Thursday and Friday at the onset of bleeding. Quite unassuming - Dr. Scherer marveled over her composure - she told us:

> "Until 10:30 p.m., a man was here (she does not want to expound further,: I knew, the man is industrious, generous, of best of will, a nature lover, but someone who lost his faith reading books like Haekl's *World Enigma*. For 25 years he has not been to confession, and now he is imploring Neumann to help him with his search for God. -Naber) we talked about religious issues, but also about little goldfish, which he is going to bring me, because he thinks I might like them.
>
> At about 11 p.m., my family had left by then, I said my evening prayer and just lay there. At that, this man came back to my mind with his plea for his soul, then the goldfish. Suddenly, pain began. At the same time, the picture of the Savior on the Mount of Olives appeared before my eyes and heart, eyes, hands, and feet began to bleed."

I must also note that Neumann is punctual, obedient and would most prefer to be alone with God.

"I'd prefer the worst pain to all these visitors and being gawked at," she told me.

The whole issue is a very precarious matter, to which I am not up to. Therefore, I appeal to his Excellency in humbleness to support me with his kind wisdom, fatherly advice and directives. We will make every effort to follow them most conscientiously.

In deepest reverence to your Episcopal Excellence, remains J. Naber, Pastor.

BISHOP'S REPLY TO FATHER NABER'S LETTER

Regensburg, May 6, 1926

In matters of Therese Neumann, this advice is rendered to Fr. Naber:

To be cautious in his judgment with the public. Next, to prevent the run of curiosity seekers. In particular, since Dr. Seidl, who retains a most strict Catholic position, believes, that certain appearances on the Neumann can be positively diagnosed. What arouses concern with myself is the naive address "Resl", which the extraterrestrial "voice" is supposed to have used. Heaven knows nothing incomplete, not even the naming of names.

The Pastor will therefore do well to be continuously guided by the advice of St. John the Apostle, "Test the spirits whether they emanate from God." He is requested to report back in 8 weeks if nothing extraordinary occurs.

Antonius

EPILOGUE

I t is fitting to take a last look at Resl, her life and its purpose. Why was it that God presented to the world this woman whose only desire was to love Him and to do His Will?

As an instrument of the Will of God, her life and phenomena, in particular her stigmata and Friday sufferings, were an admonishment to the society of her days; a society which had rejected God. Resl was a manifestation that Jesus had truly been on earth; that He had, out of love for us and for our salvation, suffered the terrifying death of crucifixion. It also showed that this suffering continued in Resl's time, it continues now in our time, and will continue until the end of time. The admonishment is as valid in our day, when religion and the supernatural are rejected, as it was in her time.

Resl was not only here to show and help oppose the Nazi powers. Her purpose on earth had a much greater scope. She was a visible testimony from God rebuking the rejection of the supernatural; this rejection which embraces atheism.

How very much our present times need her affirmation of the presence of God! The conceit of our intellectuals who reject God while at the same time making themselves and science the new God smacks of a repeat of Lucifer's infamous deed.

Let us who believe and love our Lord and His Church join our prayers with those of His beloved servant Resl, that His Will be done. Let us also pray that the process for Resl's beatification be started now, so that all may see a light through this ominous darkness we live in.

PRAYER FOR THE BEATIFICATION OF THERESE NEUMANN

Almighty God, our Father in Heaven, with infinite love You give us signs to stir our dull minds when we consider the lives of Your Saints. To recall our Lord's Passion You granted Therese Neumann to bear His sacred wounds visibly on her body. You enabled her to see much of His life on earth in her visions. You allowed her to make amends for the sins of men by suffering with the Savior. Likewise You reminded us of the lasting value of the Sacrifice of the Mass and the abiding presence of Christ Your Son in the Most Holy Sacrament of the Altar by permitting her to live for over 30 years solely through receiving the sacred host in daily Holy Communion! We beg to further distinguish Therese Neumann by granting our prayer to have her raised to the Honors of the Altar, that more people may through knowledge of her love for You and Your laws draw nearer to You. We ask this through Christ our Lord. Amen.

- The Konnersreuth Circle

REFERENCES

1. L. Witt
    Konnersreuth im Lichte der Religion und Wissenschaft   1930
    (Konnersreuth In The Light of Religion and Science)

2. Dr. Fritz Gerlich
    Die Stigmatisierte Therese Neumann von Konnersreuth   1929
    (The Stigmatist Therese Neumann of Konnersreuth)

3. Dr. Joseph Teodorowicz, Archbishop of Lemberg
    Konnersreuth im Lichte der Mystik und Psychologie   1936
    (Konnersreuth in Light of Mysticism and Psychology)

4. Cardinal Lambertini, (Pope Benedict XIV)
    *Treatise on The Beatification and Canonization
    of the Servants of God. 3 Vols.*

5. Bishop Dr. S. Waitz
    Die Botschaft von Konnersreuth   1957
    (The Message From Konnersreuth)

6. Father Joseph Naber
    Tagebuecher und Aufzerchnungen ueber Therese Neumann   1987
    (Diary and Reports about Therese Neumann)

7. Helmut Witetschek   1985
    Father Ingbert Naab, OMF

8. Albert Paul Schimberg
    The Story of Therese Neumann   1947

9. Albert Panzer
    Licht von "Drueben"   1991
    (Light From "Beyond")

10. Guenther Schwarz
    Das Zeichen von Konnersreuth   1994
    (In The Sign of Konnersreuth)

11. Elizabeth von Guttenberg
    A Message From The Beyond   1978

12. Johannas Maria Hoecht
    Traeger der Wundmale Christi   1964
    (Carriers of the Stigmata of Christ)

13. Paul Siwek S.J.
    The Riddle of Konnersreuth   1953

14. Hilda Graef
    The Case of Teresa Neumann   1950
    From Fashions to the Fathers, The Story of My Life   1957

15. Joseph Hanauer
    Wunder Oder Wundersucht   1991
    (Miracle Or Miracle Craving)
    Konnersreuth - Lug und Trug - mit Kirchlichen Segen   1994
    *(Konnersreuth - Lie and Deceit - with Ecclesiastical
    Blessing)*

16. Von Skorpio
    Therese von Konnersreuth

17. Rev. Charles M. Carty
    Padre Pio   1955

Who Is Teresa Neumann   1956
Padre Pio and Terese Neumann   1956

18.   Maria Valtorta
      The Poems of The Man-God   1989

19.   Emmerich/Brentano
      Life Of Christ   1954

20.   Mary F. Ingoldsby
      Padre Pio, His Life and Mission   1978

21.   Anni Spiegl
      Leben und Sterben der Therese Neumann
          von Konnersreuth   1976
      (Life and Death of Therese Neumann from Konnersreuth)

22.   Rev.Dr. Alfred O-Rahilly
      "Therese Neumann - Stigmatist"   1958
      from *The Sunday Press*, Dublin, Ireland

23.   *New Catholic Encyclopedia*

24.   Dr. G. Ewald
      Die Stigmatisierte von Konnersreuth   1927
      (The Stigmatist of Konnersreuth)

Beim hl. Meßopfer wollen
wir uns mit dem Priester
am Altar vereinen und mit
ihm mitbeten und mitopfern.

Beten wir füreinander!

Therese Neumann

Taschenlehen, den 6. Oktober 1936

In Holy Mass, we will unite with the priest at the altar and pray and sacrifice with him!

Let us pray for one another!

–Therese Neumann
Taschenlehen, October 6, 1936

(Resl's inscription into the Missal of my husband, Wendell)